SIGNS OF HOPE

SIGNS OF HOPE

Thomas Merton's Letters on Peace, Race, and Ecology

Gordon Oyer

ORBIS BOOKS

Maryknoll, New York 10545

Founded in 1970, Orbis Books endeavors to publish works that enlighten the mind, nourish the spirit, and challenge the conscience. The publishing arm of the Maryknoll Fathers and Brothers, Orbis seeks to explore the global dimensions of the Christian faith and mission, to invite dialogue with diverse cultures and religious traditions, and to serve the cause of reconciliation and peace. The books published reflect the views of their authors and do not represent the official position of the Maryknoll Society. To learn more about Maryknoll and Orbis Books, please visit our website at www.orbisbooks.com.

LIBRARY OF CONGRESS CATALOGING-IN-PUBLICATION DATA
Names: Oyer, Gordon, author.
Title: Signs of hope : Thomas Merton's letters on peace, race, and ecology / Gordon Oyer.
Description: Maryknoll, NY : Orbis Books, [2021] | Includes bibliographical references and index. |
Identifiers: LCCN 2021013383 (print) | LCCN 2021013384 (ebook) | ISBN 9781626984301 (trade paperback) | ISBN 9781608338931 (epub)
Subjects: LCSH: Merton, Thomas, 1915-1968—Political and social views. | Peace—Religious aspects—Christianity. | Race relations—Religious aspects—Christianity. | Ecology—Religious aspects—Christianity. | Merton, Thomas, 1915-1968—Correspondence.
Classification: LCC BX4705.M542 O94 2021 (print) | LCC BX4705.M542 (ebook) | DDC 261/.1—dc23
LC record available at https://lccn.loc.gov/2021013383
LC ebook record available at https://lccn.loc.gov/2021013384

For Ched and Eric, Wilbur and Larry,
Michael and Brian and too many others to name,
whose ongoing wisdom and friendship expanded
my awareness of our urgent need for a transformed society.

CONTENTS

PART III
RE-VISIONING A FRAGMENTED WORLD

FOREWORD

It has been said that Thomas Merton never had a thought that wasn't published. Indeed, the monk from Gethsemani was a prolific author with fifty books and hundreds of articles published in journals and popular magazines. Because he was a monk of the Trappist order, his writings had to pass through his order's censors and be approved before they could be published. Only his journals and his correspondence were free from the censors. This is the Thomas Merton whom Gordon Oyer encountered when he did his research and writing for this book.

Oyer had plenty of primary sources for his research. Thomas Merton wrote over 12,000 letters to over 2,100 correspondents worldwide. The people he wrote to ranged from teenagers to popes. There are scores of letters that I have called "the interfaith letters" written by Merton to Jewish, Muslim, Buddhist, Taoist, and Hindu friends and acquaintances. These letters, which were often about world peace and peacemaking, formed the basis for my book *Signs of Peace*. All of the "interfaith letters" along with the vast majority of his other letters were written during the last decade of Merton's life, 1958–1968.[1] But there is so much more to be done with Merton's letters. Might there be other groupings of letters around a common theme? This is where Gordon Oyer came into my life.

Gordon contacted me nearly four years ago, asking if he might visit me at my home in Oregon.[2] He too had a strong interest in Merton's correspondence. I was delighted and somewhat intrigued that Gordon would make a trip all the way from Illinois to Oregon for our meeting. We sat together at

---

1. In his early years at Gethsemani, Merton was permitted only four letters a year. The abbot could look at those letters if he so desired. He was also free to examine Merton's incoming mail, unless it was marked "conscience matters." As Merton's reading public grew during the 1950s, the restriction on the numbers of personal letters was eventually lifted.

2. Gordon Oyer was the recipient of the 2015 "Louie Award" awarded by the International Thomas Merton Society for his book *Pursuing the Spiritual Roots of Protest*. He has since given Merton-related papers and addresses at several Thomas Merton conferences and other venues.

my home in western Oregon in the heart of the wine country with its rolling hills, and with "Our Lady of Guadalupe" Trappist Abbey nearby. It seemed to be a good place in which to discuss all things Merton. What a lovely visit for me. Gordon expressed appreciation for my work as a Merton scholar, which he had thoroughly examined. It is always good to be appreciated!

Gordon had a specific project in mind. He had carefully read my book *Signs of Peace: The Interfaith Letters of Thomas Merton.* He liked the format and general thrust of the book. He wondered if he might do a sequel. My book had been on Merton's letters concerning peace, and he wanted to do a book on Merton's letters involving issues of social justice and his vision for transforming our society into one more just and fair. Together we would have covered the "penetrating questions" that Merton spent all of his time addressing in his last decade of life.[3]

I was pleased and honored that Gordon wanted to write a book similar to mine. That result is a sequel, but it is much more than a sequel. As a theologian and spiritual biographer, I had taken an approach that focused on Merton's expansive spirituality as he was in dialogue with his interfaith friends— all for the sake of peace. As a historian, Gordon has taken an approach that is quite different from mine.

Gordon does note the spiritual grounding of Merton and the men and women whose social activism fueled the dialogue between Merton and his interfaith friends and acquaintances. But for Gordon's accounts, the focus is more on outward actions grounded in the hope that change was possible, actions that emerged from their spirituality, rather than on the inward spirituality itself. Being the excellent historian that he is, Gordon was always on the hunt for the connection and the relationships that paved the way for the things that made for just action and said no to the forces that protected an unjust status quo. He also delves more deeply into the history surrounding Merton's epistolary partners than I did.

To a large extent, *Signs of Peace* has to do with the inner journey of Merton and his epistolary partners in dialogue, with their spirituality in its formation, and in its depth dimension. These are people whose spirituality enables them to reach out to others in ways that lead to wholeness, to peace. Gordon's *Signs of Hope,* as I have said, focuses more on the outer journey, the application of the spiritual life to hopeful action, to what Bonhoeffer calls "righteous (just) actions." These actions include a call to solidarity in confronting racism, war, poverty, and ecological crises.

In Gordon's chapter on Dorothy Day, he writes of her compassionate perseverance as she lived and worked with the poor and dispossessed at the

---

3. John Moses, *The Art of Thomas Merton* (Columbus, Ohio: Franciscan Media, 2019), 71.

Catholic Worker in New York City. Everything Day did was part of her nonviolent way of life, which was an integral part of her discipleship as a follower of Jesus. Gordon, in writing about Day, could understand her nonviolent way of life existentially because of his own faith as a Mennonite, whose way of nonviolence is also derived from the life and teachings of Jesus.

Gordon's exploration of the relationship between Dorothy Day and Thomas Merton must have been challenging since they never met, and yet their relationship was special and unique. Prayer was at the very center of their relationship. This spiritual bond between Day and Merton might elude the eyes of many historians but not Gordon. He sees that it was this spiritual bond that resulted in a mutual trust which enabled each to support the other and gave each strength and courage for the journey God had set out before them. They asked each other to remember the other in prayer, a most intimate relationship indeed.

For me, Gordon's chapter on "whiteness" and racism in America is perhaps his finest, in terms of both his thorough historical research and his grasp of what the significance of the dialogue between Merton and Vincent Harding might mean for us today. As he does throughout the book, Gordon allows the reader to draw his or her own conclusions from his research and observations. So I too will draw mine. Briefly stated: we cannot read this chapter without noting how far ahead of his time Merton was in the insight he brought to his exchange of letters and to his meeting with Harding. Merton understood more than half a century ago what the "Black Lives Matter" movement has been trying to tell white people—myself included—about "whiteness." We must be conscious of what having a privileged white position means in our society, and we must understand how that attitude of superiority affects people of color, especially Blacks.

As was clear to Vincent Harding, a young African American academic and activist, Merton was the rarest of white people—one who understood what his "whiteness" was all about. Harding had become friends with Merton when they met and talked at Gethsemani in 1967.[4] He sent but one letter to Merton and that was on New Year's Day of 1968. Gordon has thoughtfully included selected quotes from Harding's letter. Merton's letter of response is printed for us at the end of the "Whiteness" chapter. Harding's words quoted here were written in the context of Merton and Harding's emerging friendship and spiritual kinship. Harding wrote: "I sensed that you [Merton] . . . were enough at peace with the scandal of your whiteness and all of its implications that you could be at peace with me and my searching. And I felt

---

4. See chapter 8, page 186.

you loved the world, and that its ragged, surging madness pained you deeply but did not totally disorient you."[5]

Building on this quotation, Gordon notes just how far ahead of his time Merton was in race relations. His awareness of his own "whiteness" was apparent as he engaged in dialogue with Harding. White people today would do well to embrace Merton's insistence that each person, no matter what their ethnic group, their gender, their station in life, has the God-given right and freedom to define themselves. This is the essential point of departure as whites and people of color enter into the kind of dialogue for change encouraged by the "Black Lives Matter" movement. Once again, we see how Gordon came to terms with his own "whiteness" as he discussed issues of race and white racism in this context. Only someone who has worked through these things for himself can have the depth of insight that Gordon has.

In relation to Merton, Gordon finds someone who, through his letters, became a "sign of hope." The issue of race among all of the social justice issues was the most challenging for Merton to address. It could not be otherwise, since it is the social justice issue that white Americans have the most trouble facing squarely with honesty and credibility. It is America's original sin, and like all sin it is most difficult for the sinner to see its reality within one's self.

Howard Thurman, the African American pastor, prophet, theologian, and mystic, taught me, as well as thousands of others, that in order to live life in its fullness, we must engage the head (intellect) and the heart (our compassionate self) in all that we do. This is Gordon's great asset. If readers of *Signs of Hope* have eyes to see and ears to hear, they will read Gordon's story of Merton and his social justice friends and the lessons it has to teach us by using both the head and the heart. What Gordon has written is long overdue. Readers, read on. You have much to ponder and act upon, if this book is given its due and as you are called to action.

— William Apel
August 2020

---

5. See chapter 8, page 191.

PREFACE

As William Apel's foreword suggests, this study of Thomas Merton's letters on social transformation owes its inspiration to Bill's study of Merton's interfaith letters, *Signs of Peace*.[1] Both books rely upon the massive body of Thomas Merton's correspondence,[2] which has long been recognized as a significant part of his literary corpus.[3] Therefore, many of Merton's reflections on social concerns as he recorded in letters are already in print.

The approach Bill has modeled, however, seeks not to simply share Merton's words, but to interpret them in the context of his relationships with correspondents. This book's shift from interfaith dialogue to U.S. social issues also required, as Bill noted, expanding his largely theological/spiritual approach to include a broader historical context. In doing so, *Signs of Hope* seeks to illuminate how Merton deployed his craft of writing to engage specific people on specific social topics and thereby expand our understanding of his overall vision for social transformation beyond what his published writings alone can provide. Exploring his personal insights into longstanding Western cultural paradigms also sheds light how those paradigms continue to drive concrete experiences in our own times.

A major challenge when addressing Merton's social concern letters involves narrowing the scope to a manageable size. In some ways, a scope for "interfaith letters" may be more direct: letters to those of other faiths. But deciding what warrants inclusion as letters on "social transformation" proves quite nebulous. It could include exchanges with those recognized as "activists," committed to directly addressing social problems and injustices. It

---

1. William Apel, *Signs of Peace: The Interfaith Letters of Thomas Merton* (Maryknoll, NY: Orbis Books, 2006), 1.

2. In the past decade about 3,800 additional letters to or from Merton have been discovered, bringing the count to about 20,350.

3. Five volumes of selected letters were published between 1985 and 1994, followed by at least two letter anthologies. Twenty-six collections of both sides of Merton correspondence have been published—eight in the last decade—with a twenty-seventh in process.

could focus on abstract concepts while minimizing real-life, on-the-ground social events. It could include *any* correspondence that captures social stances Merton expressed.

Merton often approached writing personal letters as a mission of relational connection that might further the understanding and vision of both himself and his correspondents. He did not hesitate to drop random observations and concerns about society and events in letters to a wide variety of recipients. As William H. Shannon and Christine M. Bochen observed in their introduction to *A Life in Letters: The Essential Collection*:

> Merton is inclined to talk to everyone about everything. So while writing to peace activists about their resistance to war, he may branch off and talk about issues facing the Catholic Church. Addressing fellow writers about their work and his, he shares thoughts about his life and work and the threats to freedom in the world. Writing to fellow monks about obstacles to an authentic living of the monastic life, he offers critiques of American culture. The scope and variety of his correspondents are staggering.[4]

This range within a given letter's content, from the concrete to the metaphysical, carries diverse fodder for personal reflection on relating to one another and to the planet. Since his comments bleed across neat categories like literary, religious, or social, his comments about a particular piece of literature or poetry may carry profound social implications. The book's scope, then, could have virtually no limit, and almost anyone to whom he wrote could be a candidate for inclusion.

To balance these challenges, the scope of this book has been mostly limited to correspondence with representative persons whose lives and work focused on advocacy for social change or whose correspondence with Merton engage or reflect social tensions. In doing so, *Signs of Hope* does not revisit any of the correspondents included in *Signs of Peace*, although some, such as Quaker June Youngblut, Jewish rabbi Abraham Joshua Heschel, and Vietnamese Buddhist monk Thich Nhat Hanh easily qualify for both volumes.

In his opening chapter, "Merton's Ministry of Letters," Bill offers a wonderful summary of the role correspondence played in Merton's monastic career. The introduction to *Signs of Hope* builds on some of those key observations and explores in more depth dynamics unique to Merton's social engagement letters. The following ten chapters are then organized into three

---

4. Thomas Merton, *A Life in Letters: The Essential Collection*, ed. William H. Shannon and Christine M. Bochen (Notre Dame, IN: Ave Maria Press, 2008), xiii.

parts, each with its own brief introduction to frame what follows. Part 1 includes four correspondents who in part constitute a sort of "Catholic inner circle" that offered friendship and encouragement as they collaborated to urge the American Catholic Church, and Christians in general, to embrace peace in a war-prone nation. Part 2 features four African American correspondents and displays Merton's insight and sensitivity toward those living under the generations-old yoke of racial oppression. The final part addresses Merton's exploration of larger questions about Western cultural assumptions that drive modern global structures and dominate life within Earth's biosphere.

Demographically, these chapters feature Merton's exchanges with three white women, four Black men, and four white men. They also extensively draw on fragments of letters to numerous others, and occasionally on Merton's journal entries and published writings.

Each chapter is organized around one or two key concepts that help focus the themes of Merton's exchanges with a particular person. Each concept served as a spiritual skill or "tool" to navigate the issues of Merton's times. They remain profoundly relevant to navigating our own. Therefore, *Signs of Hope* looks beyond specific social issues in themselves. It seeks to reveal how those issues and relationships fit into Merton's own pilgrimage as well as ours. Through this relational and contextual focus, *Signs of Hope* aspires to offer a unique contribution regarding Merton's posture toward social concerns.

ACKNOWLEDGMENTS

I am deeply indebted to many who helped bring this book to print. Foremost, I am grateful to Bill Apel for his gracious support, encouragement, and blessing to pursue this project, inspired by and modeled after his own study of Merton's interfaith letters—this despite having done his own initial groundwork toward such a project, which he generously shared. I am also grateful to Bill for carefully reading and commenting on each chapter and writing the book's foreword. In addition to Bill, Paul Pearson and Eric Anglada reviewed its entire content, and Joseph Flipper, Thom Moore, Malgorzota Poks, Andrew J. Stone Porter, and Mary Rademaker commented on specific chapters. Special thanks to all.

Archival support from several repositories proved crucial, especially as COVID-19 restrictions made onsite visits impossible. Foremost among these, Mark Meade and Dr. Paul Pearson, Thomas Merton Center staff at Bellarmine University, offered invaluable assistance and guidance throughout the project. During the spring and summer of 2020, when the university placed Mark on furlough, Paul provided particularly crucial support through promptly scanning and forwarding documents and making audio recordings remotely available. Other key archival support included: Shelly Barber at the Burns Library of Boston College; Vincent Barraza at Xavier University of Louisiana; Laura Mills at Roosevelt University; Maryalice Perrin-Moore at New England Conservatory of Music; Kathy Shoemaker at Emory University; Fr. Dale Cieslik of the Alexandria (Louisiana) Archdiocese; Diane Hagan of St. Thomas Parish at Bardstown, Kentucky; Kay Hackett of the Louisville Archdiocese; Thomas P. Lester of the Boston Archdiocese.

Several others informally lent special insights. Especially noteworthy, Professor Gregory Hillis of Bellarmine University generously shared materials from his research on Fr. August Thompson, and Fr. Daniel P. Horan, OFM shared from his Naomi Burton Stone research. Others shared helpful personal reflections and memories: Dr. E. Glenn Hinson; Br. Paul Quenon, OCSO; Sr. M. Camilla Roach, FMSA. Special thanks also to Emily Riley Miller for subletting to me her lovely Louisville condominium where the book was written.

Those who readily granted permission to quote from correspondence of their own, a family member, or someone whose literary rights they held include: Fr. John Dear; Jim Douglass; Jim Forest; Marc Gafni; Paula Green; Rachel Harding; Linda Orell; Marian Thompson Richardson; Irene Seeland. Special thanks to the Merton Legacy Trust and Victoria Fox of Farrar, Straus and Giroux for permission to quote from and reproduce letters to Thomas Merton.

Finally, very special thanks to Robert Ellsberg, Maria Angelini, Celine Allen, and the staff of Orbis Books for their willingness, their assistance, and their effort to publish *Signs of Hope*.

ABBREVIATIONS

Thomas Merton's Letters and Journals

CT	*The Courage for Truth: Letters to Writers*
DWL	*Dancing in the Water of Life: Seeking Peace in the Hermitage* (The Journals of Thomas Merton, Volume 5, 1963–1965)
HGL	*The Hidden Ground of Love: Letters on Religious Experience and Social Concerns*
LL	*Learning to Love: Exploring Solitude and Freedom* (The Journals of Thomas Merton, Volume 6, 1966–1967)
OSM	*The Other Side of the Mountain: The End of the Journey* (The Journals of Thomas Merton: Volume 7, 1967–1968)
RJ	*The Road to Joy: Letters to New and Old Friends*
SCH	*The School of Charity: Letters on Religious Renewal and Spiritual Direction*
SS	*A Search for Solitude: Pursuing the Monk's True Life* (The Journals of Thomas Merton: Volume 3, 1952–1960)
TMA	*Thomas Merton in Alaska: The Alaskan Conferences, Journals, and Letters*
TTW	*Turning toward the World: The Pivotal Years* (The Journals of Thomas Merton: Volume 4, 1960–1963)
WF	*Witness to Freedom: Letters in Times of Crisis*

Merton Encyclopedia

ME	*The Thomas Merton Encyclopedia*

Unpublished Archival Collection

TMC/BU	Thomas Merton Center, W. W. Lyons Brown Library, Bellarmine University, Louisville, KY. Unless otherwise noted, documents referenced reside in the Thomas Merton Center correspondence file of the Merton correspondent cited.

INTRODUCTION

SEEKING A TRANSFORMED SOCIETY THROUGH LETTERS

> The Christian hope in God...must take on visible and symbolic forms, in order to communicate its message.
> —Thomas Merton in *The Solitary Life*

When Thomas Merton entered the Abbey of Our Lady of Gethsemani in December 1941, he chose a response to the social ills around him that mirrored his fourth-century Desert Father forebears: removal to an environment that permitted closer communion with God and greater clarity of meaning and purpose.[1] During the first years of his monastic life, his vocational formation and public writings focused mostly on interior work to gain that insight. During his final decade, Merton expanded his focus to consider problematic questions that roiled U.S. society and begged for its transformation. Those questions prompted Merton to increasingly reach out for conversation with others, mainly through letters.

Thomas Merton the Letter Writer

Merton's correspondence served as both a lifeline and a bane to his monastic vocation. Even as it provided his main avenue for relationships and connection with events beyond Gethsemani's enclosure, it consumed time and energy he sometimes felt would be better spent in contemplative silence. His success at both sustaining numerous external relationships and maintaining a

---

1. Gary Peter Hall, *Communing with the Stranger: Relational Dynamics and Critical Distance between Thomas Merton and His Readers* (draft of unpublished PhD dissertation, University of Birmingham, n.d.), explores Merton's monastic vocation as his consistent response to "social crisis" throughout the last seventeen years of his life, not just a late-life "turn toward the world" often associated with his interfaith and social engagement.

rigorous contemplative practice relied in part on his uncanny ability to shape thoughts into words through his facility with a typewriter. His friend, correspondent, and biographer, Jim Forest, recounts a first-hand view of this skill during his January 1962 visit to Merton:

> He had a small office just outside the classroom where he taught the novices. On his desk was a large grey typewriter. He inserted a piece of monastery stationery and wrote a reply at what seemed to me the speed of light. I had never seen anyone write so quickly. You will sometimes see a skilled stenographer type at such speed when copying a text, but even in a city news room one doesn't often see actual writing at a similar pace.... It was a very solid, carefully reasoned letter filling one side of a sheet of paper and was written in just a few minutes.[2]

For many reasons, the abundant correspondence that flowed from Merton's typewriter (and sometimes pen) holds a special place in his body of writing. Perhaps no person other than Merton himself understood the depth and breadth of those letters better than William H. Shannon. His years editing multiple volumes of Merton's letters gave him unique insight into that correspondence. Shannon notes that "the subjects of his letters parallel, and often shed light on, the wide variety of topics in his published articles and books."[3] Shannon contrasts Merton's letters with his journals, the other primary source of his uncensored writing, which sometimes could be "overly introspective and self-occupied."[4] As communication, letters must express thoughts intelligible to and capable of reception by another, written with greater care and emotional restraint than journal entries. Conversely, though his letters often expressed his thoughts more carefully than his journals, the journals must sometimes also be read alongside the letters to appreciate the letters' complexity and nuance.

Shannon also grasped how "letters have a relational character and particularity about them. Normally they are written not for a general audience, but

---

2. Jim Forest, "Meeting Thomas Merton," posted February 2, 2011, at http://jimandnancyforest.com/2011/02/meeting-thomas-merton-2/.

3. William H. Shannon, preface to Thomas Merton, *The Hidden Ground of Love: Letters on Religious Experience and Social Concerns*, ed. William H. Shannon (New York: Farrar, Straus and Giroux, 1985), vii. Cited hereafter as *HGL*.

4. William H. Shannon, "Letters," in *The Thomas Merton Encyclopedia*, ed. William H. Shannon, Christine M. Bochen, Patrick F. O'Connell (Maryknoll, NY: Orbis Books, 2002), 256. Cited hereafter as *ME*.

for a special person."[5] They are "one-on-one: they exist for dialogue and call for reaction."[6] This aspect filled a crucial need in Merton's life. During an era before email or internet, in a setting with minimal telephone or visitor access—both available only through abbatial permission—letters provided the primary means for the cloistered monk to maintain his far-flung friendships and collegial relationships. "If he wanted to keep his friends, he could not ordinarily visit [or phone, text, email, or tweet] them. He had to write" letters on paper.[7] The same was true if he wanted to make a new friend. Given his constraints, crafting an initial letter to a stranger required him to concisely articulate the essence of his interests and concerns in an inviting manner.

Jim Forest shares another key insight about Merton's skill in connecting with others:

> Merton's voice changed all the time depending on who he was talking to. If he was talking to a Quaker, he might use Quaker vocabulary. The same if he was talking to a Muslim. He created spaces in which dialogue occurred that might not happen otherwise. Merton had this facility to study and appreciate radically different points of view and somehow integrate them into his style with some people.[8]

This often proved true of his letter writing also. When we as third parties peer over his shoulder and read his correspondence a layer of complexity is added. We must keep in mind that sometimes even his style and vocabulary were ultimately focused on communicating with that particular, original audience of one.

Merton further illuminated his approach to letter writing when Forest once encouraged him to rebut a 1967 *New York Times Magazine* article on Eastern thought in Western societies: "If I tried to do anything" about the article, Merton responded, "I would embark on a long, patient personal correspondence and try and get something like a dialogue going. . . . I see more and more that it is terribly important to try to find nuances and gradations in

---

5. Shannon, "Letters," in *ME* 255.

6. William H. Shannon and Christine M. Bochen, introduction to *A Life in Letters: The Essential Collection*, by Thomas Merton, ed. William H. Shannon and Christine M. Bochen (Notre Dame, IN: Ave Maria Press, 2008), xiii.

7. Shannon, "Letters," *ME* 255.

8. "Work Hard, Pray Hard: On Dorothy Day and Thomas Merton," interview with Jim Forest, published online October 10, 2011, at USCatholic.org, https://www.uscatholic.org/culture/social-justice/2011/09/work-hard-pray-hard-dorthy-day-and-thomas-merton.

these interminable black vs. white positions in which everything has to be one dimensional."[9]

William Apel considers Merton's letters as not just an "act of friendship" but also a "serious literary endeavor." "They were more concrete than abstract; they addressed real life situations and were generally averse to metaphysical flights of fancy."[10] For Apel, his letters still speak:

> Merton's voice can almost be heard as he responds to the immediate concern of a correspondent, or as he thinks aloud with the reader of his letter about an observation he wants to share. . . . His uncanny ability to get at the heart of a matter causes his letters, and those of his correspondents, to transcend time and place. Merton, because of his attentiveness to self and others, brings all concerned into a bigger picture —a more organic whole. God's presence becomes evident to the reader in the turning of a phrase or in a gesture of true friendship.[11]

In broad strokes, "Merton wanted and needed to be in touch with contemporary women and men as together they struggled with the questions of truth, meaning, and responsibilities that continue to trouble the human spirit. . . . Letter writing, as Merton came to see it, was an extension of his monastic vocation."[12]

The "Person" as Portal to Engaging Others

Merton's interior life revolved around contemplative practice and the pursuit of wisdom. But he anchored his exterior interactions, including letter writing, in a particular understanding of human personhood. This falls within an array of twentieth century views on "the person" loosely grouped under the heading of "personalism," which reflects a broad worldview more than a precise philosophy or theology.

---

9. Merton to Forest, February 13, 1967, James Forest Correspondence, the Thomas Merton Collection, Thomas Merton Center, W. W. Lyons Brown Library, Bellarmine University. Cited hereafter as TMC/BU.

10. William Apel, *Signs of Peace: The Interfaith Letters of Thomas Merton* (Maryknoll, NY: Orbis Books, 2006), 3, 4. Affirming the literary quality of Merton's letters, see the devotional collection compiled from his letters: Fiona Gardner, *Precious Thoughts: Daily Readings from the Correspondence of Thomas Merton* (London: Darton Longman and Todd, 2011).

11. Apel, *Signs of Peace*, 8.

12. Shannon and Bochen, *Life in Letters*, xi.

As a Catholic theological perspective, personalism emerged in Europe in response to challenges posed by the Enlightenment and French Revolution. Those events prompted some to revisit St. Thomas Aquinas's ideas on the "human person," which in turn pointed back to Aristotle. This led to distinctions between "persons" grounded in God's immanent presence and modern ideas of rational and autonomous "individuals." According to Piotr H. Kosicki's *Catholics on the Barricades: Poland, France, and "Revolution,"*[13] Catholic appeals to personhood intensified during upheavals of the late industrial revolution and two world wars.

Shortly after World War II, Jacques Maritain—a key interpreter of Aquinas and friend of Merton—counted at least a dozen versions of "personalism" in circulation.[14] Its framework helped many navigate between the poles of collective totalitarianism (found in fascist or communist states) and individualistic capitalism (integral to Western democracies). Some failed to grant non-Catholic humans, such as Jews, atheists, and agnostics, full "human personhood," while others were more expansive. Piotr Kosicki contends that the Second Vatican Council's Pastoral Constitution on the Church in the Modern World (*Gaudium et Spes*), filled with personalist language, signaled that the Church formally recognized potential personhood in *every* human. As you might expect, Thomas Merton was well ahead of them.

Merton was exposed to European Catholic personalist thinkers early in his religious life. These included Maritain, whom he met while a student at Columbia University and with whom he corresponded from at least 1949. Étienne Gilson—whose book *The Spirit of Medieval Philosophy* played a key role in Merton's conversion to Catholicism—also addressed Aquinas on personhood,[15] and Merton's 1956 journal includes notes from Emmanuel Mounier's book *Personalism*.[16]

Given Merton's focus on intimate connection with others in relationship, understanding Merton's thread of "personalist" commitments becomes key to studying his correspondence and other direct interactions, as well as his views

---

13. Piotr H. Kosicki, *Catholics on the Barricades: Poland, France, and "Revolution," 1891–1956* (New Haven: Yale University Press, 2018). This book provides a helpful overview of the emergence of Catholic personalism and its influence on mid-twentieth century European political thought.

14. Kosicki, *Catholics on the Barricades*, 10.

15. For example, Thomas D. Williams, LC, "What Is Thomist Personalism?" *Alpha Omega* 7, no. 2 (2004): 163–97.

16. Emmanuel Mounier, *Personalism*, trans. Philip Mairet (London: Routledge and Kegan Paul Ltd., 1952).

on human society in general. In *Merton and Walsh on the Person*,[17] Robert Imperato explores "the person" as Merton's "root metaphor."[18] Imperato also makes a strong case that Dan Walsh, Merton's Columbia philosophy instructor and friend, became a major influence on Merton's personalism. Walsh had studied with Gilson, and it was he who introduced Merton to Maritain. Walsh moved to Kentucky in mid-1960 and briefly lived at Gethsemani Abbey before teaching at Bellarmine College in Louisville, where he sometimes lectured on personhood. He and Merton interacted often during the sixties, and Walsh later mentioned that they sometimes discussed personhood. He once noted that "from Maritain, Merton borrowed distinctions between the notions of individual, the common or communal good, and the person in man."[19] But Walsh also suggested that Merton's views on persons were "far from" simply adopting those of Maritain and Gilson, and that he developed them along "less philosophical" and "more spiritual" lines.[20] Imperato credits Merton's monastic formation and its emphasis on "self-knowledge" with initially shaping his thoughts on personhood and framing his "personalist" development. In this, he gives a special nod to Merton's reading of twelfth-century Cistercian fathers, especially founder St. Bernard of Clairvaux, and notes Walsh's suggestion that writings of the thirteenth-century Franciscan Scholastic, Duns Scotus, also influenced Merton. Paul Pearson associates this emphasis with the "monastic theology" developed by Merton's Benedictine correspondent, Jean Leclerc.[21]

Merton's sense of the person relied on more than Catholic sources, though. He drew from Zen, Christian humanist, and Russian Orthodox "wisdom" traditions, as well as existentialist writers.[22] Christopher Pramuk asserts that Merton's attention to Eastern Orthodox wisdom theology and its imagery of Sophia, feminine divine wisdom, serves as a "golden thread" of influence that weaves throughout and holds together his final decade of writing.[23] Pra-

---

17. Robert Imperato, *Merton and Walsh on the Person* (Brookfield, WI: Liturgical Publications, 1987).

18. Imperato, *Merton and Walsh*, 120.

19. Imperato, *Merton and Walsh*, 4.

20. Imperato, *Merton and Walsh*, 4, 89.

21. Paul Pearson to Gordon Oyer, email January 10, 2020.

22. For example, Ross Labrie, "Thomas Merton and Existentialism," *The Merton Seasonal* 43, no. 3 (Fall 2018): 10–13. But Merton also told Alaskan nuns: "I think it is the Orthodox who have the key [to Christian personalism], not the French existentialists and other such groups." *Thomas Merton in Alaska: The Alaskan Conferences, Journals, and Letters*, ed. David D. Cooper and Robert E. Daggy (New York: New Directions, 1988), 87. Cited hereafter as *TMA*.

23. Christopher Pramuk, *Sophia: The Hidden Christ of Thomas Merton* (Collegeville, MN: Liturgical Press, 2009), xxiv.

muk's work implies that this tradition also helped form Merton's perspective on the human person. He attributes to it "Merton's *person*-centered Christology," which "expresses a mystery that applies not only to Jesus Christ but analogically to all human beings, to every person, by virtue of the incarnation, and the potency for *theosis* [becoming like or united with God] that the incarnation inscribes into human being."[24] Pramuk shares this Merton journal quotation of the Russian Orthodox writer Sergius Bulgakov: "Divine Wisdom, the ground source of all ideas, is the eternal humanity in God—the divine prototype and foundation of the being of man."[25]

Merton referred to himself as a personalist when addressing Alaskan nuns in September 1968,[26] but he had begun to expressly identify with personalism in the late 1950s as his social awareness grew. This emerged noticeably in *Disputed Questions* (1960) and *New Seeds of Contemplation* (1961). Here, deploying typically personalist terms, Merton distinguished between the *person*, or what he sometimes referred to as the "true self," and the *individual*, the "false self." Persons are guided by what Mounier called an "affirmation of the *unity of mankind*"[27] and what Merton described as an embrace of the shared "image of God."[28]

In a 1967 letter to Amiya Chakravarty, Merton addressed awareness of this intrinsic unity through contemplative practice, and he described it as the "hidden ground of love," a phrase William H. Shannon borrowed to title his volume of Merton's letters on religious experience and social concerns. In that letter Merton reflected on "the reality that is present to us and in us. ... By being attentive ... we can find ourself engulfed in ... the happiness of being at one with everything in that hidden ground of Love for which there can be no explanations."[29] As Shannon elaborated:

> In [Merton's] religious experience he met God and discovered his own true self in God; but more than that: he also confronted, in God, his fellow men and women—not as a faceless mass, but as persons, each infinitely precious and all linked to one another in a network of relationships, grounded in God, that made them one.

24. Pramuk, *Sophia*, 185. Emphasis in the original.

25. Pramuk, *Sophia*, 156.

26. Merton, "Workshop given at Precious Blood monastery in Alaska," Item 4, subsection E.1, typescript transcript, TMC/BU, 49.

27. Mounier, *Personalism*, 30. Emphasis in the original.

28. Merton, *Disputed Questions* (New York: Farrar, Straus and Cuhady, 1960), xi.

29. Merton to Amiya Chakravarty, April 13, 1967, *HGL* 115.

This is to say that Merton discovered God as the ground of his own being and in that same ground he found the rest of reality, especially his brothers and sisters, in a unity that was beyond separateness.[30]

In contrast to grounded "persons," modern "individuals" construct their identity through an ego-driven separation from (not unity with) others to meet the demands of what Merton termed "mass society." They are caught up in what Mounier called "a play of masks"[31] and what Merton named "illusion."[32] Merton asserted that "the person must be rescued from the individual,"[33] which mirrors Mounier's statement, copied by Merton into his 1956 journal, that "the person is only growing in so far as he is continually purifying himself from the individual within him."[34] It also echoed Maritain's 1925 comment that "the modern order sacrifices the person on the altar of the individual."[35]

Socially, again echoing Mounier, Merton contrasted "communities"—made up of mutually grounded persons relating together in love, freedom, and respect—with "collectivities"—made up of ego-driven individuals who shift their priorities with the latest mass trend.[36] Persons "work for the establishment of that 'Kingdom of God' which is the unity of all men in peace, creativity and love."[37] Significant for his ministry of letters, Merton felt that communities of persons can exist across distance as well as face-to-face. In his 1964 "Message to Poets," written for a gathering of Latin American poets he could not attend, Merton expressed this sense of extended community using the term "solidarity":

The solidarity of poets is not planned and welded together with tactical convictions or matters of policy.... [It] is an elemental fact like

---

30. William Shannon, *HGL* ix.

31. Mounier, *Personalism*, 18.

32. For example, *Disputed Questions*, vii–xii.

33. Thomas Merton, *New Seeds of Contemplation* (New York: New Directions, 1961), 38.

34. Mounier, *Personalism*, 19.

35. Jacques Maritain, *Trois réformateurs: Luther – Descartes – Rousseau: avec six portraits* (Paris: Plon, 1925), 16; quoted in Kosicki, *Catholics on the Barricades*, 40.

36. See Mounier, *Personalism*, 25–29. Merton rarely used the term "community" in this context, but contrasted collectivities to persons relating in "communion" (*New Seeds of Contemplation*, 52–63; *Disputed Questions*, ix).

37. Merton, *Disputed Questions*, xii.

sunlight, like the seasons, like rain. It is something that cannot be organized, it can only happen. It can only be "received." It is a gift to which we must remain open.... Solidarity is not collectivity. The organizers of collective life will deride the seriousness or the reality of our hope.... True solidarity is destroyed by the political art of pitting one [person] against each other and the commercial art of estimating all [persons] at a price.[38]

Merton saw the model for human personhood in the three persons of the Trinity, together holding a shared existential nature, yet each existing "unto the others, for the others."[39] And he linked that divine expression of personhood to his understanding of ultimate Truth, noting that "Truth is a Way and a Person...to be found and followed. Truth is to be lived."[40]

Understanding his view of personhood and its basis for extended community sheds light on how Merton engaged his correspondents. "When you have such a thing as a person," he counseled in his 1968 talk to Alaskan nuns:

You don't measure; you don't judge.... To live on a level of total openness to God's will is to live on a level where no one can judge you.... The one condition the Gospel gives us for this is that you have to do the same for everybody else. You have to assume that everybody that you meet is perhaps on that level.... Christian personalism is a level of respect for others which is so deep that you assume they are all living on this deep level or potentially living on this deep level in the presence of God where you cannot judge because you cannot measure.[41]

Merton's language of "the person" and his appeals to the personhood of others also surface in his published writings on peace, nonviolence, and race. He grounds his views on nonviolence, for instance, in "the truth that is incarnate in a concrete human situation, involving living persons whose rights are

---

38. Thomas Merton, "Message to Poets," *Raids on the Unspeakable* (New York: New Directions, 1966), 156–57.

39. Merton, *TMA* 87.

40. April 20, 1958, *A Search for Solitude: Pursuing the Monk's True Life. The Journals of Thomas Merton: Volume Three, 1952–1960,* ed. Lawrence E. Cunningham (New York: HarperCollins, 1996), 192. Cited hereafter as *SS*.

41. Merton, "Workshop in Alaska," 51.

denied or whose lives are threatened."[42] Merton filled his response to Vatican II's *Gaudium et Spes*, itself steeped in personalist language, with thoughts on human persons, such as:

> The progress of the person and the progress of society therefore go together. Our modern world cannot attain to peace, and to a fully equitable social order, merely by the application of laws which act upon [humanity] from outside.... The transformation of society begins with the person. It begins with the maturing and opening out of personal freedom in relation to other freedoms—in relation to the rest of society.[43]

Likewise, in one of his earliest published writings on race, Merton wrote about the "tragedy" of whites' delusions that they are free, though actually "victim[s] of the same servitudes which [they have] imposed on the Negro." He then asks, "Is there really a genuine freedom for the person or only the irresponsibility of the atomized individual members of mass society?"[44]

Merton's Letters on Social Transformation

If Merton's social writings expressed certain ideas on the implications of human personhood, his letters often embodied them. But in his letters, Merton's commitment to personalist ideals was often tested by the demands for loyalty to causes that social movements often require.

Though Merton's entry into the cloistered life had diverted his attention from events in the world beyond, his gaze toward social concerns began to reawaken during the later 1950s. It emerged as Merton participated in Abbey discussions about founding a Latin American monastery and engaged with his Latin American novices (beginning in 1957). They introduced him to Latin American poets and writers and shared their experience of the gravitational pull felt from this northern U.S. giant.[45] We also see this gaze in his

---

42. Thomas Merton, "Blessed Are the Meek," *Faith and Violence* (Notre Dame, IN: University of Notre Dame Press, 1968), 19.

43. Thomas Merton, "Christian Humanism in the Nuclear Era," *Love and Living* (New York: Farrar, Straus and Giroux, 1979), 154–55.

44. Thomas Merton, "The Legend of Tucker Caliban," *Seeds of Destruction* (New York:Farrar, Straus and Giroux, 1964), 85–86.

45. In "A Letter to Pablo Antonio Cuadra Concerning Giants" (Thomas Merton, *The Collected Poems of Thomas Merton* [New York: New Directions, 1977], 372–91), Merton used "giant" imagery for Cold War power blocs in relation to Latin America.

emerging literary correspondence with dissident writers caught in the orbit of a competing, Soviet giant—writers such as Boris Pasternak and Czeslaw Milosz (both starting in 1958). We see it as he reached out to the pacifist servant to the poor, Dorothy Day (beginning in 1959). And we see it in journal comments of the late 1950s as he revisits with refreshed eyes readings from the pens of social critics such as Karl Marx and Gandhi.

Merton's early published reflections showed his ambivalence toward movements and political ideologies in favor of human freedom grounded in Christ. He initially identified "mass movements" with totalitarian fascist and communist regimes that soaked the mid-twentieth century in waves of bloody violence and oppressive social control.[46] As his public voice on specific social issues began to address nuclear arms in 1961, Merton warmed to the potential for positive movements, and he became affiliated with a Catholic "Pax movement"[47] that he described as a "peace movement we are now starting."[48] At about the same time, his correspondence on peace concerns exploded.

But tensions between his contemplative calling with its personalist priorities and his calling to address social issues and correspond with movement activists tested him the rest of his few remaining years. Trappist censorship followed on the heels of his first anti-nuclear war publications, but Merton continued to interact and correspond sympathetically with movement figures and publish what he could as permitted. At a critical juncture in this journey, Merton's journal captured his realization that: "I can't be a militant in the peace movement and a hermit at the same time," and "I need distance for the development of a new unexplored consciousness, which has nothing directly to do with the strategies of active movements and the proving of an activist conscience—yet is not alien to their struggles."[49] Although Merton sometimes questioned social actions—he still cautioned not to "seek community in all sorts of power movements" in his final year[50]—he remained committed to addressing social concerns.

---

46. For example, he first published "Christianity and Mass Movements" in the July 1958 *Cross Currents*, then included it in *Disputed Questions* as "Christianity and Totalitarianism."

47. Merton to Ernesto Cardenal, December 24, 1961, *The Courage for Truth: Letters to Writers*, ed. Christine M. Bochen (New York: Farrar, Straus and Giroux, 1993), 130. Cited hereafter as *CT*.

48. Merton to Erich Fromm, December 1961, *HGL* 317.

49. N.d., *Dancing in the Water of Life: Seeking Peace in the Hermitage. The Journals of Thomas Merton: Volume Five, 1963–1965*, ed. Robert E. Daggy (New York: HarperCollins, 1997), 341, 342. Cited hereafter as *DWL*. The published version mis-transcribed the word "alien" as "akin."

50. Merton, *TMA* 109.

As his interpersonal encounters with others expanded through correspondence and other interactions, his commitment to engage them as "persons" also grew. One detects throughout these social concern letters Merton's commitment to engage each interaction both without judgment toward the other and as an opportunity to connect with the other's unique personhood. Unlike his interfaith letters, which reflect expanding insight into the spirituality of other traditions as grounding for peace, these letters combine incisive insight into real-world events with the nurturing of deep friendships. At the same time, especially as anti-Vietnam War protests escalated, he sought distance from popular political calculation and from the very movements in which those friends acted. Over the course of these letters, Merton at times found himself simultaneously questioning actions of his friends while still seeking to respect their human freedom and personhood without judgment. We glimpse his desire to offer respect, freedom, acceptance, and love of the other even as he challenges and encourages opening hearts and minds beyond calculated objectives or uncritical loyalty to causes.

Merton's letters to African Americans were written in a milieu of pervasive suspicion and incomprehension across racial divides of the 1960s and steeped in expectations of Blacks' deference to whites. They reflect a different sort of complexity. Whereas his interfaith and peace movement letters emerge from a comparable social status between correspondents, the writers of these letters occupied different social locations. Barriers to communication as equal persons here loomed especially large. The letters needed to bridge generations of entrenched oppression and navigate longstanding resentments that shut down meaningful relationship. As with his letters to peace movement friends, Merton sought distance from political calculation for the sake of greater human connection. To his credit, Merton grasped—decades before most—that as a white man his role was not to instruct Blacks in steps they should take but to address "the whites who refuse to trust [Blacks] or hear [them]."[51]

The letters he received from these friends both informed Merton of current events and interpreted them with insider insight. He corresponded with people living and working on the cutting edge of social change. When fed into Merton's contemplative reflection, their letters bled into Merton's own powerful insight, which could not emerge simply from either correspondence or contemplation in isolation. Each practice needed the other on which to feed and deepen. Merton also appreciated the challenges and discouragement his friends faced in day-to-day battles of resistance and advocacy toward

---

51. Merton, "From Non-Violence to Black Power," *Faith and Violence,* 129.

ends he also sought. His letters of response offered much-appreciated acceptance and encouragement. One can argue that, despite discomfort with certain movement mechanics, his letters ultimately contributed mightily to those movements. Jim Forest concurs: "What he did was mainly by letter and always had its roots in relationships. He raised such important issues."[52]

Precarious Times, Then and Now

Given that we perceive time on a human scale, we might question the current relevance of letters on social issues written more than five decades ago. Our lives are immersed in technologies that evolve at a bewildering pace and require us to perpetually update our daily routines. Modes of interpersonal communication, news reporting, and dissemination of ideas that Americans of the sixties relied on have been rendered obsolete by today's social media. Once-palpable fears that a monolithic Cold War could erupt into nuclear annihilation at any moment now seem more remote. Volunteers rather than draftees staff today's U.S. military machinery. Even that era's countercultural opposition to mainstream materialism and economic priorities now seems quaint. Such differences tempt us to dismiss the social reflections of Merton's generation.

Yet in stepping back for perspective, our times share much with Merton's. Massive nuclear warfare between superpowers seems less imminent, but increased access to nuclear technology makes its use more likely in regional conflicts or by non-state actors seeking to terrorize and disrupt. A voluntary and privatized military coupled with entrenched interests of arms contractors and uncritical post-9/11 patriotism have weakened public oversight and normalized perpetual warfare. While people of color now hold more legal rights than in Merton's day, they endure new forms of marginalization through adapted socio-economic structures, mass incarceration, and police profiling. Social media have not simply expanded our means of public expression, their algorithms fragment and parse communication into echo chambers that perpetuate rather than bridge social divisions similar to those Merton witnessed. The tensions of Merton's final decade have not been transformed; they have simply transitioned into different expressions.

Beyond this, viewing time on a scale longer than a lifetime reveals that Merton's era ultimately remains ours. Thomas Berry called it a new "Ecozoic" era, others an "Anthropocene" epoch. Regardless of what we name it,

---

52. Jim Forest email to Gordon Oyer, November 5, 2018.

both Merton and we have found ourselves at the dawn of this period when our species began to leave an indelible geological imprint on our planet, and when we in the "developed" world must come to terms with our limits and our interdependence, as well as our power. We humans now hold the capacity for our own self-destruction, either in the flash of a nuclear moment or in pan-generational climate asphyxiation and mass extinction. These forces transcend specific policies and practices. They are driven by widely held, Western and "enlightened" assumptions about our relationship to each other and our planet. Assumptions of unlimited extraction, industrialization, and economic growth. Assumptions that fetishize competition and individual wealth accumulation. Assumptions that prioritize economic efficiency and technological innovation over and above their consequences for lived human experience.

Seen from this broadened perspective, our times remain precarious due to forces shared with Merton's times. If there is a difference, it mainly lies in the degree to which those forces have deepened their hold and begun to play out in real time. Technocratic processes we invested in to preserve our way of life have become destructive of it. Indicators such as wealth inequality, species extinction, and carbon emissions track the unrelenting march of the Anthropocene. Even U.S. middle classes feel its weight bearing down, and reinvigorated patterns of reaction double down to secure systems of privilege and levels of comfort that cannot be sustained. We may laud material or technical measures of increased human wealth, life span, comfort. But seen in geological time, we resemble miners celebrating overtime pay while ignoring the canaries that litter the mine shaft floor. Our sense of loss and grief, whether for our biosphere or our democratic aspirations, grows.

What Merton continues to offer in such times is a profound awareness and critique of those forces at their root. He focused his contemplative gifts on what churns below more than on fleeting manifestations that bubble to the surface. His insights drew from the common ground of our being that unites us with all of creation, rather than from superficial cultures that fragment us into irreconcilable difference. He developed his social vision in dialogue with events of his day, but he publicly expressed it through written reflections that challenged worldviews driving those events. In this, he sought to inspire in others not just a more contemplative and interconnected *awareness*, but *actions* grounded in that awareness. Merton envisioned that through *aware actions* that are respectful of persons we might not only address concrete human needs but also resist and transform those colonial, industrial, and technological paradigms that hold captive our imaginations.

Hope and Action

Given Thomas Merton's own recurring doubts that humanity would ultimately embrace the transformation he advocated, it may seem ironic to include "hope" in the title of a book on his letters. Besides, invoking hope two
decades into the twenty-first century has fallen out of favor. There are reasons for this. Hope in unseen outcomes or a heavenly reward has too often
been misused to hinder meaningful action; calculated appeals to patiently
hope have quieted dissent and permitted oppressive machinery to grind away
unchallenged. Also, prematurely invoking hope can harm by circumventing
our need to accept and grieve loss before moving onward. As one observer
states, "We must move through the hopelessness of admitting what... can no
longer change in order to find new hope in what we can."[53] And then some
who most deeply experienced the grasp of Western domination consider it
futile to even imagine possibilities for a just, mutually shared society, let
alone act in hope toward them.[54] Beyond all this, our driven and action-
obsessed culture often overwhelms reflective, purposeful, and hope-grounded
action with a compulsion for "activism" that demands constant motion for its
own sake.

To further complicate our views on hope, we often conflate it with optimism. Assumptions of control over and certainty of outcomes reflect confident, pragmatic optimism rather than genuine hope's active pursuit of possibility. Today's actions may *influence* our collective future, but we as
individuals cannot *direct* our future with confident certainty, despite our
shrewdest calculations. The most we can do is offer up our best efforts with
our best intentions based on our best discernment and act in "hope" that they
will bear the fruit we seek. Confusion between hope and optimism seems
woven into the "case against hope" by commentator Roxanne Gay: "I don't
traffic in hope. Realism is more my ministry than unbridled optimism.
...Hope allows us to leave what is possible in the hands of others.... So
much of what is possible is, in fact, in our hands.... When we hope we have
no control over what may come to pass.... We abdicate responsibility."[55]

---

53. Lane Patriquin, "The Zeitgeist of Grief," *Geez* 54 (Fall 2019): 31.

54. Thanks to Andrew J. Stone Porter for introducing me to the critique of
"Afro-Pessimism," which posits that Black experience is so removed from dominant
Western experience that it renders impossible any possibility of real communication
and reconciliation across racial divides.

55. Roxane Gay, "The Case against Hope," *New York Times*, June 6, 2019, https://
www.nytimes.com/2019/06/06/opinion/hope-politics-2019.html.

Gay wisely resists abdication of responsibility, and her preference to act toward realizing possibilities rather than passively wait on others is crucial. But genuine hope *motivates* sober and responsible pursuit of the possible; it does not express unbridled optimism in fantasies. Hope-inspired effort to engage entrenched problems prompts action toward possible but uncertain outcomes, not toward propped-up illusions of control over them. Acting responsibly in hope requires that we transcend the memes of control and power we are socialized to embrace. History is littered with too much evidence of unintended consequences and ironic outcomes to realistically imagine otherwise. This posture reflects genuine "realism." For, as another observer suggests, "Hope grounded in realism gives birth to hopeful pessimism" rather than unbridled optimism, even as it "informs realism of the possibilities of the future."[56]

For those informed through reflection and prayer and dialogue within faith-based communities, the choice to act relies primarily on our hope that the "Great Mystery," to borrow a Lakota term,[57] will honor those offerings. As Merton grasped better than most, God receives and weaves together human actions and intentions in ways we could never have calculated or imagined. We offer our service to other beings and our resistance to forces that dominate human freedom in hope they somehow may be integrated into that larger flow of life and creativity. It is this hope that empowers us to act within human history, without optimistic or blind assumptions that outcomes we seek will magically materialize simply through good intentions and force of will. As Václav Havel stated, "Hope is not the conviction that something will turn out well, but the certainty that something is worth doing no matter how it turns out."[58] Or, in the words of Rebecca Solnit:

> To hope is to gamble. It's to bet on the future, on your desires, on the possibility that an open heart and uncertainty is better than gloom and safety. To hope is dangerous, and yet it is the opposite of fear, for to live is to risk.... Hope just means another world might be possible, not promised, not guaranteed. Hope calls for action; action is impossible without hope.[59]

---

56. Lawrence J. Terlizzese paraphrasing Jacques Ellul in *Hope in the Thought of Jacques Ellul* (Eugene, OR: Cascade Books, 2005), 199, 200.

57. "Wakan Tanka" in Lakota. Louis S. Warren, *God's Red Son: The Ghost Dance Religion and the Making of Modern America* (New York: Basic Books, 2017), 159. Also translated "Great Holy" or "Great Spirit."

58. Václav Havel, *Disturbing the Peace*, https://www.vhlf.org/havel-quotes/-disturbing-the-peace/.

59. Rebecca Solnit, *Hope in Dark Times: Untold Histories, Wild Possibilities*, 3rd ed. (Chicago: Haymarket Books, 2016), 4.

Signs of Hope

Merton would concur. Having just entered his hermitage, he penned in late 1965 that

> the Christian cannot be fully what he is meant to be in the modern world if he is not in some way interested in *building a better society*, free of war, of racial and social injustice, of poverty, and of discrimination.... On the contrary, eschatological Christian hope is inseparable from an incarnational involvement in the struggle of living and contemporary [humanity].[60]

In another reflection written near the same time, Merton ties that "eschatological" social hope back to personal human connection:

> From this basic experience [of loving and having been loved by others], one can, after all, recover hope for the other dimension of [human] life: the political.... It does not make logical sense to be too hopeful, but once again this is not a question of logic and one does not look for signs of hope in the newspapers or the pronouncements of world leaders.... Because there is love in the world, and because Christ has taken our nature to Himself, there remains always the hope that [humanity] will finally, after many mistakes and even disasters, learn to disarm and to make peace, recognizing that [we] *must* live at peace with [our sister and] brother.[61]

And, we might add, with our planet.

Though not a stereotypical "activist," Thomas Merton nonetheless saw his own monastic vocation and its withdrawal into the solitude of a hermitage as one of taking personal responsibility and acting in hope. In assessing a world infected with a pandemic "virus of mendacity," Merton considered his solitude as something that was not

> a rejection of other [people]; but it may well be a quiet and perhaps almost despairing refusal to accept the myths and fictions with

---

60. Merton, "Christian Humanism in the Nuclear Era," *Love and Living*, 156; Merton's emphasis.

61. Thomas Merton, *Conjectures of a Guilty Bystander* (Garden City, NY: Doubleday, 1966), 214.

which social life is always full—and never more than today. But to despair of the lies with which [humanity] surrounds [itself] is not to despair of [humanity]. Perhaps, on the contrary, it is a sign of hope.

So when, as in our time, the whole world seems to have become one of immense and idiotic fiction, and when the virus of mendacity creeps into every vein and organ of the social body, it would be abnormal and immoral if there were no reaction. It is even healthy that the reaction should sometimes take the form of outspoken protest.... The desert is for those who have felt a salutary despair of accepted values, in order to hope in mercy and to be themselves merciful [persons] to whom that mercy is promised. Such solitaries know the evils that are in other [people] because they experience these evils first in themselves.[62]

Merton continued this reflection by emphasizing that withdrawal in hope does not also mean absence of communication:

The Christian hope in God...must take on visible and symbolic forms, in order to communicate its message.... Some [people] will seek clarity in isolation and silence... to withdraw from the babel of confusion in order to listen more patiently to the voice of their conscience and to the Holy Spirit.... [The resulting] renewal will communicate itself to others who remain "in the world," and will help them to also have a clearer vision, a sharper and more uncompromising appreciation of Christian truth.[63]

Although Merton believed in transcendent spiritual communication with others, he took it upon himself to also communicate a clarified vision explicitly and directly through his gift of writing. As with his published work, typing his letters was not passive; it was a step of action. The content of his letters did not promote passivity. It encouraged action. These letters on social transformation therefore offer his personal "signs of hope" that our human social and political and economic actions may somehow converge to realize God's intent for our species, its society, and the rest of creation.

Merton invoked the phrase "sign of hope" twice in his letters collected within *The Hidden Ground of Love*. The first appears in a 1959 letter to

---

62. Thomas Merton, "The Solitary Life," *The Monastic Journey of Thomas Merton*, ed. Brother Patrick Hart (Kansas City: Sheed Andrews and McMeel, 1977), 152–53.

63. Merton, "The Solitary Life," 152–53.

British author John P. Harris regarding Boris Pasternak's literary protests and odes to dignity and love found in his poetry and the novel *Doctor Zhivago*. Here Merton names Pasternak as a unique "sign of hope." He goes on to elaborate: "The simplicity of this human voice speaking directly and reaching everyone, in spite of all the barriers erected around him, is a portent of immense significance in an age when men can communicate with the moon but not with one another."[64]

The second appears in a 1962 letter to Catherine de Hueck Doherty, his mentor when he volunteered in her Harlem house of hospitality before entering the monastery. In this case, Merton shares his sense of suffering following Trappist censorship forbidding him to publish on matters of war and peace. He writes, "The fact that we suffer from the things that make us suffer, the fact that we cannot find any way out of suffering, is perhaps a sign of hope." He seems to suggest that if our efforts to address social ills do *not* invoke a sense of suffering, perhaps our actions were poorly grounded to begin with. Merton then offers a sense of what that more solid grounding requires:

> What is wanted is love. But love has been buried under words, noise, plans, projects, systems, and apostolic gimmicks.... We will not see anything clear, but we must do [God's] will.... And that may mean cutting through a whole forest of empty talk and clichés and nonsense just to begin to find some glimmer of [God's] will. To obey always and not know for sure if we are really obeying. That is not fun at all, and people like to get around the responsibility by entering into a routine of trivialities in which everything seems clear and noble and defined: but when you look at it honestly it falls apart.[65]

Like Pasternak's literary output, Merton's letters on social transformation offer a "portent of immense significance." The "simplicity" of his own "human voice" that emerges from these letters encourages a sustained hopeful focus during the long haul toward social transformation. And as expressed to de Hueck Doherty, though he recognizes a need to act, he also encourages us to not "get around the responsibility" of seeking clarity through blind immersion in "activity" that buries "love" under "noise," "projects," and "gimmicks," and that obscures any "glimmer of [God's] will." He encourages us not to simplistically enter into a "routine of trivialities" that superficially may appear "clear and noble and defined." He urges

---

64. Merton to John Harris, January 3, 1959, *HGL* 385.
65. Merton to Catherine de Hueck Doherty, June 4, 1962, *HGL* 19.

that we seek in hope to obey the God of Love without knowing "for sure" if we are really obeying.

In relinquishing such certitudes and embracing the suffering of setbacks, all that remains to motivate persistent and responsible action is hope. Merton offered his activist friends and Black correspondents the gifts of respect for their freedom to act and recognition of their human personhood. Packaged into his letters, these gifts served them—and continue to serve us—as profound signs of an enduring hope in the Kingdom vision toward which they jointly aspired.

PART I

ADVANCING A CATHOLIC GOSPEL OF PEACE

This section features letters with four of Thomas Merton's friends on whom he relied and with whom he co-labored to inspire a peace witness among Catholics and across U.S. society. Their correspondence illuminates Merton's vision and priorities for that Gospel of Peace. These letters also supplement the insights of his published works on peace and help chart his pilgrimage through the turbulent 1960s landscape of militarism and faith-based resistance to it.

Merton began his exchange with Dorothy Day (chapter 1) in 1959 and his exchanges with Jim Douglass, Jim Forest, and Daniel Berrigan (chapters 2–4) in the fall of 1961. These last three exchanges began just as his public voice against atomic warfare also emerged, signified by publication in *The Catholic Worker* of his poem, "Chant to Be Used in Processions around a Site with Furnaces" (August), and updated essay, "The Root of War Is Fear" (October). That same fall Merton also engaged at least three of these four individuals on plans to establish the U.S. Catholic peace advocacy group PAX (to become Pax Christi a decade later), modeled on a British group with the same name.

Several themes interweave among these letters: the Cold War and public accommodation of nuclear proliferation; establishing PAX; treatment of nuclear arms and conscientious objection to military service in the Second Vatican Council's Pastoral Constitution on the Church in the Modern World (*Gaudium et Spes*); establishment of the Catholic Peace Fellowship; controversy over the self-immolation of Catholic Worker volunteer Roger LaPorte as a Vietnam War protest; escalating Catholic antiwar protest through draft card burning and draft board raids. The letters reveal what was involved in grappling with questions of absolute pacifism, nonviolence and nonviolent resistance, Catholic just war and social teachings, and ideals taught by Mahatma Gandhi and Jesus. They also express concern over reluctance among church leadership to publicly support peacemaking as a Catholic vocation.

Merton wrote to many others active in this circle, including Philip Berrigan, Tom Cornell, Eileen Egan, Jean and Hildegard Goss-Mayr, and Gordon Zahn. Though these exchanges also reveal much about Merton, their correspondence mostly lacks the volume and breadth of his letters to these four friends. A significant omission due to space constraints is Merton's correspondence with John Heidbrink, director of interfaith relations for the Fellowship of Reconciliation (FOR). Although Protestant, Heidbrink belongs here, perhaps under a "bridge-building" theme; they exchanged at least sixty-five letters between October 1961 and April 1967. Heidbrink worked diligently to create a Catholic FOR affiliate, intent on bridging the skepticism with which Protestants and Catholics of that era regarded each other. Toward this end he helped initiate PAX in 1961, which ultimately declined FOR affiliation, but he later succeeded in 1964 when the Catholic Peace Fellowship was founded as a FOR affiliate. Heidbrink also wooed Daniel and Philip Berrigan, Jim Forest, and Merton into FOR membership, which connected them with Protestant peacemakers and nurtured collaborative peace advocacy.

Other Merton correspondence reached beyond Catholicism and into that ecumenical peacemaking realm. His "Cold War Letters" alone—112 collected letters that critique nuclear warfare, written between October 1961 and October 1962—include 81 different recipients, with only 9 letters addressed to members of his Catholic peace circle. Most of his letters and published works hold broadly Christian, not narrowly Catholic, relevance and remain fully accessible to non-Catholics. Yet Merton deeply yearned for a specifically Catholic peace witness and nurtured that.

Consequently, his letters to these four friends explore an expansive vision for peace that speaks to yet transcends his own tradition. In them Merton models subordinating his ego to his calling as a contemplative monk and larger social needs. His voice against nuclear arms and the militarism they fostered emerged when he felt no one else in his Church—at least no one beyond the marginalized Catholic Worker movement—either grasped or addressed the urgent crisis the Cold War posed. Following Merton's censorship by his order, Pope John XXIII issued the encyclical *Pacem in Terris*, the Vatican Council in its Pastoral Constitution on the Church in the Modern World addressed conscientious objection, and other Catholic clergy began to speak out. Merton's urgency to lend his public voice then waned, and in a perpetual dance of balancing his prophetic voice with his contemplative practice, Merton welcomed the opportunity to withdraw further into solitude. Yet he did so just as friends were ramping up their antiwar activism. He then faced the challenge of increased solitude when others had come to expect his public voice, link his published words with activists' choices, or undervalue the centrality of contemplation in his life.

Merton continued to pursue that balance from his hermitage as he criticized the escalating U.S. role in Vietnam and compiled his final book on social issues published during his lifetime, *Faith and Violence*. During this period, he took care to distinguish his views from those of friends whose tactics sometimes gave him pause, even as he offered them prayers, personal support, and programmatic advice through his letters.

1

PRAYER, PERSEVERANCE, PEACE

THE MERTON-DAY LETTERS

Perseverance is not hanging to some course which we have set our minds to, and refusing to let go. . . . God . . . loves and helps best those who are so beat and have so much nothing [they] . . . gradually lost everything. . . . Hence perseverance is not hanging on but letting go.

— Thomas Merton to Dorothy Day
February 4, 1960[1]

Few figures if any loom larger in twentieth-century American Catholic social thought than Dorothy Day and Thomas Merton. When the name of one surfaces, the other often follows, as Pope Francis famously demonstrated in his 2015 address to the U.S. Congress. He named both, together with Abraham Lincoln and Martin Luther King Jr. as "great Americans" who helped "shape fundamental values which will endure forever in the spirit of American people." To the pontiff, Day exemplified Gospel-inspired "passion for justice and for the cause of the oppressed," whereas Merton "challenged the certitudes of his time" as "a man of dialogue, a promoter of peace between peoples and religions."[2] Little wonder these co-religionists and contemporaries found each other and forged a bond of friendship, mutual support, and respect.

The more one learns of each, however, the more ironic it seems for both to be heralded in the halls of Congress. Neither placed great faith in nationalist U.S. ambitions or embraced traditional American political agendas. As their letters display, they both adamantly rejected the currents of militarism that undergird American identity for much of its citizenry, and they challenged the

---

1. *HGL* 137.

2. http://w2.vatican.va/content/francesco/en/speeches/2015/september/documents/papa-francesco_20150924_usa-us-congress.html.

economic individualism that informs the daily aspirations of most Americans. The core identity of each rested instead in their Catholic faith and in their deep confidence in the power and role of prayer, not just in their personal lives but in the broad workings of human society and relationships. Both Day and Merton also viewed others through a personalist lens that saw intrinsic and holy worth in each person they encountered.

Yet despite their many common priorities, they did not always agree on the details of an engaged faith and they occasionally navigated differences. At those times their correspondence also reveals two spiritually mature and seasoned elders of the Church granting one another grace and encouragement to move forward, to persevere in living out their respective vocations. Theirs is a model sorely needed in today's poisoned milieu of acrid and bitter discourse.

Dorothy Day (1897–1980)[3]

Like Thomas Merton, Dorothy Day converted to Catholicism as an adult following a season of bohemian exploration.

She was born in Brooklyn to parents who had abandoned their Episcopalian (mother) and Congregationalist (father) traditions and raised their children unchurched. Her father covered horse racing for newspapers, a career that prompted moves to San Francisco, then Chicago, and later back to New York.

A Young Life in Motion

Several early experiences anticipated and shaped Dorothy's future vocation as writer and servant to the poor. The instinctive outpouring of assistance to strangers that she witnessed in the wake of the 1906 San Francisco earthquake left an indelible impression. Her childhood love of diverse literature included Thomas à Kempis's *The Imitation of Christ*, the work of Russian anarchist Peter Kropotkin, and Upton Sinclair's *The Jungle*. The last book, coupled with her older brother's newspaper coverage of Chicago's working poor, inspired her to explore the city's tenement neighborhoods and follow its labor movement. During her two years at the University of Illinois she learned to love Russian literature, made leftist friends, and began to write for university and local newspapers.

---

3. Details of Dorothy Day's life primarily from Jim Forest, *All Is Grace: A Biography of Dorothy Day* (Maryknoll, NY: Orbis Books, 2011) and Brigid O'Shea Merriman, OSF, *Searching for Christ: The Spirituality of Dorothy Day* (Notre Dame, IN: University of Notre Dame Press, 1994).

When Dorothy's family returned to New York in 1916, she moved with them and began to eke out a life on her own while writing for socialist newspapers. She would be arrested twice, once for participating in a suffragist march in Washington, DC, and again when caught up in a raid during post–World War I anti-communist paranoia. Dorothy fell in love, aborted a pregnancy, married, and then divorced. Observing the piety of Catholic housemates and seeking the solitude of Catholic sanctuary spaces sparked a spiritual awakening that expanded her curiosity about the Church.

Dorothy Day, ca. 1965
(Courtesy of Catholic Worker Archives, Marquette University)

Dorothy experienced her second pregnancy in 1925 as a joyful confirmation of God's presence, but her atheist common-law husband, Forster Batterham, felt otherwise. After the birth of their daughter, Tamar, Dorothy had her baptized in the Catholic Church, which created an irreconcilable rift with Forster. Day felt his parting as a profound loss, and she remained committed to celibacy for the remainder of her life.

The Catholic Worker and Spiritual Maturity

Dorothy also chose baptism for herself in 1927. This difficult decision created cognitive dissonance as an act of "going over to the opposition, because the church was lined up with property, with the wealthy, with capitalism, with all the forces of reaction."[4] While covering a December 1932 labor march in Washington, DC, Dorothy visited the National Shrine of the Immaculate Conception and offered a prayer for a way to use her talents to aid the poor. Upon her return, she was met by Peter Maurin, whom the editor of *Commonweal* magazine had referred to Dorothy as someone with similar ideas. Their meeting launched a collaboration that would end only seventeen years later with Maurin's death. The following May they published their first

---

4. Forest, *All Is Grace*, 84.

issue of *The Catholic Worker*, and by year's end its print runs numbered in the tens of thousands. In mid-1935 their community began renting space for hospitality to the homeless, and sister communities sprouted in other cities. The Catholic Worker movement was off and running.

Dorothy's and Peter's strengths complemented each other. Where Peter, twenty years Dorothy's senior, offered an intellectual and theoretical framework for the movement, Dorothy offered pragmatic, hands-dirty, on-the-street dedication to living it out, as well as the means to spread those views through their newspaper. They expressed their own brand of personalist Christian anarchism that combined reverence for each human's dignity with personal responsibility for social transformation. Unwavering commitment to pacifism during World War II cost the movement considerable popular support and staffing. But it survived the war, resumed its growth, and filled a unique niche as social conscience and gadfly in the U.S. Catholic Church.

Dorothy's rich inner life also expanded. Brigid O'Shea Merriman suggests that the essence of Day's spiritual quest focused on uniting love of God with love of neighbor, and "the meeting place for both was her ardent love of Christ: Christ as God made human and Christ within in every human being."[5] Merriman notes several spiritual streams of influence, including the controversial Lacouture Catholic retreat movement.[6] Founded by the Jesuit French Canadian Onesimus Lacouture and based on Ignatian Spiritual Exercises, it emphasized a committed ascetic lifestyle as evidence of love for God and neighbor, one grounded in "prayer, detachment, imitation of Christ's poverty, and love for those who are difficult to love."[7] Lacouture met with criticism and censure for his focus on human depravity and the supernatural over the natural. Two of his students, Fr. John Hugo and Fr. Pacifique Roy, were Day's spiritual mentors and they both surface in her correspondence with Merton.[8]

Jim Forest observed that "the Catholic Worker example of community, as Dorothy saw it, had much in common with the monastic model."[9] Aspects of St. Benedict's Rule, such as its call for hospitality and grounding in disciplines of work and prayer, especially appealed to Day. Her early appeals for financial support in the 1930s led to relationships with various abbeys. She

---

5. Merriman, *Searching for Christ*, 166.

6. For an inside perspective of the impact Fr. Hugo and this movement had on Dorothy and the Catholic Worker community, see Kate Hennessy, *Dorothy Day: The World Will Be Saved by Beauty. An Intimate Portrait of My Grandmother* (New York: Scribner, 2017), 125–32.

7. Merriman, *Searching for Christ*, 134.

8. Merriman, *Searching for Christ*, 165, 167.

9. Forest, *All Is Grace*, 135.

became an oblate—a lay person affiliated with a Catholic monastic order—
of one monastery and closely related to another.[10] Dorothy also saw the earliest Desert Fathers as models and resonated with Fr. Charles de Foucauld, a
Trappist-formed hermit who lived among indigenous Muslims in the Sahara
during the early twentieth century. For a time, Dorothy related to a secular
fraternity inspired by Foucauld. Merton shared her interest in all these
monastic expressions.

Thomas Merton's Relationship with Dorothy Day

Dorothy Day and Thomas Merton regarded each other with respectful deference during their decade of friendship through letters. Day was Merton's senior by seventeen years and had joined the Church twelve years before his
own conversion. Though Merton admired her dedication to peace and the
poor, as well as her spiritual maturity, he lamented that most Catholics con-
signed Day to the Church's margins, someone "whom everybody dismisses
with a shrug of the shoulders."[11] From Day's view as a devout Catholic
layperson, Merton held institutional stature as both priest and monk, plus
considerable status as a popular spiritual writer.

Along with the contents of their letters, their salutations and signatures
show a growing familiarity that shrank the barriers often raised by formal
status. Day consistently addressed Merton using his monastic name, "Father
Louis"; yet after signing her first two letters "Dorothy Day," she mostly
signed them "Dorothy." Merton signed his first four letters "Father Louis,"
then "Tom Merton," with an occasional "Tom." Following his first letter to
"Miss Day," he addressed all others to "Dorothy."

The pair never met face-to-face, though they briefly planned to in late
1963. A Trappist monk named Father Charles—previously Jack English, a
trusted member of her New York Catholic Worker community—had suffered
a heart attack during his December 1963 visit to Gethsemani Abbey. Dorothy
considered traveling to visit him, and Merton as well, but with news of Father Charles's speedy recovery, she opted against the trip.[12]

---

10. Oblate of St. Procopius Abbey in Lisle, Illinois, which sought to reconcile
Eastern Orthodoxy with the Roman Catholic Church; close relationship to English Benedictine congregation in Portsmouth, Rhode Island. Merriman, *Searching for Christ*, 104.

11. Merton to Ernesto Cardenal, December 24, 1961, *CT* 130.

12. Jim Forest (*Living with Wisdom* [Maryknoll, NY: Orbis Books, 2008], 135)
suggests they met when Day visited St. Bonaventure where Merton taught (fall 1940
through fall of 1941), but clarified otherwise in a January 21, 2019, email to Gordon

Prior Awareness and Initial Contact

Merton and Day knew of each other prior to corresponding, though. In one letter, Merton suggests pre-monastic awareness of her in relation to his brief 1941 service at Catherine de Hueck Doherty's Harlem house of hospitality, which was not affiliated with the Catholic Worker movement: "To me the *Catholic Worker*...stands for my own youth and for the kind of influences that shaped my own life thirty years ago. It happened that I went to Friendship House rather than CW because I was at Columbia, FH was just down the hill and so on."[13] Following the 1948 publication of *Seven Storey Mountain*, Merton sent several copies to the New York Catholic Worker, some of which Day distributed to old leftist friends.[14] In his first letter to Day, sent in April 1959, Merton acknowledged: "It occasionally happens that I see a copy of the Worker."[15] And a week before he typed that initial letter, he had advised a colleague, who inquired about preparing for the role of novice master, to include Day in his background reading.[16]

Two decades before she corresponded with Merton, Day had struck up another letter-based friendship with Gethsemani's Abbot Frederic Dunne,

Oyer (confirmed by Robert Ellsberg email to Jim Forest, January 21, 2019). Regarding Jack English, see Merton to Day, December 4, 1963, *HGL* 148; Day to Merton, [December ?]; *American Catholic Pacifism: The Influence of Dorothy Day and the Catholic Worker Movement*, ed. Anne Klejment and Nancy L. Roberts (Westport, CT: Praeger, 1996), 112; December 3, 1963, journal entry, *DWL* 42; Br. Paul Quenon email to Gordon Oyer, January 16, 2019. Paul Elie (*The Life You Save May Be Your Own* [New York: Farrar, Straus and Giroux, 2003, 412–13) notes that Merton and Day missed each other while in Washington, DC, in August 1968 when Day attended a liturgical conference and Merton visited the Indonesian ambassador regarding his Asian journey. But the conference was held during the week (Day attended a Monday night performance of Merton's "Freedom Songs") whereas Merton arrived Friday night, so it's doubtful both were in town at the same time. Neither their journals nor correspondence suggest either was aware they could have met.

13. Merton to Day, December 29, 1965, *HGL* 151.

14. Day to Merton, Feast of the Sacred Heart [June 4,] 1959, *All the Way to Heaven: The Selected Letters of Dorothy Day*, ed. Robert Ellsberg (Maryknoll, NY: Orbis Books, 2012), 255. Day indicates she received the copies "some years ago"; the *Daily Worker* ceased publication in January 1958.

15. Merton to Day, April 22, 1959, original in Dorothy Day Papers, Special Collection and Archives, Marquette University, Milwaukee, WI.

16. Merton to Mark Weidner, OSCO, April 15, 1959, *The School of Charity: Letters on Religious Renewal and Spiritual Direction*, ed. Brother Patrick Hart (New York: Farrar, Straus and Giroux, 1990), 119. Cited hereafter as *SCH*.

presumably as an outgrowth of her fundraising efforts.[17] But beyond Day's receipt of Merton's autobiography, her early awareness of Merton is demonstrated through excerpts from his poems and published writings reprinted in *The Catholic Worker* during the decade before they corresponded. The earliest appeared in January 1948, prior to publication of *Seven Storey Mountain*: his poem "Clairvaux Prison" accompanied by a review of his poetry volume that contained it, *Figures for an Apocalypse*.[18]

Merton kicked off their relationship in April 1959 by forwarding some gifts received for his novices unbefitting their ascetic enclave, such as "scented soap, fancy toothpaste and other articles of that nature." He stated in his accompanying letter that he thought the Worker might find a good use for them, and he commended Dorothy's paper as "one of the few Catholic publications in this country" possessing "the breath of the Holy Spirit." He lamented that "so few religious men should take seriously the idea of praying, doing penance, and practicing non-violent resistance in the cause of peace," and commended her community as "among the very very few who use any spiritual means at all." Merton closed asking prayers for him and his novices, describing her prayers as "of far greater worth in God's sight than ours."[19] The correspondence this initiated lasted until Merton's death. They exchanged at least one letter, usually more, in each of the following years—except perhaps for 1964, part of a unique, seventeen-month gap in the archival record. Thirty pieces of correspondence from Merton have survived, two of which he included in his Cold War Letters. Twenty-two from Day remain, although their letters allude to another five or six from her.

An array of shared interests helped to solidify the bonds of friendship thus launched. In addition to their common background as Catholic converts and writers, their mutual commitment to nonviolence, and their opposition to war and racism, they also shared a love of literature (especially Russian writers) and an appreciation for Eastern orthodoxy and indigenous peoples. Their shared respect for monastic experience often dovetailed, especially regarding that tradition's commitment to a life of prayer. They also endured similar frustrations and disappointments over limited openness to their social views within the Catholic Church.

---

17. Merriman, *Searching for Christ*, 108.

18. Merriman, *Searching for Christ*, 109. Other excerpts were from *Seeds of Contemplation* ("Poverty," April 1949); *Sign of Jonas* (September and October 1956); *Thoughts in Solitude* (June 1958).

19. Merton to Day, April 22, 1959, Dorothy Day Papers.

Spiritual Encouragement and Prayer

Dorothy's status as Merton's senior in both age and mature faith was unique among his circle of correspondents on social concerns, many of whom were younger than he. Merton saw her as a spiritual mentor, and the tone of his letters reflects deference. Jim Forest concurred that "Merton probably had less influence on Dorothy than she had on him."[20] But respect certainly flowed both ways, with Dorothy perhaps benefiting from Merton's published writings at least as much as through their correspondence. She regularly affirmed to him the value of what he published, though in her diary she critiqued his perspective on a couple of occasions. In her first two letters she noted, "We are all intensely grateful to you for all your writings and it delights me especially to see them in bus stations and drug stores as I travel bout the country,"[21] and "Your books are regarded as treasures around the CW and keep circulating."[22] She shared examples of how those in her community benefited, reporting that one troubled member had exclaimed, "Thank God for Thomas Merton," in reference to material in *The Thomas Merton Reader*.[23] Three years later Dorothy reported back that although the same person had been "going bad" with "men and marijuana," she was now "fine—has a good husband, a child and has retreated to the countryside."[24] Once they began to correspond, many original pieces by Merton appeared in *The Catholic Worker*, and it continued to print excerpts from and reviews of his books. In the years following his death Dorothy would return to his writings in her personal reading and listen to tapes of his lectures.

If asked, though, one suspects that Day may have named Merton's prayers as the source of his greatest benefit to her life and work. Her letters are filled with detailed prayer requests. Jim Forest also attests to her faith in the power of prayer, with her copious lists of names of people for whom to pray. He quotes her comment that, "If an outsider who comes to visit us doesn't pay attention to our praying and what that means, then he'll miss the whole point" of their service to the poor.[25] On occasion, Day pours out to Merton her frustrations with the challenges and dysfunction that accompany hospitality to the poor. She made special note of young mothers in her midst

---

20. Forest, "Work Hard, Pray Hard."
21. Day to Merton, June 4, 1959, *All the Way to Heaven*, 255.
22. Day to Merton, June 20 [1959], *All the Way to Heaven*, 255.
23. Day to Merton, November 12 [1962], *All the Way to Heaven*, 289.
24. Day to Merton, December 2, 1965, *All the Way to Heaven*, 320.
25. Forest, *All Is Grace*, 322.

abandoned by the men who had fathered their children. She was also quick to correct Merton's perception that cultural "beats" staffed her programs, and she dismissed the few who did as a "fly by night crew." They

> despised and ignored the poor around us and scandalized them by their dress and morals. I am afraid I am uncharitable about the intellectual who shoulders his way in to eat before the men on the line who have done the hard work of the world, and who moves in on the few men in one of the apartments and tries to edge them out with their beer parties and women. . . . Unfortunately we are left with the women who are pregnant, for whom I beg your prayers.

She added her gendered perspective that, "As far as I am concerned, I must look on these things as a woman, and therefore much concerned with the flesh and with what goes to sustain it."[26]

For his part, Merton also regularly asked for prayers, and he often expressed to her and others his admiration for Dorothy and her legacy. He told her the movement she had birthed was "a real sign of life . . . full of a certain truth that one looks for in vain in many other quarters,"[27] and "something absolutely unique and alive in the American Church," adding, "If there were no Catholic Worker and such forms of witness, I would never have joined the Catholic Church."[28] In praise of her to Dom Gabriel Sortais, the Trappist abbot general in Rome, he asserted: "Dorothy Day, who founded this [Catholic Worker] movement and this paper, is one of the holiest persons among us,"[29] and to an unnamed nun he shared, "I think Dorothy Day is there as an example of what it means to take Christianity seriously in the twentieth century."[30]

Respectful Difference

Merton sometimes lagged in grasping Day's perspective, however. She seemingly overlooked his faux pas in an early letter that showed him unaware of her claim to Christian anarchism. When Merton shared his emerging social concerns with her in mid-1961, he wrote: "I find myself more and more drifting toward the derided and probably quite absurd and defeatist

---

26. Day to Merton, June 4, 1962, *All the Way to Heaven*, 287.
27. Merton to Day, March 21, 1962, *HGL* 144.
28. Merton to Day, December 29, 1965, *HGL* 151.
29. Merton to Sortais, May 26, 1962, *SCH* 144.
30. Merton to Sister K., March 10, 1967, *SCH* 329.

position of a sort of Christian anarchist. This of course would be foolish, if I were to follow it to the end."[31] Dorothy did not challenge the comment, and six years later Merton shared a more evolved stance with Protestant historian Martin Marty that, "My position is on the Christian non-violent left, particularly that segment of it which is occupied by Dorothy Day, the Catholic Peace Fellowship and people like Joan Baez. We are not liberals. We are still, I suppose, Christian anarchists, except that the term has no political relevance whatever."[32]

They also diverged in more substantive ways. Day fiercely adhered to most Catholic doctrine, especially regarding the personal responsibility of confirmed members, and she took the words and instructions of Christ at face value. Merton, in his preference for concrete persons and situations over rigid doctrine, was more open to dialogue and compromise on applying formal teachings. For example, in a letter to Jim Forest, when reflecting on Catholic divorce and remarriage, Merton commented: "I think I take a much more flexible view of it than Dorothy does, though I am no 'underground priest.'…Dorothy is a person of great integrity and consistency and this hits one between the eyes in the way she sums it up, hard as it may be."[33] He later shared, "I tried to say things that even Dorothy would have to accept"[34] on the topic, also showing he recognized their differences.

Sometimes these contrasts in perspective and life experience prompted misunderstanding. Merton found he needed to explicitly name which of his letter enclosures were only for their edification rather than publication. But, more significantly, though Merton admired Dorothy's unflinching views on pacifism, he did not fully share them. He considered "pacifism" an ideology that could lead to error if held too absolutely and, unlike Dorothy, he refused to formally abandon Catholic just war doctrine. This divergence is further explored below.

Despite such differences, this relationship through letters played a special role in Merton's life. Day reminded him of the realistic, non-idealized trials and dysfunction that accompany a life of hands-on service in the streets. She enlightened him on the unromanticized realities of involuntary poverty, even as she reinforced his appreciation for the spiritual power of voluntary poverty. She encouraged and deepened his commitment to nonviolence and peace. In response, he confided his doubts and frustrations, trusting

---

31. Merton to Day, July 23, 1961, *HGL* 139.
32. Merton to Martin Marty, September 6, 1967, *HGL* 458.
33. Merton to Forest, March 21, 1967, *HGL* 301.
34. Merton to Forest, June 17, 1967, *HGL* 303.

that the prayers and goodwill of this spiritual elder remained with him, even as he sometimes gently prodded in an attempt to expand Day's perspective.

Prayer, Perseverance, Peace

Prayer and Inspiration to Persevere

During their early correspondence, Merton's willingness to share his doubts and the challenges he was facing elicited Day's encouragement to persevere. She addressed "perseverance" in three different letters to Merton, though each time she invoked not its general meaning but the particular idea of "final perseverance."[35] In Catholic parlance, this refers to being in a state of grace at the moment of death and alludes to Matthew 10:22, which states in part, "The one who endures will be saved."[36] Though Day expressed a desire for her own final perseverance, she did so in response to Merton's suggestions that he might leave Gethsemani. Her words indirectly implore Merton to retain his vow of stability for his own final perseverance, which his departure might compromise.

She first used this term in response to Merton's increasing sense that "the only final solution to my own desires will be something like getting permission to go off and live among Indians or some such group, as a kind of hermit-missionary. . . . I do very earnestly and imploringly ask your prayers for this."[37] Merton was then lobbying the Vatican for permission to explore options as a hermit. Ernesto Cardenal's invitation to affiliate with his Nicaraguan colony especially interested Merton. Dorothy's response arrived five months later as a holiday greeting in which she reminded him that God, not we, must choose our destination: "A very Happy New Year to you and may you be faithful unto death. My constant prayer is for final perseverance—to go on as I am trusting always the Lord Himself will take me by the hair of the head like Habbakuk and put me where he wants me."[38]

Merton's response six weeks later described perseverance as something beyond rigid clinging:

---

35. This may have been a theme of Fr. Hugo's Lacouture retreat program. Hennessy recounts that Hugo once quoted Day as saying his retreat "was a foretaste of heaven, that it gave her courage to persevere." Hennessy, *World Will Be Saved*, 127.

36. "Final Perseverance," Catholic Online, https://www.catholic.org/encyclopedia/view.php?id=4677.

37. Merton to Day, July 9, 1959, *HGL* 136.

38. Day to Merton, December 23 [1959], *All the Way to Heaven*, 257.

Perseverance—yes more and more one sees that it is the great thing. But there is a thing that must [not] be overlooked. Perseverance is not hanging to some course which we have set our minds to, and refusing to let go. It is not even a matter of getting a bulldog grip on the faith and letting the devil pry us loose from it.... Really, there is something lacking in such a hope as that. Hope is a greater scandal than we think. I am coming to think that God...loves and helps best those who are so beat and have so much nothing when they die that it is almost as if they had persevered in nothing but had gradually lost everything, piece by piece, until there was nothing left but God. Hence perseverance is not hanging on but letting go....As you say so rightly, it is a question of [God] hanging on to us, by the hair of the head, that is from on top and beyond, where we cannot see or reach....If we reach it...we stand a good chance of interfering with God's grip.

Merton saw Dorothy and her poor in this relinquishing of all but God and asked her to "intercede for me, a stuffed shirt in a place of stuffed shirts."[39]

Day closed her next letter with this theme: "I am begging your prayers and be assured I pray for you as I hope you do for me. I am often full of fears about my final perseverance."[40]

Merton's next response followed a visit to the Little Sisters of the Poor in Louisville and expands on the relationship between perseverance and poverty. "We (society at large) have lost our sense of values and our vision," and "[I] can't help sharing its guilt, its illusions....I am not poor here. I wonder if I am true to Christ, if I have obeyed His will." He then returns to perseverance as relinquishment of control, linked to the power of poverty:

We should in a way fear for our perseverance because there is a big hole in us, an abyss, and we have to fall through it into emptiness, but the Lord will catch us....He will catch you without fail and take you to His Heart. Because of the *prayers of the poor*. You are the richest woman in America spiritually, with such prayers behind you.... The mighty prayers of the poor will embrace you with invincible strength and mercy and bear you in spite of everything into

39. Merton to Day, February 4, 1960, *HGL* 137.
40. Day to Merton, June 4 [1960], *All the Way to Heaven*, 266.

the Heart of God. . . . I have immense faith in the prayers of the poor: ask them for me too please.[41]

Day responded from the Catholic Worker farm, outlining their nightly prayer routine "in our little chapel over the barn, heavy with the smell of the cow downstairs" and its "bulletin board there with names of those who ask prayers," adding, "Yours is there." She closed by once more prodding for Merton's perseverance without using the term: "Your writing has reached many, many people and started them on their way. Be assured of that. It is the work God wants of you, no matter how much you want to run away from it. Like the Curé of Ars."[42] Here she referred to a nineteenth-century French parish priest, confessor of the masses, who four times ran away from his post in the desire for a more contemplative life, only to return each time to his calling.

Day's last explicit reference to final perseverance came two-and-a-half years later in the context of "friends who are always worrying about your leaving the monastery," which "does irritate me to hear these woeful predictions." She took comfort that his letters assured he would "hold fast," yet added, "I myself pray for final perseverance most fervently having seen one holy old priest suddenly elope with a parishioner. I feel that anything can happen to anybody at anytime." She assured him that his current position held great value: "As for your writing so much . . . it is a gift of God."[43] Merton's response confirmed Dorothy's trust with his characteristic humor:

> You often mention my perseverance: I am no stronger than anybody else, but . . . here is one place where they will have me and feed me and tolerate my presence permanently. . . . This is sufficient inducement, even if there were not the question of heaven. . . . I am here and unless the Lord pulls me out by the hair of my head (and there is no hair left) I will probably remain here. . . . I have no other plans.[44]

At the point of his death five years later, Day's *Catholic Worker* tribute to Merton seems designed to assure readers that he had in fact attained this "final perseverance." She devoted considerable space to discounting "gossip" he intended to leave his monastery, "discontented" with Trappist life.[45]

---

41. Merton to Day, August 17, 1960, *HGL* 138. Emphasis in the original.

42. Day to Merton, October 10 [1960], *All the Way to Heaven*, 268.

43. Day to Merton, March 17, 1963, *All the Way to Heaven*, 293–94.

44. Merton to Day, September 5, 1963, *HGL* 147–48.

45. Day, "Thomas Merton, Trappist, 1915–1968," *The Catholic Worker* 34, no. 10 (December 1968): 1, 6.

In these exchanges, Merton expressed what it means to persevere in re-linquishing control of outcomes, in the poverty that may require, and in hope as the only thing left to sustain us. His is no "prosperity gospel." He linked these interwoven themes with Dorothy Day's vocation to serve the poor. Be-yond explicit references, an undercurrent of perseverance pervades their cor-respondence, especially in their repeated pleas for prayer for themselves and their particular challenges. Their encouragement in the rightness and power of the other's vocation also urged perseverance. These letters offer powerful "signs of hope" to persevere in service against social ills, even as they urge release of our ego-driven grasp after power and illusory control over out-comes.

Peace, Pacifism, Protest

Their shared commitment to nonviolence and peace provides another thread running throughout these letters. Merton raised the topic more often than Day, periodically commending her for her stance. In return, Dorothy's letters offered Merton glimpses of the tenor and flavor of the era's peace activism. Her earlier letters shared frustration with what she considered the question-able morality and attitude of "rebellion" she sometimes encountered among younger activists. She also briefed him on peace organizations like PAX.

But their differences offer greater insight into their peace theologies, such as Day's embrace and Merton's skepticism of traditional pacifism. In an April 1962 letter Dorothy alluded to Merton's mimeographed Cold War Let-ters, which he had begun to circulate: "I understand from your 'letters' ... that you are not a pacifist and that you are speaking in terms of modern war." She failed to make it a point of contention, though, adding, "This may draw the Catholic layman further along the way of peace."[46] As the letter re-produced below illustrates, Merton responded similarly, acknowledging this difference yet affirming her stance: "In practice I am with you, except inso-far, only, as a policy of totally uncompromising pacifism may tend in effect to defeat itself and yield to one of the other forms of injustice. And I think that your position has immense importance as a symbolic statement that is ir-replaceable and utterly necessary."[47]

Merton and Day also disagreed regarding the burning of draft cards, though again without notable tension. Dorothy asserted she was "certainly behind the boys who burned their draft cards"[48] in the fall of 1965, because

---

46. Day to Merton, June 4 [1962], *All the Way to Heaven*, 285–86.

47. Merton to Day, June 16, 1962, *HGL* 145.

48. Day to Merton, November 15, 1965, *All the Way to Heaven*, 317.

"they are young men liable to the draft." She saw Merton's contemplative vocation as different, to "bring the suffering world and individuals in it before the Lord in prayer."[49] Day pointed him toward the November 1965 *Catholic Worker*, where draft card burners had articulated their position. Merton responded with diplomatic humility, saying the November issue "gave me a much clearer view of the motives behind the burning of draft cards," and conceding that "some protest and civil disobedience may be perfectly right." Still, he asserted, "I would not be prepared to say anyone and everyone who burned his card was necessarily doing a good thing,"[50] and his published essays consistently withheld support for the act.

The Gospel Way of Jesus versus Natural Law

Perhaps they muted their differences on pacifism and draft card burning seeking to mitigate the greater tension that preceded each of these conversations. In the months before Day's comments on Merton's "modern war" pacifism, sharper tensions had emerged surrounding the second essay Merton submitted to *The Catholic Worker*, titled "The Shelter Ethic."[51] Merton's initial *Catholic Worker* essay, "The Root of War Is Fear,"[52] had alluded critically to the idea of violently defending one's place within a fallout shelter in the event of nuclear attack, whereas Jesuit theologian L. C. McHugh had recently published an *America* magazine article expressing a theological rationale for exactly that. When "The Root of War Is Fear" appeared in *The Catholic Worker*, its staff issued a press release that explicitly contrasted the two positions.[53] Perhaps fearing the risk of being drawn into an intra-Church theological debate, Merton quickly whipped out "The Shelter Ethic" and submitted it. The article seems designed to tread a fine theological line that grants validity to McHugh's position as meeting a "minimum" requirement of Christian behavior according to natural law, while also asserting that the teaching of Christ calls for a higher standard of nonviolence. In seeking to justify both positions, it comes across ambiguously and fails to capture the personal disgust Merton had exhibited toward the shelter scenario in a letter to Jim Forest.

---

49. Day to Merton, December 2, 1965, *All the Way to Heaven*, 319.

50. Merton to Day, December 29, 1965, *HGL* 151.

51. This essay and Day's response are examined in William H. Shannon, *Silent Lamp: The Thomas Merton Story* (New York: Crossroad, 1992), 216–17.

52. *The Catholic Worker* (October 1961).

53. See Jim Forest, *The Root of War Is Fear: Thomas Merton's Advice to Peacemakers* (Maryknoll, NY: Orbis Books, 2016), 29–36.

But the article struck a raw nerve with Dorothy, on a couple of levels. For one, it failed to reflect her absolute adherence to pacifism. And for a second, Merton's appeal to natural law echoed the natural law appeals that grounded criticisms of the Lacouture movement so dear to her heart. She apparently debated publishing "The Shelter Ethic" at all. This led Forest to advocate in favor,[54] and it appeared in the November 1961 issue. Rather than directly challenging the monk on his position, Day spoke indirectly through her December column. Without naming either Merton or McHugh, she lamented that "we now have a priest defending the right of man to defend his life" from air raid shelter intruders. She countered with the "Gospel way" of Jesus's "new commandment (not a counsel)" to love and forgive enemies in nonviolent response. Perhaps seeking to invoke Merton's first article against his second, she advocated for "overcoming fear" that would "lead a man to take to any implement handy to wipe out his opponent's threat." She closed her argument by saying bluntly, "The theologians who justify a man's right to defend himself, are preaching *casuistry*, dealing with *cases* which should be dealt with in the confessional, not in the pulpit or the press."[55]

Merton got the message. He promptly devoted a single-spaced, two-page letter entirely in response to her published comments, clarifying, expanding, and perhaps backpedaling a bit. "I have read your latest 'On Pilgrimage' in the December CW," he begins, "and I want to say how good I think it is. In many ways it is about the best thing I have seen that came out of this whole sorry shelter business." What follows is a lengthy explication of Merton's views on natural law as it relates to the Sermon on the Mount, stating that he holds a view that aligns more with the "Greek fathers" than with Thomist "scholastics." He grounded it in the "person" as God intended rather than a "jungle" law in support of violence toward others. "I want with my whole heart to fulfill in myself this natural law, in order by that to fulfill also the law of grace to which it leads me.... I must rise above nature, I must *see the person*...and I must see the person in Christ, in the Spirit." He also asserts that his own words on self-defense were "based entirely" on Gandhi. Merton closed his letter by saying, "These words are to explain and apologize for the totally insufficient tone of my last article in CW which seemed in so many ways to fall short of your editorial standards," adding, "I am offering my sec-

---

54. Forest, "Work Hard, Pray Hard." He does not name this article but it seems the likely candidate: "I can remember having to argue Dorothy into publishing articles by Thomas Merton in *The Catholic Worker* because he wasn't taking the pacifist position that Dorothy took."

55. Day, "On Pilgrimage," *The Catholic Worker*, December 2, 1961. Emphasis in the original.

ond Christmas mass for you all. Do pray for me, I value and need your prayers."[56]

Day's next letter to Merton has not been preserved, so we don't know if it included any direct response to Merton's explanation, though based on Merton's reply Dorothy seems only to have shared happenings among her Workers. But her following letter reports that "I am sending the letter you wrote me to Father Hugo, since, in a way, it seems to concern the whole controversy concerning nature and grace and I thought that he would be interested. . . . He might have time to clarify for me some of the points you made in your letter."[57] In follow-up (reproduced below) to yet another missing letter, Merton further explains how, "I have always felt that Fr. Hugo's 'natural-supernatural' division suffered from being oversimplified and too much based on the scholasticism against which he instinctively reacts."[58]

As a whole, this exchange suggests that Dorothy had read Merton's "Shelter" article through the lens of her Lacouture experiences as much as her pacifism, and together those themes had created tension that required at least a couple of exchanges to smooth. But they permitted Merton to express his views on natural law in relation to his personalism. They also highlight shared deference and respect, even amid disagreement. Dorothy never directly confronted or contradicted Merton, choosing a subtle and indirect way to express her point. For his part, once Merton "got" her reading of his article, he scrambled to mend the breach in vulnerable humility and to assure her of his continued commitment to prayerful support.

Reaction and Reconciliation

Later letters provide more details on the November 9, 1965, self-immolation of Catholic Worker volunteer Roger LaPorte. That event created another point of tension for Merton and Day to navigate. Various Catholics perceived Merton as having undue influence on peace movement activism, and as news of LaPorte reached Merton, he was gripped with concern over how backlash might affect him and therefore his monastery and his order. In a pique of overreaction, he sent two telegrams, one to Jim Forest asking that his name be removed as a Catholic Peace Fellowship sponsor and a second to Dorothy expressing "shock" and "concern" over "current developments in [the] peace movement." He asked her, "Do they represent a right understanding of

---

56. Merton to Day, December 20, 1961, *HGL* 140–43; Dorothy Day Papers. Emphasis in the original.

57. Day to Merton, June 4 [1962], *All the Way to Heaven*, 286.

58. Merton to Day, June 16, 1962, Dorothy Day Papers.

non-violence? I think not."[59] In doing so, he implied Catholic Worker complicity in LaPorte's action.

Day's response was impressively measured and calm, sandwiching her perspective on the controversy between news items regarding Worker happenings, as though it was just another event to be dealt with in the chaotic flow of Catholic Worker life. She engaged the topic nondefensively with her assertion that "we are so glad you know about our tragedy, being assured you are praying for us." She recounted LaPorte's brief, marginal relationship to the Worker and explained that she personally had never spoken with him. In response to Merton's comments, she casually shared:

> I am only hoping that your reaction, as evidenced by your telegram, that is, holding us responsible, is not general, but I am afraid it may be. We have already received two bomb threats and I myself have been threatened at a public meeting at N.Y. Univ[ersity]. Of course, as members of one Body we are all responsible for each other.[60]

Without formal rebuke, Day forcefully reminded Merton that he did not fully understand the context and that the event had radically disrupted their lives far more than his. She also reminded him of the larger issues at stake and of her own protest legacy. "In view of the terrible things that are happening," she added, listing recent news of U.S. violence toward Vietnamese civilians, "there [are] bound to be increased protests. I am glad there are so many now. The Catholic Worker has borne the burden for 33 years—protesting war, Chinese-Japanese, Ethiopian, Spanish, World War II, Korean, Algerian and now this."[61]

Merton again perceptively grasped her message and offered thanks for her "warm, wise letter. You are well experienced in this kind of upset, over the years, and I was grateful to hear your human voice stating what you know, and not magnifying it any further."[62] During the following month they each sent two letters to the other, and over their course, a sense of normalcy, trust, and reassurance of like-mindedness returned to their correspondence. But the incident greatly wounded Day, a wound that never quite healed. When reading *The Sign of Jonas* ten years after Merton's death, she reminisced about Merton in her diary, recalling the 1962 visit of Catholic Work-

---

59. Merton to Day, November 11, 1965, TMC/BU; from Merton's handwritten draft.

60. Day to Merton, November 15, 1965, *All the Way to Heaven*, 317–18.

61. Day to Merton, November 15, 1965, *All the Way to Heaven*, 317–18.

62. Merton to Day, November 22, 1965, *HGL* 148.

ers to Gethsemani and "how TM wrote to urge me not to urge our young men to [self-immolate]. Hard to forgive him this stupidity!"[63] Despite this wound, Day continued to engage Merton's writings and tapes of his lectures ("first time I ever heard his voice") after his death, once commenting after watching a film of his lecture in Bangkok: "I must pray to him for aid, now, and patience, and 'diligence' in my work."[64]

These threads of peace and perseverance weaving throughout the Day-Merton exchanges cast more light on Merton's person-centered peace theology and reveal his willingness to reach out in deference for prayer and support and perspective. They capture his challenge to balance movement relationships with the burdens of a public figure who symbolized for many the Catholic Church and its monastic traditions. Above all, they display commitment to not let differences divert mutual encouragement in a common pursuit of peace, a commitment that inspires perseverance to imitate Christ in a broken world.

Thomas Merton wrote the following letter soon after he learned that Trappist censors had prohibited further publication on war and peace; he included it as letter #86 in his Cold War Letters. It demonstrates the diverse topics he and Dorothy Day discussed, Merton's reasoning on pacifism and just war, thoughts on natural law, and his desire to persevere in a time of uncertainty. An abridged version of this letter appears in The Hidden Ground of Love, *145–46. The original letter is held in the Dorothy Day Papers, Special Collection and Archives, Marquette University.*

June 16, 1962

Dear Dorothy,

I have just come from saying Mass for the intentions of the Catholic Worker, especially all yours and Deane Mowrer's.[65] May the Holy Spirit fill you all

---

63. October 31, 1978; *The Duty of Delight: The Diaries of Dorothy Day*, ed. Robert Ellsberg (Milwaukee: Marquette University Press, 2008), 616.

64. *The Duty of Delight,* January 17, 1973, 519; July 30, 1976, 561.

65. Mowrer, for whom Day requested prayers, was on the Catholic Worker editorial staff, nearly blind and undergoing eye surgery.

with His peace and light, and shape you according to His ineffable designs. He has blessed you with a wonderful simplicity and honesty there at the Worker. I am sorry that I was confused enough to take the boys who came down here as typical, but that the Holy Spirit brings them to you also, is important.[66] Even though they may have been wild and untamable, and even though they could not stay. But of course I appreciate the solid and faithful ones even more. The things blessed by God today are the hidden things of this world, the simple, the not even romantically little, but the more or less ordinary, but not of this world.

It is true that I am not theoretically a pacifist. That only means that I do not hold that a Christian may not fight, and that a war cannot be just. I hold that there is such a thing as a just war, even today there can be such a thing, and I think the Church holds it. But on the other hand I think that is pure theory and that in practice all the wars that are going around, whether with conventional weapons, or guerilla wars, or the cold war itself, are shot through and through with evil, falsity, injustice, and sin so much so that one can only with difficulty extricate the truths that may be found here and there in the "causes" for which the fighting is going on. So in practice I am with you, except insofar, only, as a policy of totally uncompromising pacifism may tend in effect to defeat itself and yield to one of the other forms of injustice. And I think that your position has an immense importance as a symbolic statement that is irreplaceable and utterly necessary. I also think it is a scandal that most Christians are not solidly lined up with you. I certainly am.

It is good to hear from you that the articles have been read and reprinted. I do not get much of the backwash here, and do not hear too many comments. I know a high school teacher, a priest in Duluth, picked up the Jubilee article[67] and on the basis of that and some other material made up a study outline on the morality of nuclear war which he took up with the seniors. That is a hopeful sign.

I'm glad you sent the article, rather than the letter, on to Father Hugo. In reality the matter is one of terminology and theological outlook, rather than one of essence. I have always felt that Fr. Hugo's "natural-supernatural" division suffered from being oversimplified and too much based on the scholasticism against which he instinctively reacts, so that it seems to me that he cannot say all he would like to say, and cannot say it fully effectively. I think the whole question needs a lot of study, and do not pretend that I have any answers that are startlingly new. I just approach the question from the viewpoint of the Fathers and the Bible, regarding nature as God meant it to be and not in its fallen state, still less in its abstract state.

---

66. Several Catholic workers had visited Gethsemani on "retreat" in January 1962. See also chapter 4.

67. Most likely Merton's "Religion and the Bomb," published in the May 1962 *Jubilee* magazine.

Yesterday I mailed you a copy of the book which is not to be published: "Peace in the Post Christian Era."[68] My Superiors, having been alerted by zealous individuals in this country, felt that I was "going too far" and getting away from the contemplative vocation into "dangerous ground" etc. etc. The book has not even been censored, just forbidden. I accept this with good will and I think humor, because there is a lot of irony in it after all. Have you seen the news release about the fallout shelter which our monks in upper New York[69] have built for themselves? What a grim joke that is! In all their innocence. Where is the "prudence of serpents" that sees through the lies and nonsense with which the world surrounds and seduces us, especially the Catholics who are so lamentably involved in worldly interests? The fallout shelter at that monastery is to be seen in the light of the "monks bread" ads. It is the same monastery which gets royalties from the bread formula which is used by some big bakeries in the East. It all hangs together, doesn't it? It becomes part of the same "image" (that fatuous, unintelligent monkface in the ad, and the fatuous shelter in which monks say, with all seriousness, "No, we will probably not have the Blessed Sacrament there permanently"). Monks bread. Bl. Sacrament temporarily in the shelter with the monks. Etc. One shudders a little.

I am so happy you are going to Brazil.[70] Amorosa Lima is the translator of one of my books, and I met him some years ago. Is Aime his wife? If so I met her also, and she is charming, as were their children, then quite young. I saw one of his sons recently, with his wife. They are a lovely family and wonderful people of whom I am very fond, but he has an altogether exaggerated idea of my powers as a writer I am afraid. Do be sure to give them my most cordial messages. In fact, before you go, please let me know and I will send you a couple of things to take to them. I have an awful time trying to get things through to Brazil by mail.

I will be sending you a copy of the Cold War Letters[71] too.

Since I am not writing anything about war anymore, I have gone back to the Fathers, to Cassiodorus, Cyprian, Tertullian, etc. I will try to type out bits of things they say that could be used in a box here and there by CW and will send them along. I will probably do a few translations, and maybe write some prayers. I have to do a book on Cassian some time, and thanks again for the translation you sent. We always use it.

It is no use speculating too much about the world situation, but it is certainly a very risky one. The whole world is under judgment, and one feels it

---

68. Merton's book *Peace in the Post-Christian Era* was published forty-two years later, in 2004, by Orbis Books.

69. Abbey of the Genesee, Pifford, New York.

70. Day never made the trip; Aimee Amorosa Lima was translating her book, *The Long Loneliness*, into Portuguese.

71. Merton's book *Cold War Letters* was published forty-four years later, in 2006, by Orbis Books.

keenly. Without saying that I think something is going to happen, I think I can say reasonably that there is just no reason in the world for it not to happen. I think the evil in us all has reached the point of overflowing. May the Holy Spirit give us compunction and inner truth and humility and love, that we may be a leaven in this world. And that we may help and bring light to those who need it most: and the Lord alone knows who they are, for the need of all is desperate.

All blessings to you, Dorothy, and to all at the Worker. Your presence and your example are precious to all of us, and especially to me.

Ever yours in the Holy Spirit,

2

NONVIOLENCE

THE MERTON-DOUGLASS LETTERS

The human personality of the individual marchers is totally lost in the mass-effect. . . . Was it, on all their parts, a real, fully developed non-violence . . . completely and maturely personal?
— *Thomas Merton to Jim Douglass*
April 17, 1967[1]

As Jim Douglass embarked into the world following high school, few would have envisioned a life dedicated to the theology of nonviolence and acts of nonviolent resistance. Indeed, he seemed well on his way in the opposite direction. Douglass aspired to design nuclear-armed missiles when he enrolled in the University of California's nuclear physics program at Berkeley in 1955, but he quickly dropped that for a six-month Army stint. The following year, in a freshman rhetoric class at Santa Clara University, he denounced Dorothy Day and others for refusing to participate in city-mandated Civil Defense drills—their response to the delusion that such drills could help survive nuclear strikes.

But Day's resistance so impressed Douglass that he began to read *The Catholic Worker*, which pulled him into her Gospel logic of peace. Five years later, Thomas Merton's critique of nuclear war further rocked his worldview when it burst onto the scene in Day's periodical. He contacted Merton, and soon the monk joined Day as a pivotal mentor in his pilgrimage toward Gandhian nonviolence. By the mid-1960s Douglass had become a significant Catholic theologian of nonviolence. He collaborated

---

1. *HGL* 165.

with Merton to encourage Vatican II opposition to nuclear war and its sup-port of conscientious objection, and together they wrestled with questions of when acts of resistance crossed a line from nonviolence to violence. Though sporadic, their correspondence captures important facets of Thomas Mer-ton's quest for wisdom to consistently live out nonviolent commitments in a violent world.

James Wilson Douglass (1937–)[2]

Douglass was born in British Columbia to American parents as a dual citizen and spent his first five years in Canada. He then moved with his family to the United States, where he attended Catholic grammar and high schools. Fol-lowing his false starts at Berkeley and in the Army, he enrolled at Santa Clara University to study English and philosophy, and he obtained his degree there in 1960. His four years at Santa Clara fostered a dramatically changed perspective.

Toward the Embrace of Nonviolence

Douglass credits his freshman rhetoric professor, Herbert Burke—who be-came another friend and mentor—with introducing him to Day and *The Catholic Worker*. By the time Douglass was a sophomore, he had rejected the morality of total nuclear war as taught by his ethics professor, Father Austin Fagothey, because of its indiscriminate destruction, and he debated Fagothey in the school literary magazine and at a public lecture. As a student Jim pub-lished two pieces in *The Catholic Worker*.[3] He married his first wife, Sally

---

2. Biographical details in this section and the opening paragraph are compiled from: personal conversations with Douglass (May 3, 2018, in his Birmingham, AL, residence; May 19, 2019, via telephone); "Acts of Resistance and Works of Mercy: Street Spirit Interview with Jim Douglass, part 2," *Street Spirit* 21, no. 7 (July 2015): 10–14; "Americans Who Tell The Truth" website, https://www.americans whotellthetruth.org/portraits/james-douglass; "Confronting the 'Auschwitz of Puget Sound': Street Spirit Interview with Jim Douglass," *Street Spirit* 21, no. 6 (June 2015): 7–10, 12; Douglass, "Foreword," in *Cold War Letters* by Thomas Merton (Maryknoll, NY: Orbis Books, 2006), x; James W. Douglass, *JFK and the Unspeak-able: Why He Died and Why It Matters* (Maryknoll, NY: Orbis Books, 2006), xiii; James W. Douglass, *The Nonviolent Coming of God* (Maryknoll, NY: Orbis Books, 1992), 99–103, 181–204.

3. The first, "Dante, Envy and Us" (25, no. 44 [November 1958]: 3, 7) was de-rived from a class paper; the second was "Nuclear Challenge to Conscience" (26, no. 3 [October 1959]: 3, 6).

Cotton, while in college. After graduation he studied English at the University of Kansas and then at the University of Notre Dame earned a master's degree in theology. Notre Dame professor John Dunne then recommended him to the Gregorian University in Rome to study the theology of war and peace.

He arrived in Rome to pursue a licentiate degree in the fall of 1962 as the first session of the Second Vatican Council prepared to convene. But after two semesters he pivoted to serve as a theological advisor to the Council, where he lobbied bishops to condemn nuclear war and support conscientious objection to military participation. Jim also encountered his former professor, Fr. Fagothey, attending Gregorian University to prepare a dissertation that rationalized total nuclear war. The Council eventually embraced more of Douglass's position than Fagothey's in its Pastoral Constitution on the Church in the Modern World. Though it failed to explicitly condemn nuclear war or nuclear proliferation as a deterrent, it condemned a broader concept of "total war" that indiscriminately killed civilians, and it supported conscientious objection to war by Catholics. In the summer of 1964 Douglass also greeted a tour of U.S. churchmen led by the Fellowship of Reconciliation (FOR) when they arrived in Rome. He joined their trip to the Christian Peace Conference in Prague and participated in a discussion among the tour's Catholics, including Jim Forest and Dan Berrigan, who committed to forming the Catholic Peace Fellowship.

Before the Council closed, Douglass returned to the United States and taught religion at Bellarmine College in Louisville, Kentucky, during the 1965 calendar year. But he revisited Rome in September for three weeks that year to continue promoting key peacemaking provisions. In early 1966 Douglass retreated to the British Columbia mountains of his childhood to write the first of four books on nonviolence, *The Non-Violent Cross: A Theology of Revolution and Peace*.[4]

Embarking on Nonviolent Resistance

From early 1968 through mid-1969, Douglass taught religion at the University of Hawaii, where his first act of nonviolent resistance occurred. In the spring of 1968, following Martin Luther King Jr.'s assassination, students in his peace theology course burned their draft cards and organized as the "Hawaii Resistance." Douglass discouraged public disobedience, feeling that the timing was poor and would alienate too many. But when they chose to act, Douglass joined them in solidarity, and all were arrested for

---

4. New York: MacMillan Publishing, 1968.

blocking trucks that transported Hawaiian National Guardsmen activated for Vietnam duty.

Douglass next taught in Notre Dame's program for the study and practice of nonviolence, and married his current wife, Shelley Hall Smith, his ongoing inspiration and partner in peace and social justice advocacy. They moved to British Columbia, where their son, Thomas Merton Douglass, was born,[5] as Jim began his second book, *Resistance and Contemplation: The Way of Liberation.*[6] Returning in the fall of 1971 to again teach religion at the University of Hawaii, Jim with Shelley helped found Catholic Action of Hawaii. The next year, Catholic Action launched a Lenten campaign at Hickam Air Force Base, the Pacific Air Force Headquarters, in resistance to the U.S. bombing of Indochina. In March 1972, Douglass and high school religion teacher Jim Albertini were arrested for pouring blood on Hickam's electronic warfare files, which ended both men's formal teaching careers.

The Douglasses returned to British Columbia and in 1975 launched the next phase of their collaboration: resistance to the submarine-deployed Trident nuclear missile program. That work endured for fifteen years and led them to Birmingham, Alabama, in 1989, where their resistance work soon shifted toward the Palestinian-Israeli conflict and the First and Second Gulf Wars. In 1992 they also founded Mary's House, a Catholic Worker house of hospitality. Jim published two more books on nonviolence[7] followed by two others that delve into the underbelly of governmental complicity in the assassinations of John F. Kennedy and Mahatma Gandhi.[8] Throughout his writings and interviews, Douglass names his relationship with and study of Thomas Merton as foundational to his career of action and scholarship.

---

5. Jim and Shelley had one child together; each had three children prior to their marriage.

6. New York: Dell Publishing Co., 1972.

7. *Lightning East to West: Jesus, Gandhi, and the Nuclear Age* (New York: The Crossroads Publishing Co., 1983; *The Nonviolent Coming of God.*

8. *JFK and the Unspeakable*; *Gandhi and the Unspeakable: His Final Experiment with Truth* (Maryknoll, NY: Orbis Books, 2012). Douglass is currently writing a volume that explores the assassinations of Malcolm X, Martin Luther King Jr., and Robert F. Kennedy.

Thomas Merton's Relationship with Jim Douglass

The relationship began at Jim's initiative. Douglass recalled how Merton's poem "Chant to Be Used in Processions around a Site with Furnaces," published in the September 1961 *Catholic Worker*, "electrified me when I read it.... What it meant was that a silent monk had shattered a larger silence. The greatest spiritual writer of our time had suddenly joined Dorothy Day and the Catholic Worker community in breaking the silence of the American Catholic Church on the threat of nuclear holocaust."[9] "In response, I wrote him immediately. He answered my letter quickly."[10] With that beginning, six years of correspondence followed.

Early Letters and Conversation

The first four years of these letters have not survived. As Douglass recounted, "From 1962 to early 1965, during most of which time I was in Rome, I did correspond intermittently with Thomas Merton. As I recall, the correspondence was of little substance—primarily an exchange of manuscripts with cover notes."[11] But during that span, Merton mentioned Douglass to others. In December 1962, he told Herbert Burke, Douglass's former rhetoric professor, that "I got a letter from Jim Douglass this morning. It was a good one."[12] Merton had recently shared some manuscripts with Burke, then at St. John's University in Minnesota, and Burke in turn shared a letter he sent *Ave Maria* magazine editors to defend an anti-nuclear war piece Douglass had published, "The Guilt of Hiroshima."[13] Merton also mentioned Douglass to John Heidbrink of the FOR in March 1964: "Jim Douglass wrote recently and I was glad to hear from him. There again I would be keeping up a more lively correspondence if I had more time to think and compose intelligible letters."[14]

Their surviving correspondence begins in mid-1965, an intense and pivotal year for both. It was the year Douglass returned from Rome to teach at

---

9. Douglass, "Foreword," *Cold War Letters*, x.

10. Douglass, *JFK and the Unspeakable*, xiii.

11. Douglass to William H. Shannon, April 21, 1983, TMC/BU.

12. Merton to Burke, December 11, 1962, *Witness to Freedom: Letters in Times of Crisis*, ed. William H. Shannon (New York: Farrar, Straus and Giroux, 1994), 96. Cited hereafter as *WF*.

13. Burke to Merton, November 15, 1962, TMC/BU.

14. Merton to Heidbrink, March 11, 1964, *HGL* 414.

Merton with Father John Luftus, dean of
Bellarmine University, and Jim Douglass, 1965
(Photo by Sally Cotton Douglass)

Bellarmine College, just an hour from Merton's abbey, and the year his domestic life began to show the stresses of disintegration. For Merton, 1965 was the year he retired from ten years as novice master and began permanent residence in his hermitage to pursue greater solitude. For the world beyond, 1965 was the year the Second Vatican Council held its final session, mainly to finalize its last working document, Schema 13, issued that December as its Pastoral Constitution on the Church in the Modern World. It was also the year of escalating U.S. violence in Vietnam and escalating protest that erupted in draft card burning and self-immolation. All these matters converged as content in that year's fourteen surviving Merton-Douglass letters.[15]

Douglass's proximity that year also led to at least three face-to-face meetings with Merton. In reflecting on those visits, Douglass later commented: "Tom Merton prayed, listened, and wrote furious essays against the powers of destruction which he glimpsed first of all in himself. Merton seemed to know the way as no one else did. He took joy in it. At the hermitage he shared that way and joy, and without saying much, showed the roots of resistance."[16] He further observed: "The Catholic Worker opened the way [to writing *The Non-Violent Cross*], as did my reading of Thomas Mer-

---

15. This included seven from Douglass and seven from Merton, with another four alluded to.

16. Douglass, *Resistance and Contemplation* (New York: Dell Publishing, 1972), 9–10.

ton and my visits with him. The power of contemplation in the world is what one learns from Merton, almost unwillingly."[17] He conceded as much directly to Merton in a March 1967 letter from British Columbia: "During this year or so in the north woods working away on this book, I've thought often of the contemplative vocation, of you in particular, how necessary the silence and the loneliness (which, on the other hand, is communion) is in order to arrive at anything."[18]

Vatican Advocacy

Their first extant letter came from Merton to Douglass in May 1965, but it suggests that Douglass had written Merton two previous times that year. "I had no idea you had been in Louisville since January," Merton shared. "Apparently you wrote to me about it and the letter did not get through, a common occurrence." Douglass had asked that he and Dan Berrigan visit Merton to strategize over lobbying bishops at the next Vatican Council session, and Merton welcomed their visit: "There is no question at all that some rather representative portions of the US Church have simply identified the Pentagon line with Christianity and are blind to the moral consequences of such an attitude," which he considered "apocalyptic" and "so huge a mistake that one cannot be dramatic enough [about it] however hard one tried." He raised doubts about pacifist labels as he had with Dorothy Day: "At the moment the fact that those who protest against total war are regarded as pacifist creates a certain amount of confusion" among U.S. bishops. But "for our part, I think that we can still do something, and perhaps the European bishops can still exert their power."[19] Merton's journal confirmed that Douglass and Berrigan, together with Oklahoma City priest Robert McDole, visited the following Monday and "talked a bit about Schema 13" and its "article on war."[20] This was their first meeting.

The collection's next two letters originated from Douglass and confirm a second abbey visit on July 14, this time accompanied by his wife Sally and Bellarmine College dean Father John Loftus. They inform Merton

---

17. James W. Douglass, *The Non-Violent Cross: A Theology of Revolution and Peace* (Eugene, OR: Wipf and Stock, 2006), viii.

Douglass to Merton, March 29, 1967, TMC/BU.

19. Merton to Douglass, May 26, 1965, *HGL* 160, TMC/BU.

20. June 3, 1965, *DWL* 253. McDole was active in southern civil rights protests during the early sixties.

of upcoming visits to the United Nations by Pope Paul VI and President Johnson, as well as a hoped-for audience with the pope by several church-men eager to encourage his opposition to the Vietnam War. Douglass added hopefully that "Pope Paul seems many steps ahead of the Council and the Schema 13 revisionists."[21] The early October letter which follows, again from Douglass, reports on his three-week trip to Rome in late September for intensive appeals to numerous bishops, and it thanks Merton for his open letter to the U.S. bishops on the matter. Dorothy Day had also trav-eled to Rome that month in a group of twenty women to likewise encour-age opposition to nuclear war. Douglass kept Merton apprised of Vatican deliberations during November, and when the Pastoral Constitution was re-leased in December, Merton expressed his overall satisfaction with it to Douglass.

Nonviolence

No single thread ties together the relationship of Merton and Douglass better than nonviolence. Beyond their work to influence Vatican Council delibera-tions, they wrestled in parallel during the mid-sixties to reconcile what it means to be nonviolent during a precarious time of tumultuous change while remaining within the bounds of Church doctrine. During a period spanning late 1965 through 1967 they collaborated to explore the implications of non-violence and its love of enemies—first as they responded from remote Ken-tucky to the real-time escalation of Catholic antiwar protest in New York, and later as Douglass grappled to work out his own theology of nonviolence. Both exchanges allowed Merton to apply and express his ideals of person-centered nonviolence.

Responding to Nonviolence in Crisis

A late October 1965 letter from Douglass to Merton portends the controversy soon to erupt among Merton and his Catholic activist friends in New York and real-world tensions between nonviolent theory and practice. The letter opens innocuously, offering thanks for Merton's third reception of Douglass at the Abbey a couple of days earlier, this time accompanied by Austrian peace advocate Hildegard Goss-Mayr, another Merton correspondent. But it closes ominously, referencing clippings with "this morning's reports on what is becoming a deep polarization on Vietnam. In a way the situation in the US

---

21. Douglass to Merton, June 19, 1965, TMC/BU.

is becoming even more dangerous than in Vietnam. I fear the reverberations of the Times News Service piece on David Miller and the Berrigans especially. It will certainly not reduce any pressures."[22]

That piece, subtitled "A Study in Pacifism," explored the context around Catholic Worker David Miller's recent choice to publicly burn his draft card in protest of the Vietnam War. It described how Miller had become a pacifist "under the influence" of Daniel Berrigan as a student at Le Moyne College, Dorothy Day and her Catholic Worker movement, and the Catholic Peace Fellowship (CPF). "Father 'Dan'" had arranged with his brother, "Father 'Phil,'" for Miller to work on a Mississippi project to teach catechism and take a census of Black Catholics in Natchez. The article went on to quote his "perplexed" mother; provide a short history of Day and the Catholic Worker; describe Miller's prior arrests, including one for a racial justice demonstration; and explain that the CPF had "propelled Mr. Miller toward pacifist demonstrating." It gave short biographies of CPF leaders Philip Berrigan, Martin Corbin, and Jim Forest; named Forest along with Tom Cornell as staff members; and described its work to counsel Catholic conscientious objectors. The article closed with a quote from Dorothy Day: "'Our boys and our priests have been tearing up draft cards for years,' the tall white-haired woman said quietly. 'I don't know why the press is so excited now about David.'"[23]

Perhaps the article's only omission was how closely Thomas Merton related to most of those it named and how his writings inspired them—something well known among many Catholics. It implied close collaboration among the Berrigans, the Catholic Worker, and the CPF in New York's protest activity. In providing the only context for Douglass and Merton to interpret subsequent New York happenings from distant Kentucky, the article also helps explain how Merton might conclude that Day and the CPF were complicit in what transpired.

Just ten days after he sent Merton the Miller article, Douglass shared with increased alarm that "the apocalyptic symbols deepen." Another news item described how Quaker Norman Morrison had burned himself to death in front of the Pentagon, barely dropping the infant daughter he held in time for her to avoid the flames. Douglass's commentary intensified the news report's impact: "I was shocked by this. But now the mass media broadcast it ...and next week several more desperate people will be doing it." He also pointed Merton toward a *Commonweal* story about an upcoming rally

---

22. Douglass to Merton, October 24, 1965, TMC/BU. The letter is dated October 24, but internal evidence confirms it would have been written in September.

23. Edith Evans Asbury, "David Miller and the Catholic Workers: A Study in Pacifism," *New York Times*, October 24, 1965, 76.

planned by New York Catholic Workers where "fifty or more" would burn draft cards, quoting a Worker that "We've never felt so much power." "There is an utterly wild note in the air," Douglass concluded, and he implored, "Please write on these things. We need your vision."[24]

Merton's November 6 response three days later is packed with fascinating reflections. He agreed that those actions were "disturbing," but conceded that he failed to fully grasp them. Merton speculated that they reflected some "new and more monstrous" pattern of "logic" emerging from dynamics "changing more and more rapidly and no one knows quite where we are going." He feared the onset of "a kind of political vertigo that could be in part demonic in origin." Yet he acknowledged: "The deepest symptoms are still those of the massive and official irrationality which provokes everything else." Merton supposed Morrison's self-immolation may prompt some to question the war, but he anticipated it would soon be forgotten. He judged the draft card burning "an act of provocative violence, a moral aggression" that resisted what he at that point considered an objectively "just" draft law. Still, not having discussed it with those who acted, he conceded "no way of seeing what they see" amid his doubts.[25]

Regarding Douglass's request that he write about it, Merton offered to "say something about the basic principles that may be involved when I can, as I can." But as for specific actions like these, he wrote,

> I am too out of contact, never hear of anything until it is all over, almost never have a chance for reasonable discussion or debate, and when I have made up my mind about something I discover that the whole situation has radically changed and calls for a new decision. Hence I am confined to questions of more or less abstract principle, if anything.

He closed this candid and perceptive letter by offering a typically profound synthesis of where he felt U.S. society stood. It lacked rationality in its deployment of "huge technological resources" without long-range plans or objectives, which led toward "motiveless violence." More broadly, the economic pursuit of "better refrigerators for more people," coupled with "clichés about faith and liberty," failed to "cloak our essential emptiness," which was itself "the great danger."[26]

---

24. Douglass to Merton, November 3, 1965, TMC/BU.

25. Merton to Douglass, November 6, 1965, *HGL* 161.

26. Merton to Douglass, November 6, 1965, *HGL* 161–62.

With Douglass's next letter, sent special delivery, the distant turmoil crashed into Merton's personal world with resounding force. It reported five new draft card burnings, including one by his colleague in nonviolence, Tom Cornell, a former Catholic Worker and on staff with the CPF that listed Merton as a sponsor. And it gave Merton his initial report of another self-immolation, this time by Catholic Worker volunteer Roger LaPorte.[27]

Several key dynamics framed the responses of Douglass and Merton to these events. Both were geographically removed and initially learned of the events through media reports. Merton, doubly removed in his hermitage, shared that, "At present you are the only one sending me any info."[28] Beyond that, both were nearing the culmination of years nudging bishops in Rome to oppose nuclear warfare, and as he later put it, Merton feared those acts would "give ammunition to American bishops and Catholics in general who oppose conscientious objection."[29] In addition to Douglass's plea that he write on these events, Hildegard Goss-Mayr, an esteemed correspondent, encouraged him to write on nonviolence,[30] and Bellarmine dean John Loftus encouraged his instinct to articulate "a genuinely non-violent appeal to conscience."[31] As countervailing pressure, Merton's recent peace advocacy had been poorly received by many Catholics such that, as he shared with Jim Forest, "There is no question that people, at least in this area, tend to hold me responsible for what you guys do. I know this because I am told it.... They are associating the card burning with my ideas about peace."[32] Balancing these vectors of pressure in real time from a wooded hermitage cloaked in silence presented a bewildering challenge.

On the same day he learned of LaPorte, Merton wrote Douglass to share that he had telegrammed Dorothy Day and Jim Forest to withdraw as a CPF sponsor and drafted a letter to Forest about that decision. He invited Douglass to send more information or suggestions for what to write, adding, "This suicide business is surely demonic."[33] Douglass affirmed Merton's draft to Forest as "painful but necessary" and suggested he develop it into a *Catholic Worker* article.[34]

---

27. This letter not extant; Merton recorded reading it in his journal, November 11, 1965, *DWL* 314.
28. Merton to Douglass, November 6, 1965, TMC/BU.
29. Merton to Forest, November 11, 1965, first draft not sent, TMC/BU.
30. October 23, 1965, *DWL* 308.
31. Douglass to Merton, November 16, 1965, TMC/BU.
32. Merton to Forest, November 19, 1965, *HGL* 288.
33. Merton to Douglass, November 11, 1965, *HGL* 162.
34. Douglass to Merton, November 16, 1965, TMC/BU.

Merton and Douglass exchanged five more letters that November and December, four from Merton and one from Douglass. They mostly discuss further developments in their parallel negotiations—one between Merton and Forest regarding CPF sponsorship, the other between Douglass and the bishops in Rome. "It would seem that patience," Douglass concluded, "in the sense of a suffering labor which works in, with, and through the community —in all its limitations—is essential to non-violence."[35] Chapter 3 shares more details of Merton's negotiation with Jim Forest, but by the end of the first week in December, Douglass reported that "the atmosphere itself seems a good deal calmer than it was a month ago. I feel that your action raised the right questions in a quiet way and has put us on firmer ground." He added that the "latest Berrigan Affair"—referring to Catholic leadership's hostile response to Dan Berrigan's homily at Roger LaPorte's funeral (see chapter 4) —"will all be for the good in the end, purging us of some of the dishonesty and power techniques which continue in the Church."[36]

The significance of these letters for Merton's pilgrimage with nonviolent peace activism cannot be overstated. Douglass was Merton's only direct, personal source of information about these events as they happened. He also provided a strong voice reinforcing Merton's own concerns and—with Hildegard Goss-Mayr and John Loftus—became a primary goad to write about them. They tested Merton's theoretical nonviolent ideals and provided hard lessons on the complexities of public advocacy on controversial issues. But the mix of Merton's move to his hermitage, calls to write on nonviolence, and public opposition to his stance also yielded significant output on his principles for nonviolent protest and prompted powerful letters to Jim Forest and Dan Berrigan that expressed his vision for movements and nonviolent resistance. Merton had previously written on nonviolence, but perhaps to help clear his order's censors, he couched his thoughts mostly as reflections on the work of others, such as Gandhi and various resisters to Nazism. But between November 1965 and February 1966 he wrote five essays for publication that expressed his own ideals.[37] They include Merton's penulti-

---

35. Douglass to Merton, November 16, 1965, TMC/BU.

36. Douglass to Merton, December 7, 1965, TMC/BU.

37. The five essays are: (1) "Peace and Protest: A Statement," written November 1965; reprinted in Thomas Merton, *The Nonviolent Alternative*, ed. Gordon C. Zahn (New York: Farrar, Straus and Giroux, 1980), 67–69. (2) "Christian Humanism in the Nuclear Era," written December 1965; reprinted in Thomas Merton, *Love and Living* (New York: Farrar, Straus and Giroux, 1979), 151–70. (3) "Blessed Are the Meek: The Christian Roots to Non-Violence," written January 1966; reprinted in Merton, *Faith and Violence*, 14–29. (4) "Peace and Protest," written February 1966; reprinted in *Faith and Violence*, 40–46. (5) "Events and Pseudo-Events," written February 1966; reprinted in *Faith and Violence*, 145–64.

mate statement on nonviolence, "Blessed Are the Meek: The Christian Roots of Non-Violence," published at least four times during his lifetime. This block of writing often invoked Gandhi and King as models, and it raised questions about actions he felt communicated ambiguously, like draft card burning. Merton also emphasized that nonviolence pursues dialogue that honors the freedom and human personhood of both victim and oppressor, not coercion. (See also chapter 9, section on "Language and Communication.")

The Non-Violent Cross

When they closed out that 1965 correspondence, Douglass shared that he and Sally were separating as she pursued an acting career while he, with their children, returned to British Columbia to write a book on nonviolence. Douglass and Merton's letters ceased during 1966 but resumed in 1967. These mostly discussed chapters of that book, *The Non-Violent Cross*, and captured additional nuances of Merton's outlook on nonviolence. The initial letter from Merton was prompted by his friend W. H. "Ping" Ferry, who had forwarded a chapter to Merton. Douglass originally shared it with Ferry to pursue financial backing from the Center for the Study of Democratic Institutions for which Ferry served as vice-president.

Merton read only five of the book's eleven chapters in draft form, and his comments ranged from insights on modern society to interpretation of Church history. Ferry had supplied the text of chapter 2, "From Bonhoeffer to Gandhi: God as Truth," in which Douglass built his foundation for a "cross-centered theology" that offers "a moment of contemplation under the chaos and at the root of things." Douglass added, "You must know... that the chapter you read and much else keys largely off Merton." Its material echoes Merton themes and lays out Douglass's sense of modern secular culture and how faith-based public engagement must shift from ethereal "God" language toward politically addressing concrete circumstances. Like Merton, Douglass saw modern culture as technological in nature and drew on Jacques Ellul to emphasize resisting an obsession with means that fail to reflect the ends toward which they point. His primary example: seeking world peace through modern war. Also, like Merton, he saw Gandhi's "experiments in Truth" as a model for engagement, and he viewed Gandhi as key to navigating activism without "capitulating through either involvement [in modern "totalist" systems] or retreat."[38]

Merton was impressed. "This is far and away the best and most important thing you have ever written, or that I have seen of yours." He praised

---

38. Douglass to Merton, March 29, 1967, TMC/BU.

Douglass for making "the right qualifications about technology while fully accepting secularity as it must be accepted." Merton chastised much of contemporary Christianity as "simply bustling to catch up with the status quo: affluence, gimmickry, the Muzak-supermarket complex and all that" which seemed to think that "Los Angeles is the New Jerusalem. There has to be an element of further looking protest if the absent God is somehow to be realized as present in the supermarket." Merton noted how Gandhi was "in the end non-modern," just as Camus, then his object of study, was "essentially a 'conservative,' in the sense of consciously keeping alive the continuity with a past wisdom stated in contemporary terms." Merton's main caution was to not place great hope in politics. Merton feared that by provisionally "slipping history and politics into the old base position once occupied by metaphysics" we might "in the end just contribute to the big slide into technical totalism." He proposed "a radical rethinking of politics and political relevance, to find something else besides the brutal authoritarian manipulation of the establishments and the quietism or nihilism of the [religious] minorities."[39]

Douglass forwarded his next chapter, "From Gandhi to Christ: God as Suffering Love," sometime within the next couple of weeks, for on April 17 Merton penned his response (reproduced below). While the previous chapter had addressed an increasingly secular culture, this one grappled with a Christianity that took its cues more from that culture than from a living Christ—or a living cross. Using Church responses to both Nazism in Germany and slavery/segregation in the United States, Douglass denounced what he called a "Milieu-Catholicism" which sought to accommodate the surrounding culture rather than challenge its denials of justice and truth. Merton encouraged Douglass to further clarify this Milieu-Catholicism's "incarnational heresy," which relies more on cultural forms than suffering love, and explain more about how a narrow focus on doctrine can offer "an excuse for staying remote from reality."[40]

They resumed their letters two months later when Douglass forwarded chapters 4 and 5, though Merton only addressed the latter, "Toward a New Perspective on War: The Vision of Vatican II."[41] Douglass feared this Council material might be overly technical, but he felt it was "important to show the convergence of the two streams of thought, just-war and non-violence, in the Council and the emergence of just one as the authentic Gospel wit-

---

39. Merton to Douglass, March 24, 1967, *HGL* 164–65.

40. Merton to Douglass, April 17, 1967, TMC/BU.

41. Chapter 4, "The Non-Violent Power of *Pacem in Terris*," explored Pope John XXIII's 1963 encyclical.

ness in our time" and to address "serious misinterpretations of the Council statement" on nuclear weaponry.[42] Merton responded with even greater enthusiasm: "The one on the Council is really first-rate, one of the best things in the book." He had learned much from it and felt that for the first time he could see the Council's Pastoral Constitution as "an admission that the Church cannot pretend to talk to the world in that way: that she just can't claim to have answers the world really needs to listen to. The efforts of those people to tell everybody what God's mind about the bomb is are just a little shocking."[43]

Merton's comments in this collection's last surviving letter from October 1967 address "Christians and the State" (chapter 8), "one of the best" he had read with "splendid points." He offered minor suggestions about the "Constantinian transition" from an oppressed early church to a Roman state church and on the tenth century's first crusade.[44] Beyond manuscript comments, these 1967 letters offer several personal thoughts, such as Douglass's mention of Joan Baez's visit to Merton and a Canadian television performance where "she sang and talked non-violence," which struck him as "terrific: purity."[45]

Nonviolence and the Person

Merton's 1967 feedback on *The Non-Violent Cross* offers his clearest expression of person-centered nonviolent principles within the Merton-Douglass letters. In his chapter "From Gandhi to Christ," Douglass included a lengthy press account detailing the horrific beatings that repeated waves of Gandhi's nonviolent resisters met in 1930 as they approached the Dharasana salt works to freely access that resource. Merton's response (below) questioned this account's value as an "ambiguous" message that lost "the human *personality* of the individual marchers." Second, "*Was* it, on all their parts, a real, fully developed non-violence? Was it in other words completely and maturely personal, or did they in fact move as a mass, impelled by the will of a leader?" His comments reveal the centrality of human freedom and personhood in Merton's nonviolence and his concern that nonviolent protest not reflect the illusions of a superficial mass-mind, but the integrity of a grounded person, "completely and maturely personal."[46]

---

42. Douglass to Merton, June 16, 1967, TMC/BU.

43. Merton to Douglass, June 30, 1967, *HGL* 166.

44. Merton to Douglass, October 3, 1967, *HGL* 166.

45. Douglass to Merton, March 29, 1967, TMC/BU.

46. Merton to Douglass, April 17, 1967, *HGL* 165.

Merton's response to Douglass's salt works example also anticipated another perspective on nonviolence that emerged more clearly during his final year, as nonviolence faded from African American activism in favor of Black Power. He predicted that inclusion of the salt march narrative would be "repudiated lock stock and barrel by SNCC [Student Nonviolent Coordinating Committee] and the Negro movement in general."[47] Merton later expanded this deference to African American self-determination in "From Non-Violence to Black Power," published the following year as a chapter in *Faith and Violence*.[48]

Douglass retained the extended quote on the salt march, but he affirmed Merton's personalist foundation in "Blessed Are the Meek," published in the United States for the first time that year,[49] with its foundational premise of "respect for the human person without which there is no deep and genuine Christianity."[50] He commended Merton for that "beautiful article," which he judged to be "the finest statement of the meaning of Christian nonviolence I have ever seen." He found it "clearer and more concise" than a recent book on the topic,[51] yet with "at least as much metaphysical substance." He praised its uniquely Catholic (personalist) perspective on humanity, often omitted by "Protestant commentators on non-violence, whose theological traditions seem somehow unable to prepare them for a statement on [humanity] which would avoid either a facile optimism or a withdrawal from the arena."[52] He also commended Merton's distinction between the "nature-oriented mind" and "person-oriented thinking," which parallel distinctions between Gandhi and the just war theology of natural law. Merton's thoughts in fact had proved to be "of immediate help" in developing Douglass's chapter on just war.[53]

---

47. Merton to Douglass, April 17, 1967, *HGL* 165.

48. Merton, *Faith and Violence*, 121–29.

49. *Fellowship* (May 1967).

50. Merton, "Blessed Are the Meek," *Faith and Violence*, 14–29.

51. Raymond Régamey, *Non-Violence and the Christian Conscience* (London: Dartman, Longman & Todd, 1966), for which Merton wrote the preface; originally published in French in 1958.

52. Douglass most likely refers to Reinhold Niebuhr's "realism" and similar liberal Protestant peace theologies on the one hand, and certain historic peace church perspectives, such as Mennonite theology, on the other. Regarding the latter, see note 10, page 213, in *The Non-Violent Cross*.

53. Douglass to Merton, June 16, 1967, TMC/BU.

An Ongoing Pilgrimage with Nonviolence

These letters exchanged between two apostles of nonviolence illuminate their ideals of nonviolence and the challenges faced in translating them into practice, as well as how each nudged the other along their paths. But their relationship has continued beyond these letters and into the present. As Douglass later reflected: "Those were illuminating times with Merton, but after his death he reached me more deeply with his writings."[54] He shared that "Merton had a deep influence on my understanding of nonviolence, to the point I was hugely influenced by him in writing my book called *Resistance and Contemplation*. Merton put together the contemplative life with nonviolent resistance as nobody else did. Not even Dan Berrigan did it as deeply as Merton did."[55] Douglass saw Gandhi's command to "have nothing to do with power" imbedded in Merton's life as "a paradigm of that politically scandalous tenet of nonviolence, a continuous following of a spiritual instinct which withdrew him from even the most subtle forms of spiritual power."[56]

Merton's imprint remains within Douglass's books. He considered *Resistance and Contemplation*, dedicated to Merton, a "delayed response to his death" and *Lightning East to West* "an exploration of where he was pointing (when integrated with Gandhi and Jung)" in his final year.[57] He liberally quoted Merton in both books. Douglass's two most recent works on the John Kennedy and Gandhi assassinations channel Merton's *Raids on the Unspeakable* to anchor his tectonic theses of government-sanctioned assassinations of popular leaders. He drew upon Merton's critique of the vacuous illusions that drive modern political ambition.

"The Unspeakable" is a term Thomas Merton coined . . . in the midst of the escalating Vietnam War, the nuclear arms race, and [U.S. political assassinations]. In each of those soul-shaking events Merton sensed an evil whose depth and deceit seemed to go beyond the capacity of words to describe. . . . [They] were all signs of the Unspeakable. . . . When we become more deeply human, as Merton understood the process, the wellspring of our compassion moves us to confront the Unspeakable. Merton was pointing to a kind of systemic

---

54. Douglass, *Gandhi and the Unspeakable*, xi.
55. Douglass, "Acts of Resistance," 11.
56. Douglass, *Lightning East to West*, 8.
57. Douglass to William H. Shannon, June 12, 1983, TMC/BU.

evil that defies speech. For Merton, the Unspeakable was, at bottom, a void. . . . The Unspeakable is . . . not somewhere out there . . . foreign to us. The emptiness of the void, the vacuum of responsibility and compassion, is in ourselves.[58]

In life, letter, and legacy, Thomas Merton's relationship with Jim Douglass uniquely displays his enduring impact as a mentor of nonviolence.

The following letter provides Merton's feedback on a draft of chapter 3, "From Gandhi to Christ: God as Suffering Love," in Jim Douglass's book The Non-Violent Cross: A Theology of Revolution and Peace. *An abridged version of this letter appears in* The Hidden Ground of Love, *165–66.*

April 17, 1967

Dear Jim:

Thanks for sending the new chapter (which I return). I like it, and find the last part especially powerful and convincing. But I find it more uneven than the other.[59] Around p. 7 and 8 I think it needs to be tightened up, as you are not completely clear, and especially since you use the idea of "incarnational heresy" in close conjunction with an ecclesiological heresy. I think you have to be very clear there, and perhaps spell it out more forcefully. Especially where you want to get over the idea that a purely ontic concept of Christ is an excuse for staying remote from reality: and make more clear what the existential concept is[60] (the part about the Servant[61] is fine).

The long quote from Webb Miller of the non-violent march on the salt works[62] is dreadful and perhaps essential. But there are difficulties. This kind of massive

---

58. Douglass, *JFK and the Unspeakable*, xv, xvii.

59. Merton had previously reviewed chapter 2 of *The Non-Violent Cross*, titled "From Bonhoeffer to Gandhi: God as Truth."

60. Merton appears to be referencing what became page 60 in the published book.

61. Merton refers to Douglass's discussion of the Jewish understanding of the "Suffering Servant," pages 61–66 in the published book.

62. Pages 66–69 in the published book.

beating down of wave after wave of marchers will tend for many reasons to make your message quite ambiguous, not only because it is so "Asiatic" and remote from what we conceive to be our kind of experience (though not as remote as all that), but because 1. The human personality of the individual marchers is totally lost on the mass-effect, they become cattle, though certainly they were not by any means. But the reader can't help looking at them as remote, cattle-like, less than human, and consequently can hardly identify with anyone there (while he can easily see the point of Gandhi's fast because there is a person right in focus).

2. When the suffering is not only passive but massive, it ceases to be really comprehensible by a critical western reader (acceptable only to the one who forces himself to say "this is the right way"). Without questioning the undoubted heroism of these people, was it, on all their parts, a real, fully developed non-violence? Was it in other words completely and maturely personal, or did they in fact move as a mass, impelled by the will of a leader? This is one of the great difficult questions of Indian non-v[iolence] and it raises its head here. I am being perhaps over fussy about this, but I do think that this quote here will not really help your thesis on voluntary acceptance of suffering. I think it would be much better to get examples of individuals or very small groups. There it will be abundantly clear to Americans, and these are the ones you must reach. The Webb Miller example will be repudiated lock stock and barrel by SNCC [Student Nonviolent Coordinating Committee] and the Negro movement in general. The thing has come round in a circle in this country. In the South, to let yourself be beaten does not convey the message of human dignity so much as the message that you are a Negro and therefore naturally take a beating, thereby proving you are inferior... etc.[63] For all these reasons I would suggest being careful about the long quote, though certainly it has to be brought out somewhere in your book I suppose.

I must close now: with all my best wishes and love to you both.

In the Lord,

---

63. Merton's ellipsis.

3

MOVEMENTS AND CONSCIENCE

THE MERTON-FOREST LETTERS

The trouble with movements is that they sweep you off your feet and carry you away with the tide of activism and then you become another kind of mass man. . . . So be careful.

> — *Thomas Merton to Jim Forest*
> *April 29, 1962*[1]

The real issue then is the recognition of the individual conscience. . . . To say that the clergy can tell the laity they are obliged to fight because the Pentagon or Time magazine say so, this is to me . . . a handing over of the Christian conscience in servitude to nefarious and anonymous secular power.

> — *Thomas Merton to Jim Forest*
> *November 7, 1962*[2]

It takes courage to face the fears that shape entrenched, malevolent social patterns. It takes compassion to identify with those who suffer under their weight. And it takes a refined conscience to discern actions that transform rather than perpetuate them. In Jim Forest, Thomas Merton found a young friend who possessed all three, and one who offered him an intimate view of the shifting dynamics and hard lessons learned in service to a social movement. In Merton, Forest found a spiritual mentor who offered grounding to balance reactive urgency with a long view—a grounding that sustains personal integrity in the face of pressures to simply fit in.

Loretta Ross, a seasoned Black feminist activist, reinforced the value of such mentoring. She recalls how "patient elders" had helped her address con-

---

1. *HGL* 266; TMC/BU.
2. *HGL* 272.

flict both within movements and with those holding power. Ross contrasts their wisdom to a current penchant for ostracism. She asks whether "contemporary social movements have absorbed the most useful lessons from the past about how to hold each other accountable while doing extremely difficult and risky social justice work." She suggests "a much more effective way to build social movements" that "happens in person, in real life" and not anonymously through media, ways where people "work together to ascertain harm and achieve justice without seeing anyone as disposable."[3] The mutual mentoring and accountability of Merton and Forest expressed through letters displays a relational collaboration across generations that aligns with Ross's vision.

James Hendrickson Forest (1941–)[4]

From Daily Worker *to Catholic Worker*

Jim Forest seems born to the role of persistent advocacy for unpopular causes. His parents had relinquished their faith commitments before he was born and replaced them with fidelity to a Communist Party agenda, so Forest learned the wages of political nonconformity early. He was weaned on selling *Daily Worker* subscriptions door-to-door with his mother, FBI interviews of neighbors (and its appearance at his door to fingerprint him and his brother while his mother was away), and the fallout at age ten—as McCarthyism reigned—from publicity surrounding his father's arrest and incarceration on conspiracy charges. Born in Salt Lake City, he moved east at age four with his newly divorced mother and younger brother, and they settled in a poor, mostly African American neighborhood of Red Bank, New Jersey. At fifteen he moved to Hollywood, California, dropped out of high school, returned east, and joined the Navy—not the most predictable destination for a child of radical leftists.

Forest's spiritual journey also proved unpredictable. Despite renouncing her Methodist faith, his mother, a psychiatric social worker, remained open to the spiritual curiosity of her children and allowed for Jim's intermittent Methodist, Dutch Reformed, and Episcopal church attendance, as well as

---

3. Loretta Ross, "I'm a Black Feminist. I Think Call-Out Culture Is Toxic," *New York Times*, August 17, 2019, https://www.nytimes.com/2019/08/17/opinion/ sunday/ cancel-culture-call-out.html?.

4. The following information is based on Jim Forest, *Walking Straight with Crooked Lines: A Memoir* (Maryknoll, NY: Orbis Books, 2020) and author's telephone interview with Forest (May 29, 2010).

Jim Forest, in New York City, 1963
(Courtesy of Jim Forest)

his Episcopalian baptism at age nine. Jim's early burst of spiritual interest faded until his eighteenth year. While studying at the Navy weather school, he experienced a spiritual awakening and joined the Catholic Church in 1960. This commitment deepened over time and eventually led him to the Orthodox tradition in 1988.

His earlier Catholic conversion also led to a social conversion. While stationed at the U.S. Weather Bureau in Washington, DC, Jim encountered a stack of *Catholic Worker* newspapers at a parish library and read them along with Day's autobiography, *The Long Loneliness*. They introduced new perspectives to his fledgling faith and inspired him to visit the New York Catholic Worker and protest the CIA-supported Bay of Pigs invasion—which he later realized benefited from Navy Weather Bureau data. After he processed these convictions with his superiors, the Navy discharged him as a conscientious objector in June 1961. From there, Forest entered Day's movement in New York, and a month later she appointed him managing editor of *The Catholic Worker*.[5]

Life in Movement Activism

Thus began Forest's immersion in the Catholic wing of the peace movement and his emergence as a journalist and writer. He moved out of the Catholic Worker community in early 1962 following a kerfuffle involving more culturally radical, "beat" volunteers and his conflicting commitments. But Forest retained close ties to the Catholic Worker throughout his life, and in the years that followed he became immersed within the broader peace movement. He helped found the U.S. PAX organization in 1961, and three years later laid

---

5. Forest appears in *The Catholic Worker* masthead from November 1961 through February 1962.

groundwork for the Catholic Peace Fellowship (CPF). This included joining John Heidbrink's 1964 Fellowship of Reconciliation (FOR) tour of East/West European Christendom, during which the initial conversation to form the CPF occurred. Forest served as a key CPF staff member for several years. During the 1960s he also worked as volunteer or staff for the Committee on Non-Violent Action (CNVA), Catholic Relief Services, the War Resister League, and as FOR special projects coordinator for its Vietnam program.

Forest married twice during the sixties, meeting both women in movement circles. First, in early 1962, he married Jean Morton, a poet he met while at the Catholic Worker; in 1967 he married Linda Henry, New York coordinator of a program to reduce poverty in the South. Forest also developed his craft as a writer and editor, working with newsletters of various peace organizations, serving as assistant editor of the movement-oriented journal *Liberation*, and spending a year as a journalist with the *Staten Island Advance*. He honed his movement credentials through ongoing participation in antiwar and civil rights protests and direct actions—his most consequential, perhaps, as part of the September 1968 Milwaukee Fourteen draft board raid, which led to a fifteen-month prison term.

He resigned from U.S. FOR staff in 1977 and moved to Holland to head the International Fellowship of Reconciliation as its general secretary, a position he held for twelve years. After joining the Orthodox Church he served the Orthodox Peace Fellowship as its international secretary and journal editor. Forest has authored numerous books on peace/nonviolence and Orthodox Church themes; biographies of Thomas Merton, Dorothy Day, and Dan Berrigan, plus his own memoir; and children's books, among others. He married his current wife, Nancy Flier, in 1984, and they continue to live in The Netherlands.

Thomas Merton's Relationship with Jim Forest

Getting Acquainted

Newly converted to Catholicism, Jim was a mere nineteen-year-old, living at the New York Catholic Worker community and working on its newspaper, when he first exchanged letters with Merton in the late summer of 1961. Day had given Forest access to the poem Merton sent her, "Chant to Be Used in Processions around a Site with Furnaces," and Jim wrote to Merton to thank him for the poem, share that it would appear in the next issue, and express admiration for his writing. Although Merton had promised the poem elsewhere and responded quickly asking Jim not to publish it, the poem had already gone to press. But this introductory snafu failed to prevent a close and lasting friendship between them from quickly gelling.

They twice met in person, first during Jim's weeklong retreat at Gethsemani Abbey that began in the last days of February 1962. Dorothy Day had commented to Merton how, following his Navy discharge, Jim had been rebuffed by two monasteries upon learning he was a conscientious objector. Merton offered to arrange for "anybody there who wants to make a retreat," since at Gethsemani, "c[onscientious] o[bjectors]'s and sit-ins and all sorts of people who are struggling hard to swim against the stream ought to be able to find silence and rest and understanding."[6] Jim's often-told account of that first meeting remains memorable:

> When at last we arrived at the monastery and were shown to adjacent rooms in the guesthouse, [fellow Catholic Worker Bob Kaye] collapsed on his bed while I found my way through a connecting passageway to a balcony in the back of the monastery's barn-like church.... The Church's silence was soon broken by laughter, a sound so intense and pervasive that I couldn't fail to be drawn to it. ...I quickly discovered the source was Bob's room. I pushed open the door, and indeed Bob was laughing, but the sound was mainly from a monk on the floor in his black and white robes, knees in the air, face bright red, hands clutching his belly. [It was Merton.] And laughing about what?...The smell! Bob, after three days of rough travel without a change of socks, had taken off his shoes. The room was like the Fulton Fish Market in a heat wave.... It was, in a way, the Catholic Worker's social gospel incarnate.... It made Merton roar with pleasure until the need to breathe took precedence and there could be a shaking of hands and a more traditional welcome.[7]

Their second meeting came at a November 1964 retreat of interdenominational peace activists Merton hosted at Gethsemani.

But their relationship deepened through their letters. The ebb and flow of this extensive collection[8] over the course of their seven-year friendship reveals their growing mutual trust and reliance. These exchanges may not match the prayer-focused spirituality of Merton's correspondence with Day,

---

6. Merton to Day, August 23, 1961, *HGL* 140.

7. Jim Forest, *The Root of War Is Fear: Thomas Merton's Advice to Peacemakers* (Maryknoll, NY: Orbis Books, 2016), 37–39.

8. The Thomas Merton Center collection includes about 100 transmissions from Merton to Forest and 47 from Forest to Merton, with at least another 30 from Forest mentioned in Merton's journal and correspondence.

but he perhaps shared more intimately with Jim his monastic frustrations and his hopes and concerns for the state of the Church, the world, and the peace movement.

Navigating Censorship

This intimacy becomes apparent as Merton expressed frustration with Trappist censors—initially because they slowed publication of his material on nuclear war and later when they forbade it altogether. Merton tested with Forest strategies for side-stepping this hindrance, noting that neither published letters[9] nor publication in small-circulation periodicals needed to be censored. So, Merton suggested, if he published a long article in one of these, why not summarize it, with citation, in a major publication?[10] Forest assured he would at least circulate copies of Merton's letters to interested and influential parties.[11]

Merton's lengthy letter explaining his response to the censors' decision reveals his deep commitment to obedience in the face of profound frustration and concern over its implications. Their verdict reflected "an astounding incomprehension of the seriousness of the present crisis" and "insensitivity to Christian and Ecclesiastical values." These "authoritarian minds" placed monastic reflection in "the rear guard with the baggage" to simply pray for the "purposes and objectives of an ecclesiastical bureaucracy" and justify "the already predecided rightness of the officials." Quite an impressive display of personal venting to a twenty-year-old, newly converted Catholic known for only nine months! But Merton reconciled that frustration with "true obedience (which is synonymous with love)." To "just blast the whole thing wide open" in belligerent resistance would backfire and simply

> witness *against* the peace movement and would confirm these people in all the depth of their prejudices and their self complacency. It would...make it even more impossible for them ever to see any kind of new light on the subject.... [My point is one] simply of saying what my conscience dictates and doing so without seeking my own interest...but out of love for God who is using these things. ...I find no contradiction between love and obedience...[as] the only sure way of transcending the limits and arbitrariness of ill advised commands.[12]

---

9. Merton to Forest, December 20, 1961, *HGL* 260.
10. Merton to Forest, November 14, 1961, *HGL* 258.
11. Forest to Merton, May 15, 1962, TMC/BU.
12. Merton to Forest, April 29, 1962, *HGL* 266–68; TMC/BU.

Mutual Education

Their friendship got an early boost through Forest's presence in Day's community. She often shared letters with those around her, so Forest also "received" several of Merton's letters to Day, and Merton soon sent *Catholic Worker* submissions directly to Forest as managing editor. Reading Merton's letters to Day alongside those to Forest gives a fuller sense of his relationship to both. Though Dorothy's letters also granted Merton glimpses into the Catholic and broader peace movement scenes, that pales compared to the steady stream of clippings and articles Forest provided, filled with news of the world and opinions on peace and war and race. Forest's material proved especially helpful during 1964 in apprising Merton of growing United States involvement in Vietnam before it erupted as a public concern.

Merton responded with items he had written, other religious pieces, and current affairs clippings of his own. As editor of newsletters and magazines, Forest became a conduit for publishing and disseminating many Merton pieces. While a *Liberation* associate editor, for example, Forest solicited Merton's first foray into publishing on race (see Part 2, introduction). Over the years Forest peppered Merton with requests for material or statements of various sorts. Merton often complied, but as he moved toward hermit life, he increasingly declined, explaining his inundation with writing tasks and his need to cut back on articles and public statements to focus on his vocation.

Times of Tension

Their bonds of intimacy and support become especially evident on occasions when Forest navigated personal issues such as marital transitions and other matters that strained his relationship with Day. Merton treads a fine line to sustain both of these vital relationships without alienating the other. In contrast to Day's firm and narrow expectations for personal behavior, Merton granted leeway to the young convert. At the point of Forest's departure from the Worker community in early 1962, Merton voiced pleasure at having met Forest and described him to Day as "exceptional."[13] And when Day felt Forest's first marriage lacked Catholic grounding, Merton voiced support for them.

The most awkward of these tensions arose in 1967 when Jim and Jean mutually agreed to separate and Jim began his relationship and later marriage to Linda. Dorothy asserted that this transition did not befit a CPF leader, and she indicated she would resign as sponsor if it persisted. When Forest

---

13. Merton to Day, March 21, 1962, *HGL* 143.

reached out to Merton for counsel, the monk found himself in a doubly ironic bind. For one, the matter reversed roles from two years earlier, when he sought withdrawal as a CPF sponsor over the LaPorte incident, for which Day gently reprimanded him. But for another, unknown to either Forest or Day, Merton himself had engaged in a clandestine romance the year before,[14] one that Day surely would have rejected with even greater vigor. Merton credited Day's concerns with "great integrity and consistency," but in his "much more flexible view" on it, he declined to "in any way judge" Forest and encouraged him to invoke Catholic theological writings that might help sway Dorothy. But he came down on the side of CPF viability: "If [resigning] means the collapse of the CPF, which it well might, then you should not do so. Let her withdraw her name if she must. But this in turn will be a grave blow."[15] Over time this tension also eased.

The most intense and arguably consequential phase of these letters occurred in late 1965 and early 1966 surrounding the Roger LaPorte affair. Though Merton's letters to others in this circle reveal much about his views on the incident, his six letters to Forest spanning November 1965 to February 1966 especially illuminate Merton's evolving ideals for the roles of social movements, individual conscience, and his own place among them. But he expressed the seeds of those perspectives and ideals to Forest from the start.

Social Movements and Individual Conscience

Engaging the Peace Movement

Well before he met Forest, as noted in the Introduction, Merton viewed "movements" skeptically, especially the era's totalitarian communist and fascist movements. But as he weighed in on the morality of nuclear war, he warmed to the term and sympathized with anti-nuclear resistance as "the most small and neglected of 'movements' in the whole Church," serving as sponsor to help found the Catholic "Pax movement."[16] He also reflected on how the broader "peace movement is a great potentiality," though somehow "terribly superficial."[17] But he identified with it enough to support the 1962 independent Senate campaign of Harvard historian H. Stuart Hughes, who

---

14. Merton had an affair with a twenty-five-year-old student nurse during the summer of 1966. For a brief treatment of this see the entry "M." in *ME* 276.

15. Merton to Forest, March 21, 1967, *HGL* 301–302.

16. Merton to Ernest Cardenal, December 24, 1961, *CT* 129–30.

17. Merton to Forest, August 27, 1962, *HGL* 270.

ran on an anti-nuclear platform, by offering two of his manuscripts and a cal-
ligraphy sketch for a fundraising auction. As he told Forest: "I have become
a professional abstract artist: abstract drawing of mine knocked down sixty
bucks in an auction of artists and writers stuff for Hughes Peace campaign.
This was more than a manuscript I also sent, got."[18]

But he also felt the peace movement needed to mature:

> We have to have deep and patient compassion for the fears of men,
> for the fears and irrational mania of those who hate or condemn us.
> ...Really we have to pray for a total and profound change in the
> mentality of the whole world.... Vastly more important [than Christ-
> ian penance] is the complete change of heart and the totally new out-
> look on the world of [humanity].... The great problem is this inner
> change, and we must not be obsessed with details of policy that
> block the deeper development in other people and in ourselves.[19]

These concerns deepened as the year progressed. He told Forest in late
September how "the peace movement needs a more substantial ideology: it
needs an ideology period. And ideology isn't enough, either. It seems to me
that the [movement] is centered mostly on the fact that these people don't
like war. The answer to that is a lot of rich people and powerful people and
crackpot people like war, and they are in the majority. This is no answer and
no dialogue."[20] For Merton, mere moral outrage was no grounding for a
credible movement; it required communication. He reaffirmed these concerns in December, advising Forest, "The prime duty of all honest movements is to protect themselves from being swallowed by any sea monster that
happens along.... Once the swallowing has taken place, rigidity replaces
truth and there is no more possibility of dialogue."[21]

But in early November that same year, Merton encountered a "fine new
book" on nonviolence and conscientious objection that seemed to offer him a
handle with which to focus his movement advocacy. Written by the French
Dominican Raymond Régamey, *Non-Violence and the Christian Conscience*
would be translated into English and published four years later, with a pref-

---

18. Merton to Forest, December 8, 1962, TMC/BU. After Hughes lost the election, he transitioned his campaign into a peace advocacy organization, which the following year awarded Merton its PAX medal. See John P. Collins, "Thomas Merton
and the PAX Peace Prize," *Merton Seasonal* 33, no. 1 (Spring 2008): 3–14.

19. Merton to Forest, January 29, 1962, TMC/BU; *HGL* 262.

20. Merton to Forest, September 22, 1962, TMC/BU.

21. Merton to Forest, December 8, 1962, TMC/BU. Merton responded to Forest's account that Communist activists had tried to co-opt CNVA speakers at a rally.

ace penned by Merton himself.[22] He described to Forest its treatment of conscientious objection as "a most essential issue, one of the cardinal moral issues of our time, one on which the witness of the Church will depend." For Merton, "the ambiguity of so many Catholics on the war question, or worse still the frank belligerency of the majority of them, is a very serious symptom of the spiritual sickness of our society." Even worse, clergy encouragement of deference to military and media assessments constituted "a handing over of the Christian conscience in servitude to nefarious and anonymous secular power," a "crass betrayal" by Church leadership.[23]

In these 1962 letters to Forest—five included in Merton's Cold War Letters, more than any recipient—Merton's nascent posture toward movement activism emerges: movements should facilitate dialogue to refine and inform the conscience of individuals, church, and nation. This conscience must be grounded in truth and freedom rather than political calculations of self-interest. "Honest movements" engage with a hope to transform the "mentality of the whole world."

Moving into Solitude

During the years following that initial outburst of engagement, Merton often signaled his need to pull back. He felt the weight of censorship, the burden of administrative tasks, and the limits of his cloistered seclusion. As he worked on his "Letters to a White Liberal" essay for *Ramparts* magazine (see chapter 6) in mid-1963 Merton told Forest, "It perhaps does not make too much sense my sounding off from here where I don't really see what is going on and am not really involved in it directly. Sooner or later I will probably get completely shut up on all these issues."[24] Then that fall: "I am having to cut down on blurbs, prefaces, and various minor statements, for the obvious reason that I am just snowed under," and to "reserve my striking power for something essential."[25] More antiwar involvement by other clergy also encouraged him to reduce his public role. In October 1964 he noted to Forest that, "With Dan and Phil [Berrigan] and people like that getting in there more...perhaps I can just be more of a monk." Yet in the same letter he agreed to be listed as a sponsor of the fledgling Catholic Peace Fellowship,

---

22. *Non-Violence et Conscience Chrétienne* (Paris: Les Editions du Cerf, 1958); *Non-Violence and the Christian Conscience* (London: Darton, Longman and Todd Ltd., 1966).

23. Merton to Forest, November 7, 1962, *HGL* 271–72.

24. Merton to Forest, July 15, 1963, TMC/BU.

25. Merton to Forest, October 19, 1963, *HGL* 277; TMC/BU.

though with noticeably more reluctance than when agreeing to serve as a PAX sponsor three years earlier:

> I suppose you might as well use my name for the Peace Fellowship ... [though] it is sort of a useless gesture.... I think this will proba-bly be my last time at it. It is true that if one has that illusory thing "a name," it might as well be used for its illusion value.... I think this had better be the last illusion of this particular kind.[26]

By the following spring, such convictions had deepened. He confided in Forest to feeling "no trust at all in my judgment of trends and events," since:

> I just can't see things in perspective from here, though I may come out with an occasional intuition about the general climate.... It is one thing to be somewhat dramatic and quite another to be perti-nent. And it is always easy to talk, but not always easy to say some-thing that makes real sense (instead of just sounding reasonable).[27]

Yet Merton continued to counsel Forest behind the scenes, especially re-garding the CPF program. The day before he formally began his hermit sta-tus in late August 1965, Merton forwarded several suggestions for a CPF statement on Vietnam that Forest was drafting. He also mentioned his open letter to American bishops, which suggests Merton at least felt *that* topic was "essential" enough to expend some "striking power." As he permanently crossed his hermitage threshold, Merton shared his need to avoid "the public eye for a while, at least while sounding off when I can," especially since his abbot continued to receive complaints about his advocacy. But he assured Forest that "the Peace Movement and the race struggle are all included al-ways" in his prayers.[28]

Refinement through Crisis

Merton would not have long to enjoy his new life as a hermit, though. Just two months in, as chapter 2 recounts, he began to receive those disconcerting reports of dramatic turns in Catholic peace advocacy from Jim Douglass. Chapter 1 treats their impact on his relationship with Dorothy Day, but these events brought even more pressure to bear on his friendship with Jim Forest, especially since word from elsewhere questioned the stability of CPF leader-

---

26. Merton to Forest, October 2, 1964, *HGL* 282.
27. Merton to Forest, March 13, 1965, *HGL* 284.
28. Merton to Forest, August 20, 1965, *HGL* 285; TMC/BU.

ship.[29] These dynamics increasingly led him to regret his choice to identify so closely with the peace movement,[30] and his response to this bubbling cauldron of concerns unfolded in letters to Forest over the next few months. It evolved from immediate knee-jerk reaction, to negotiated compromise, to clarified objectives for Catholic peace activism. This last focus culminated in what became Merton's best-known letter, his "Letter to a Young Activist" that offered advice for sustaining an activist's commitment over the long haul, in the midst of movement pressures (summarized below).

Following the November 11 special delivery letter from Douglass and telegrams whisked off to chide Day and withdraw his CPF sponsorship, Merton drafted his letter of elaboration to Forest. In fact, he drafted two versions that day, noting that he had written the second to make the first "shorter and clearer."[31] While that first draft may be ten lines longer than the second, whether it is less clear remains debatable. But it is certainly gentler. In it, Merton framed his concerns mostly as questions and clearly enumerated them, asking (1) whether LaPorte's act and draft card burning reflected genuine Gandhian nonviolence, suggesting the public would feel threatened by their antagonistic nature, which surely disqualified it as "non-violence"; (2) whether they were truly Christian expressions of God's will, though assuring he did not question the card burners' sincerity nor judge LaPorte; and then asserting that (3) those actions would "inevitably prejudice" the gains of "viewing conscientious objection favorably" toward which Vatican II had "painfully progressed." Merton noted his lack of hands-on involvement in the movement, the use of his name with acts he questioned, and a movement going in a direction with which he could not agree. In light of this mix, Merton requested withdrawal of his name as sponsor lest "an emotionally immature Catholic might conceivably get himself involved in thoughts of self-immolation through the influence of that name." He closed this draft with multiple assertions of goodwill: "I know this will hurt you"; "I am not withdrawing any offer of friendship or support"; "I am not blaming you or the CPF"; "this is one very painful letter to write. I'm sorry, but I have to."[32]

---

29. For example, Justus George Lawler to Merton, November 18, 1965, TMC/BU: "I don't know what is with the CPF, tho I suspect it is a combination of dumb-kind youthfulness, prophetic OT simplism, and general discontent with the status quo—represented respectively by Forest, Fr. Dan, and the middle-aged Catholic Workers." Lawler was based near Chicago and editor for Herder and Herder press and *Continuum* magazine.

30. *DWL* 320, 343, 348.

31. Noted on file copy of first draft, Merton to Forest, November 11, 1965 draft, TMC/BU.

32. File copy of first draft, Merton to Forest, November 11, 1965, TMC/BU.

Later that day, Merton typed his second version to Forest. Given the turmoil that ensued, it may have been better had he stuck with the first. His rewrite takes a sharper, more judgmental tone and deploys harsher, more apocalyptic language. Whereas his first effort uses more space to explain his own position, the second expresses more criticism of the movement and the country in general. What had gently closed as a "painful" letter now opened bluntly as "a bitter letter to write." The three points he had enumerated clearly and sequentially were still there, but scattered throughout and sharper. Despite conceding his lack of direct knowledge and asserting he did not question motives or sincerity, as in his first draft, this version more directly stated that the CPF was caught up in a movement that appeared "a little pathological," from which he concluded: "Jim, there is something terribly wrong here." He expressly named it "un-Christian," with a "very different smell from the Gandhian movement, the non-violent movement in France, and the non-violence of Martin Luther King." Merton asserted this would "neutralize" all the work done and gains made and asked rhetorically: "What on earth are the American bishops going to make out of that?"[33]

He described the self-immolations as "demonic" and the state of the country using words like "terribly disturbing," with a "crazy" atmosphere and "an air of absurdity and moral void." In short: "The joint is going into a slow frenzy. The country is nuts." He closed with a brief assurance to do "anything I can to be of help" and that his withdrawal did not signal "a complete repudiation of the CPF or anything of the sort." He also had meantime offered Mass for the peace movement that morning. But in the context and tone of the whole, these closing reassurances come across as weak afterthoughts rather than considered reassurance. In short, this letter does not rank among Merton's finest pastoral efforts.[34]

Several key New York friends—Dorothy Day, Dan Berrigan, John Heidbrink, Tom Cornell, and of course Forest himself—responded with letters that sought to sooth his anxiety and clarify their local dynamic. For his part,

33. Merton to Forest, November 11, 1965, *HGL* 285–87.

34. Merton to Forest, November 11, 1965, *HGL* 286–87. Merton's journal entry that day shows increased anxiety and alarm and echoes his rewrite to Forest: "I cannot understand the shape of things in the Peace Movement or the shape of things at all in this country. What is happening? Is everybody nuts? . . . I am so disturbed by the events, and especially the suicide at the U.N., that I sent [telegrams to Day and Forest] . . . but afterwards I wondered if I had been too hard on Jim and the Catholic Peace Fellowship. But with things as crazy as they are I cannot let my name be used by an outfit as unpredictable as that is, with kids likely to do anything at any moment. The CPF is right in the middle of the draft card burning and now this. Five from the Catholic Worker burned their cards. One burnt himself. Totally awful, the suicide at least. . . . The world has never been so sick." November 11, 1965, *DWL* 314–15.

Forest's four-page, single-spaced letter carefully yet firmly and clearly responded to each of Merton's various concerns. He explained how LaPorte acted in secrecy, knowing that those around him would try to thwart him and assured that Catholic hierarchy showed no signs of using the events as leverage against Vatican II deliberations. Forest also pushed back to say responsibility lay not with a pathological movement or country per se, but with "a fratricidal war in Southeast Asia which can in no way be reconciled with even the most modest Christian judgments." Through examples and enclosures Forest offered ample evidence of the CPF's positive impact on many, and he asserted that it was "playing an extremely important role in helping to develop a more informed conscience, a more sensitive and braver conscience in the American religious community." In light of this, Forest asked Merton to reconsider withdrawing his sponsorship.[35]

That wave of context and perspective certainly eased Merton's mind and softened his stance, but it failed to fully reverse his concern. Though responses to these writers reflect more deliberation and restraint than had his withdrawal letter to Forest, his journal entries betray lingering anxiety. There he conceded his error of initial overreaction but lamented that his friends still fully grasped neither his personal need to pursue solitude nor the extent to which his peace movement attachments hindered that. He also expressed considerable regret over getting so entangled with the movement to begin with. At one point he asserted that, "I trust Jim Forest to respond intelligently anyway: but there *is* this question of their interest in using my name, and to this they will cling mightily."[36] But he eventually reached a point where, despite asserting he was "through with any playing with peace movements," he could nonetheless concede that "I suppose it is not important for me if they insist on keeping me (for my name). I don't want to quarrel with them and Jim Forest at least is an excellent and competent person. I think they are doing good work—apart from card-burning which they do not 'sponsor.'"[37]

In his initial response to Forest's request that he stay, Merton apologized and retracted some of his more extreme statements. He again reassured that his decision only addressed personal vocational needs and was neither political nor a repudiation of the CPF. But he expressed dissonance with what transpired and shared accusations that he inspired draft-card burnings through his peace writings. He would "leave the thing hanging in the balance for a while," but reasserted his need to make clear which actions he did not

---

35. Forest to Merton, November 16, 1965, TMC/BU.
36. Not dated, *DWL* 341.
37. November 21, 1965, *DWL* 318.

advocate.[38] They ironed out their compromise in several late-November and early-December 1965 exchanges: Merton would remain a CPF sponsor if Forest would distribute a statement that clarified Merton's role as a hermit and his distance from decisions and actions of the CPF and its members.

As Merton transmitted his statement to Forest for CPF release, he began to articulate what would become of his evolved posture toward the peace movement. He could support the CPF "insofar as you are implementing the teaching of the Church on peace" and, as long as they respected his "curious decision" to embrace monastic solitude, he would "gladly give you all the moral support I can for your pastoral work." He also counseled Forest to avoid acts which "strike the average Catholic as a needless provocation."[39] Forest heartily agreed to these terms and distributed the statement, leading Merton to confide in his journal: "The business with Jim Forest and the Catholic Peace Fellowship is settled charitably. . . . These are authentic Christians."[40]

Prioritizing Conscience over Causes and Myths

Though Merton emerged from this crisis resolved not to re-entangle himself in movement details, he remained committed to share, publicly and interpersonally, his principles on peace and nonviolence. The resolved conflict and distributed statement also converged with the Vatican Council's December 7 publication of its Pastoral Constitution on the Church in the Modern World. Together these events helped refocus and energize Merton's peace agenda. His next two letters to Forest express this energized vision, heavily weighted toward nurturing personal conscience.

The first, written December 29, responds to Forest's news that he had distributed Merton's statement. Forest felt that it, coupled with the Pastoral Constitution, would help frame CPF's mission. He suggested "the integrity and tone involved, the lack of self-seeking" would define the value of CPF's work rather than any "provocative" qualities.[41] Merton liked what he read. He launched into lengthy reflections that read like his personal manifesto for CPF. This letter (reproduced in full below) outlines how the CPF might now lead a Catholic-based movement for peace. "Crucially important," the CPF should ground its work in the Pastoral Constitution's theological logic. Drawing on "basic principles" of "personalism and the unity of the human family," the Council provided the CPF its "big chance . . . to really do something im-

---

38. Merton to Forest, November 19, 1965, *HGL* 288.

39. Merton to Forest, December 3, 1965, *HGL* 289.

40. December 30, 1965, *DWL* 328.

41. Forest to Merton, December 22, 1965, TMC/BU.

portant for the Church" by "reaching a lot of people and helping them to change their mind." Their mission was "simply to get the Constitution across, not even worrying about whether or not it gets the CPF better known."[42]

Merton also addressed the place of "provocative" action, and he contrasted the Catholic Worker's "prophetic" role with the CPF's "apostolic" mission. Despite his "immense respect" for the Worker, it "remains more or less a symbol that everyone admires and stays away from," whereas the CPF's "more colorless and less dramatic job" was "much more important than what the CW can do." He defined the "provocative witness" Forest alluded to as having an "aggressive, challenging nature *over and above* the simple question of conscience." He affirmed occasional need for it, especially in a "serious moral situation," but provocation should be limited to "one or two reasonable people" rather than something "irresponsible" by those who just "want something to do to prove themselves." But for Catholics at this particular juncture, a "dramatic and provocative type of witness" was much less helpful than "massive and undramatic apostolic work to clarify the Church's teaching," a "first step toward an abolition of war or a renunciation of the war mentality by everyone." The next step required study of pervasive violence within a national culture "addicted to images of violence, brutality, sadism," and the like. Still, after rendering two solid pages of advice on how he felt the CPF should advance its public program, he restated his desire for personal withdrawal: "I would prefer in my present position not to have each utterance announced by a trumpet blast of some sort or anything that would give people the idea I was out there mixed up in a lot of action. Just what is necessary to get the truth out."[43]

Several days later, when forwarding examples of press coverage on Merton's statement, Forest enclosed a draft CPF pamphlet on conscientious objection and asked for comment. Merton's response expanded on his vision. Though he found the pamphlet well-grounded in the Pastoral Constitution, he encouraged Forest to double down on the topic of political noncooperation from a "Catholic viewpoint" using "specifically Catholic arguments." He advocated more explicit comments about the existing law's deference to historic peace church priorities and lack of accommodation for those whose conscience distinguishes between just and unjust wars, as Catholic doctrine teaches.[44]

Merton wrote his best-known entry in this sequence of letters a month later, in late February 1965. He crafted it in response to Forest's discouraged

---

42. Merton to Forest, December 29, 1965, *HGL* 290–91.

43. Merton to Forest, December 29, 1965, *HGL* 291–92; TMC/BU; emphasis in the original.

44. Merton to Forest, January 17, 1966, *HGL* 293.

plea for advice on the lack of impact he saw in his work. Forest had taken Merton's "Peace and Protest: A Statement," written the previous November immediately after the LaPorte incident, as a resource to "type out a few thoughts" on "effective means of getting across our ideas to the public." But he had given up, wondering, "Who is listening?"[45] Merton took great care in his response, offering sympathetic perspective, consolation, and encouragement. He told Forest not to "waste time writing notes on my peace and protest bit," especially since he had just rewritten it into a longer article for *Continuum* magazine. He instead shared a new essay for him to consider, one that explored superficiality in public discourse titled "Events and Pseudo-Events."[46]

But more specifically, Merton offered his young friend nearly three pages of sensitive counsel on surviving the ups and downs of movement activism, focused more on service to the Catholic community than the Herculean task of single-handedly altering U.S. policy. It was normal, Merton assured him, to have been "sustained by hopes that are now giving out," so one must "learn to expect it and cope with it when it comes." This means, Merton famously advised: "Do not depend on the hope of results," but look toward "the value, the rightness, the truth of the work itself." He counseled that "it is the reality of personal relationships that saves everything" and warned of common movement pitfalls like getting swept up in "words," "ideals," "causes," "ideas," "slogans," "myths," or the temptation to "yell louder" in hopes it might "make the meaning be there again by magic." He encouraged Forest to see his work as an apostolic service to the "average everyday 'Catlick'" who had been reared on simplistic rules rather than on cultivating moral reasoning "in this whole area of war and peace."[47]

Merton also cautioned against simply feeding off of personal disgust over brutalities done in the name of country and God. Submitting to emotional outrage can seduce us into the same mentality that produced those brutalities: "the myth of 'getting results'" that grew from "the *obsession* of the American mind with the myth of knowhow, and with the capacity to be omnipotent." That myth was now unraveling in Vietnam and driving the country "half nuts." Beware the trap of assumptions that "you and I and our type have a special answer" that seems to "make us sane" and leads us to "prove to ourselves that a) we at least are sane and decent people [and] b)... *our* sanity and decency ought to influence everybody else." The CPF would not of itself end the Vietnam War. Forest's best work was simply to "*begin* the laborious job of changing the national mind and opening up the national con-

---

45. Forest to Merton, February 15, 1966, TMC/BU.

46. Merton to Forest, February 21, 1966, TMC/BU.

47. Merton to Forest, February 21, 1966, *HGL* 294–95.

science," and trust he had "contributed *something* to a clarification of Christian truth in this society." Then perhaps "a *few* people may have got straight about some things and opened up to the grace of God." To succeed, Forest must "be free from the need to prove yourself," to "not pour out your life in the service of a myth," and to resist an impulse to "turn the best things into myths." Rather, "get free from the domination of causes and just serve Christ's truth," for: "The real hope, then, is not in something we think we can do, but in God who is making something good out of it in some way we cannot see. If we can do His will, we will be helping in this process. But we will not necessarily know all about it beforehand."[48]

With this "Letter to a Young Activist,"[49] a crucial chapter in Merton's letters to Forest—and in the evolution of his relationship to social movements —closes. His attempt to withdraw into solitude was temporarily thwarted by the intrusion of events in New York, events tinged with residue from prior commitments and relationships. But working through those consequences, as he absorbed the Vatican Council's statement, forced him to more clearly assert his limits and define his place within the movement's flow.

Final Exchanges

Their stream of letters continued through the monk's last two years of life. Following Merton's "Young Activist" letter, their correspondence waned for several months in 1966, perhaps reflecting his preoccupation with having found romantic love that summer, but picked up again in 1967. Most letters from that year address either personal matters or logistics of publishing Merton's writings, including several requests by Forest for Merton to write something—which he often, but not always, did. They also corresponded about the 1967 publication of Merton's "Blessed Are the Meek" essay by the CPF as a separate booklet,[50] illustrated with artwork by Sister Corita Kent and dedicated at Merton's request to Joan Baez. Few of these later letters, though, approach the intensity or capture Merton's theological and political state of mind as profoundly as those that flowed in the wake of LaPorte's self-immolation.

These final letters do note some later choices to lend his public voice. He added his signature to a public statement that critiqued Catholic Relief Services'

---

48. Merton to Forest, February 21, 1966, *HGL* 295–997; emphasis in the original.

49. This letter was first given this title and published in *The Catholic Worker* 43, no. 9 (December 1977): 3. It has been reprinted elsewhere numerous times. For an edited version, see *HGL* 294–97 or Forest, *The Root of War Is Fear*, 192–96.

50. The booklet is a recurring topic in letters from when Forest requests permission to publish it in November 1966 to when he announces its printing in July 1967.

cooperation with the military in Vietnam, and after initially declining, he at the last minute signed onto a telegram to the Vatican, spearheaded by Dan Berrigan, to oppose U.S. Vietnam policy. He wrote a statement for Forest in support of aiding Vietnamese war victims, a program Forest administered for the FOR, and he shared his short commentary on the Pastoral Constitution's position regarding personal conscience. Their letters also mention a couple of instances when Merton wrote letters of support for Catholic conscientious objectors.[51]

On occasion these later letters reflected more on movements and conscience. One, written in late February 1967, responds to a CPF "dossier" Forest had shared. Merton writes with surprising force and urgency to restate the vision for CPF he had shared a year earlier. "I am convinced that now is the time for CPF to really catch on if it is going to," he asserted. "This is the kairos. It must not be missed." Once again, Merton sought to cultivate the conscience of everyday Catholics: "Get them specifically talking and acting where they are, and explaining the fundamentals of a Catholic Peace Movement in the simplest and most universal terms: *Pacem in Terris*, the [Vatican] Council on War, Jaegerstaetter, Pope Paul, etc." He urged Forest to also ensure that the CPF newsletter provide a dialogue forum, since "in the CPF everyone should feel that his initiative and ideas mean something—and be willing also to adjust them to the movement and growth in the ideas of others." Once again, education on the history of modern violence and the "objective, not preachy" reply of nonviolence was crucial. And the CPF must have "the moral issue spelled out":

> This is a world in which power rules by indiscriminate nihilistic terror and depends on the cooperation of "ordinary decent people" to do it, and the "ordinary decent people" come through with flying colors, giving their docility and even their lives, in order that brutality may continue and grow worse—threatening the survival of the human race itself.[52]

That assessment holds even greater import for today's precarious times. Merton offered to draft material, send copies of his published writings, and arrange for cheap distribution of his book *Gandhi on Non-Violence*. Though Forest shared this letter with CPF colleague Tom Cornell, he never directly responded to its outline for seizing the moment. One gets the impression that Forest's focus at the time on the FOR program to aid Vietnamese war victims

---

51. Merton to Forest, June 17, 1967, regarding letter for Gary Gagner, a former novice; February 27, 1967, Religious News Service press release noting Merton's support of James Mulloy, both in TMC/BU Forest Correspondence.

52. Merton to Forest, February 23, 1967, *HGL* 299–300.

and on resolving personal tensions with Dorothy Day over his marital status may have consumed his attention.

By 1968, Merton's own distractions redirected his focus from CPF and movement concerns, and their correspondence ebbed. With the installation of a new abbot, Merton looked toward travel opportunities and compiling the four issues of his poetry magazine, *Monks Pond*. Yet in the midst of this he found time and attention to publish his final book on social thought, *Faith and Violence: Christian Teaching and Christian Practice*, which he co-dedicated to Forest and Phil Berrigan.

But in April 1968 Merton penned a short letter to Jim's wife, Linda, that reads like a postscript to his earlier "Young Activist" letter. She had written the monk as a "confused soul" who, as a practicing Catholic, was also navigating the decade's many streams of popular cultural influence, such as "humanism" and "Zen-pantheism-Allan Watts" views, all in a milieu where Vietnam was "draining the hell out of everyone in the movement." She closed, "but the wellsprings are deep and full of hope and that never runs out."[53] Merton responded to Linda just two days after the assassination of Martin Luther King Jr., commiserating that "These last months I have had a very deep sense of the dry rot that is coming out in everything. . . . I never had such a tidal wave of hopelessness coming in from the world on my radar: and all of it or a lot of it labeled 'optimism' [or] 'Christian hope' and even claiming to be turned on real high." He lamented how not only were too many "caught in the media machinery," but perhaps those in her own circles compounded matters by becoming "too dependent and too dominated and too pushed around, not by the squares but by each other." Merton suggested she turn inward, since "obviously one cannot expect to get anything from 'outside' whether it comes labeled 'God' or 'Zen' or 'radical Christianity.'" Rather than sink into the shared sense of sickness that clouded their social horizons, "conscience rebels," and those wellsprings Linda mentioned "are *your* wellsprings, first of all, and if you keep your own springs available, you can't die of thirst: and you can even help others to find theirs."[54]

Concerning Movements and Conscience

The seven-plus years of Merton's exchanges with Jim Forest defy easy summary. Through these letters, Merton invested heavily in a young activist whom he trusted and in whom he saw potential to nurture a movement that sought

---

53. Linda Forest to Merton, n.d., TMC/BU.

54. Merton to Linda Forest, April 6, 1968, TMC/BU; emphasis in the original.

goals and values Merton shared. But the letters' greatest value to us rests in the insight they provide on Thomas Merton's sometimes sympathetic, sometimes hostile posture toward social movements as lived out in a 1960s context. They help clarify his criteria for both movement objectives and the personal mindset he asked of movement activists, and they accent Merton's interest in moving hearts and minds within his Church so that it might then influence broader society. He saw movement vocations more as pastoral and apostolic than as social or patriotic expressions of ideological or political loyalties.

Merton did not oppose efforts to reach and influence others on a mass scale, and he felt prophetic and provocative acts have their place. But he refused to let those measures overshadow the centrality of human personhood and individual conscience. He emphasized movement building through dialogue and education of "ordinary decent people" to disrupt their dependence on myths perpetuated by a cultural mass mind. But disrupting did not mean evoking fear or provoking further retreat under the comforting shelter of those illusory myths. Activists who launch and animate such movements must draw from the wells of their *own* refined conscience rather than personal outrage. This means keeping one's sight trained on a greater truth and refusing to let ego, self-interest, or needs to prove one's goodness drive their motives. It also means guarding conscience against toxic mass mentalities and assuring that all involved feel heard and needed. This translates into an unglamorous posture of service, not showmanship, and a commitment to "the value, the rightness, the truth of the work itself," regardless of apparent results.

Helpful movements, from Merton's view, stimulate and awaken both individual and collective conscience. But movements that refuse to distinguish between harmful structures and the human persons caught up as cogs that drive structural machinery will ultimately fail. The same applies to movements to replace one coercive system with another, or those that coerce members into conformity with scripts or lack respect for members' personal conscience and freedom.

Over a half century later, as the juggernaut of an increasingly destructive and schizophrenic "mass mind" propels us closer to social, political, and biospheric collapse, the growth of a countervailing "mass mind" to push against it may seem warranted. Our milieu begs questions about whether Merton himself might not judge this a sufficiently "serious moral situation" to compel "dramatic and provocative witness." Our times have perhaps moved beyond simply the problem of decent ordinary people passively stepping aside to let the powers freely act, since our mere daily routines now perpetuate destruction already underway. Only rapid and massive systemic change can alter that. Temptation mounts to ignore Merton's personalist counsel. As we face these stark realities and prepare to respond, this relationship between a middle-aged contemplative monk and a dedicated young activist offers us a special gift. Their dialogue in letters provides a model to reflect upon as we seek our own place amid the perpetual tensions between mass movements and personal conscience.

This letter illuminates how Merton felt movements and conscience intersect. Written following Roger LaPorte's self-immolation, Merton shared his vision for movement priorities and offered personal support to Forest in his movement role. An abridged version is found in The Hidden Ground of Love, *290–93.*

Dec. 29, 1965

Dear Jim,

Your letter, statement,[55] Christmas wishes and all reached me yesterday, no doubt held up while officially scanned, and then also it is the Christmas rush. But I was glad to get all of it. No objection to any slight change in the statement, no problems. I liked your covering letter. I am glad that if and when this is a story in the press we will both have contributed something and it will be for the benefit of CPF and also a churchly act—wherever two or three are gathered in my Name . . . Etc.[56] So everything has worked out fine so far.

As a matter of fact I have just finished quite a long commentary on the Constitution on the Church in the World.[57] Had to do it for Burns Oates, they are bringing out the peace part of Seeds of Destruction only, in England, and this needed to go with it.[58] When I get a mimeo I'll send it along. But my typist is sick now, and I am also having trouble with this machine. We'll see what comes. I think the Constitution is great, but the English translation is abominable, murky, heavy, it stupefies the reader, is not in the language of modern man, etc.

I am very glad you are going to do something about this. This is crucially important. Here the Church has spoken as clearly and authoritatively as one

---

55. Forest to Merton, December 22, 1965, TMC/BU, with copy of CPF cover letter for press release of Merton's statement on protest.

56. Merton's ellipsis.

57. Pastoral Constitution on the Church in the Modern World, or *Gaudium et Spes* ["Joy and hope," the opening words of the document], published by the Second Vatican Council on its closing day, December 7, 1965.

58. *Redeeming the Time* (London: Burns and Oates, 1966).

would want, and it is an obvious apostolic duty of everyone to get down to work and interpret and apply the Constitution. Obviously the Hannons and Spellmans[59] are not going to do much with the parts that have any bite and call for any substantial change of thought. This is a big job of the CPF in the Church in America: it is what you are called to do now. I think for one thing you ought to publish something: perhaps a collection of comments and statements from bishops and theologians. I'd be glad to do a leaflet which you could mimeograph or anything you like, simply spelling out the Council teaching on war. And when you get my long commentary, you can use it in so far as you don't conflict with any magazine who might need it first (I have already mentioned it to Continuum). The only problem would be publication of it in book form. The commentary goes over the whole Constitution and stresses the basic principles, personalism and the unity of the human family, on which the whole thing is built up.

You want to get to the colleges, the seminaries and the clergy, and maybe you will need three separate approaches. I am not too smart about all that, so I won't suggest anything. You will know. I am personally convinced that this is the big chance for CPF to really do something important for the Church. More important than CW can do. I mean it. I share your immense respect for CW and its prophetic quality, but precisely because it is prophetic it remains more or less a symbol that everyone admires but stays away from. Your more colorless and less dramatic job is apostolic: simply reaching a lot of people and helping them to change their minds. You will at this present juncture be much more likely to have a deep transforming effect on the American Catholic Church than the CW ever will, if you use your opportunity. I think you need to get all your priests on the job in their milieu. The thing about this particular task is that it is not in the least ambiguous, it is the straight teaching of the Church which everybody is bound to listen to or else. Of course there will be all kinds of attempts at evasive interpretation. I think your job is in this case simply to get the Constitution across, not even worrying about whether or not it gets CPF better known and so on. Just get people thinking in terms of that Constitution. That alone will be enough to justify any one man's existence in this life. Any help I can give, I will gladly give, within my limitations.

An important point in your letter: the question of "provocative" witness. That calls for clarification, I think. Maybe I did not use the right word. Here is what I mean by it.

1. By provocative actions I mean actions that have an aggressive, challenging nature over and above the simple question of conscience that is involved. For

---

59. "Hannon" may refer to Philip Hannan, an auxiliary bishop of the Archdiocese of Washington, DC, from 1956 to 1965, a strong anti-Communist and friend of the Kennedy family, then the archbishop of New Orleans from 1965 to 1988. "Spellman" refers to New York Archbishop (1939–1967) Cardinal Francis Spellman, outspoken supporter of the U.S. war in Vietnam.

that reason I do not consider Jagerstatter's refusal of military service provocative.[60] It was straight business: a refusal to commit a crime. Naturally this had an aspect that could not help being regarded as "provocative," but this did not flow from the essential nature of the act. It did not have a provocative character and intention. Also I would say that the Peace March in Washington in November,[61] from what I heard about it, was not in any sense provocative, though it was a determined statement against the war in Vietnam.

2. Certainly there must be some provocative witness, especially now in a serious moral situation. I have changed my view of the draft card burning in the last weeks since only now am I fully informed. Before I had no idea of the existence of the law that one had to carry the card, etc. I thought that the burning was just a protest against the draft law as such. It is much more easy to see that the law about having to have that card is unjust and repressive, and aimed at silencing protest. The law itself is an example of provocative use of authority. It is a challenge, and if someone takes up the challenge, that is understandable. In this sense I think that the card burning was right, and I would go along with it in the case of one or two reasonable people. But I still would not (as you would not) back an irresponsible resort to card burning by a bunch of kids who want something to do to prove themselves.

3. I still do not think that the dramatic and provocative type of witness is what we most need now, in the sphere of Catholic peace witness. On the contrary, I think what we need is massive and undramatic apostolic work to clarify the Church's teaching and get it thoroughly known. In this I think we should avoid as far as possible any dramatization of conflict between conservatives and liberals, subjects and Superiors, and so on. The more we can work along on the assumption that the whole Church is united (until someone provocatively proves otherwise) the better chance we have of getting this Constitution understood, and making the first step toward an abolition of war or a renunciation of the war mentality by everyone. The job is titanic, and I think a few dramatic demonstrations that simply get people excited will not do much to start it, at this point.

At the moment, you know it better than I, the country is full of sincere people who are honestly bothered by the killing in Vietnam and cannot see it as a just war, yet cannot identify themselves with a specifically pacifist protest. These people are morally in no man's land, under pressure from both extremes. These are the ones who need help in articulating their objections in terms of the Church's teachings. I think they must be reached in such a way that their

---

60. Franz Jägerstätter, an Austrian peasant Catholic who refused induction into the Nazi army despite urging to do so from his parish priest and bishop. He was beheaded for his refusal.

61. March on Washington, November 27, 1965, sponsored by the antiwar organization SANE (initially the National Committee for a Sane Nuclear Policy).

refusal to be identified as pacifists is fully respected, above all because the Constitution's position is simply Catholic, and nothing else. No further label is required. People should understand this first of all. The next thing is I think to begin a study of the pervasive violence that is everywhere in our thinking. This is the thing that I think is most dangerous, and humanly speaking I think it makes one almost despair of this nation being a peaceful one: we are a nation addicted to images of violence, brutality, sadism, combat, self-affirmation by arrogance, aggression, and so on. That is another reason why the "provocative" is ambiguous as soon as it gets into such a context. On the other hand, behind all this aggressiveness is fear. Once these people are sure they are not being attacked, undermined and ruined, they are willing to listen to reason. The job is to get a hearing, a real hearing.

This letter has gone on too long, but I hope some of it may make sense. I would be glad to help with bits of commentary and clarification that you can use. I would prefer in my present position not to have each utterance announced by a trumpet blast of some sort or anything that would give people the idea I was out there mixed up in a lot of action. Just what is necessary to get the truth out.

Where's Dan [Berrigan] now?[62] How is he getting on? He's been gone almost a month already so he ought to be back before too long. Say hello if you write him, and say I am praying for him anyway. He will get back and be more valuable than ever.

I got some Masses for Christmas so on January 2 I will offer Mass for the CPF for the New Year and for the work to be done.

God bless all of you, and peace be in your hearts anyway. Ping Ferry seems gloomy about the war outlook. I don't have much of a picture of Vietnam except diffuse horror and inhumanity: but the sinister thing is that both the Chinese and the Pentagon concur in wanting this crime to continue without hindrance, and the Chinese for their part are making a great point of brave little Vietnam doing it by herself, which is pretty sad. If only somewhere there were a government one could really respect. I see no hope from that quarter. The Church is really in a position to do something now. So let's trust and do what we can. God bless you again.

Ever yours in Christ,

[PS] Jim Douglass is moving out to British Columbia and will write a book on non-violence.

---

62. Following his sympathetic homily at Roger LaPorte's memorial service, Catholic leaders criticized Daniel Berrigan for appearing to condone suicide and his Jesuit superiors sent him on a four-month tour of Latin America to remove him from the center of peace movement attention. See also chapter 4.

4

RESISTANCE

THE MERTON - DANIEL BERRIGAN LETTERS

*The moment of truth will come when you will have to resist the
arbitrary and reactionary use of authority in order to save the
real concept of authority and obedience, in the line of renewal.*
— *Thomas Merton to Daniel Berrigan
February 14, 1966*[1]

Among Thomas Merton's many friends and correspondents, Daniel Berrigan
stands out as a genuine peer. Born within five years of each other, they held
common roles of teacher, poet, writer, and priest within religious orders of
the Roman Catholic Church. Under vows of obedience to Church and order,
they encountered censure when expressing their gifts and responded creatively to surmount those obstacles and share prophetic insights. They also
held similar visions to usher forth God's Kingdom on Earth, visions that
combined respect for the integrity of human persons with nonviolent resistance to forces that impede it. The impediments they resisted took varied
forms: institutional church inertia, political and social structures, and destructive worldviews.

Persons of faith often rely on spiritual community, human society, and
guiding paradigms to navigate life. Yet each realm imposes claims to authority
and demands for obedience that beg an array of questions. Obedience to which
authority under what circumstances? Toward what end? Within what limits? In
what relation to one's interior authority and conscience? Merton and Berrigan
grappled with these questions as they engaged the world and commiserated in
resistance to ecclesiastical inertia. But their distinct vocations sometimes

---

1. *HGL* 91.

prompted differing responses. Berrigan prioritized direct resistance against social and political mechanisms; Merton focused more on transforming the paradigms that drove them. Yet as they pursued their visions inspired by scripture, tradition, and personal experience, they faced similar challenges raised by society, peers, and their unique personalities. And in this each gifted the other with affirmation, discernment, and accountability expressed through intimate friendship.

Daniel Joseph Berrigan (1921–2016)[2]

Daniel Berrigan was born in Minnesota as the fifth of six children (all boys) to a second-generation Irish-Catholic father and a mother of German descent. When Daniel was five the family moved to Syracuse, New York, where his parents spent their remaining years. His father supported the family as a laborer and trade union member, and the *Catholic Worker* newspaper became a fixture in their household. Following high school graduation in 1939, Dan entered the Society of Jesus, or Jesuits, and over the next fifteen years progressed through the order's rigorous program of formation. Ordained a priest in 1952 he culminated his formation with a year of study and priestly service in France that ended in the autumn of 1954. While abroad he encountered cutting-edge Catholic theological thought and "worker priests" committed to solidarity with France's working poor. Those experiences helped nudge his commitments toward a life of resistance to oppression and violence. During his first three years back from France, as a Brooklyn prep-school teacher, he connected students with poor urban workers and Puerto Rican communities in Manhattan's Lower East Side, and he formed ties with Dorothy Day and the Catholic Worker movement.

Beginning to Resist

The year 1957 marked a significant transition for Berrigan as he joined the theology faculty of Le Moyne College in Syracuse, New York, and published his first book of poetry, *Time without Number*, a National Book Award nomi-

---

2. Biographical information from: Daniel Berrigan, *To Dwell in Peace: An Autobiography* (San Francisco: Harper and Row, 1987); Murray Polner and Jim O'Grady, *Disarmed and Dangerous: The Radical Lives of Daniel and Philip Berrigan* (New York: Basic Books, 1997); Daniel Berrigan, *Essential Writings*, ed. John Dear (Maryknoll, NY: Orbis Books, 2009); Jim Forest, *At Play in the Lions' Den: A Biography and Memoir of Daniel Berrigan* (Maryknoll, NY: Orbis Books, 2017).

nee and Lamont Poetry Prize winner. At Le Moyne Berrigan challenged unjust social machinery and elicited its pushback. Both the Syracuse bishop and local Catholic Le Moyne benefactors bristled when he questioned city housing structures and, with a pacifist war tax resister, co-founded a house of hospitality for the poor. Le Moyne's president backed Berrigan under pressure to fire him, and he continued to push the local social envelope.

Among other efforts, Berrigan founded a campus Latin American House where he lived with students immersed in preparation for service in Mexico. Meanwhile, Daniel's younger

Daniel Berrigan, SJ, ca. 1968
(Photo by Bruce Anspach)

brother Philip had been ordained to priesthood in the Society of St. Joseph of the Sacred Heart, or Josephites, an order that served African Americans. Philip helped expand Dan's awareness of racial injustice. The brothers' 1960 attempt to join a Freedom Ride together was thwarted by their respective orders, but working together they sent Le Moyne students south to confront segregation and enrolled southern Blacks at Le Moyne. Daniel also worked ecumenically during the early sixties to co-lead joint retreats of Catholics and Protestants with John Heidbrink of the Fellowship of Reconciliation (FOR).

Nineteen sixty-three became another key year for both brothers. Their jointly authored book manuscript—in which Daniel addressed social implications of Catholic liturgy and Philip critiqued Catholic racial segregation—was rejected by censors of both orders. Philip's persistent challenges to racism in the South prompted his reassignment to a high school in Newburgh, New York, that June. In response to Dan's agitation for social justice in Syracuse, the Jesuits sent him on a European sabbatical that summer and reassigned him to the editorial staff of *Jesuit Mission* in New York City when he returned. His year abroad deepened Dan's antiwar sentiments and political skepticism. He learned from European critiques of the growing U.S. role in Vietnam, visited apartheid South Africa, and joined John Heidbrink's FOR tour of European

Christendom, where he participated in the conversation that launched the Catholic Peace Fellowship (CPF). Following his return that autumn he joined the FOR's Merton-led "spiritual roots of protest" retreat at Gethsemani Abbey.

These 1963–1964 experiences laid solid grounding for Dan's opposition to U.S. military action in Vietnam and the draft. The Gethsemani retreat helped Berrigan associate St. Paul's "principalities and powers" with dominant social and economic structures, a perspective strengthened by friendship with William Stringfellow beginning in 1965. Berrigan's resistance grew more prophetic and apocalyptic as the decade progressed.

National Emergence

As the whirlwind of war and antiwar resistance gained momentum during the latter half of the sixties, the Berrigans often found themselves at its center. When the interfaith Clergy Concerned about Vietnam[3] formed in the fall of 1965, Dan served as co-chair. During upheaval around Roger LaPorte's self-immolation in early December, Berrigan's sympathetic funeral homily created a firestorm of criticism that prompted his three-month "exile" to visit Latin American Catholic communities, which only enhanced his antiwar credentials. In early 1967, in defiance of Jesuit superiors, he joined FOR plans to deliver medical supplies to Vietnamese civilians, but their failure to obtain visas thwarted the trip. The next year he accompanied historian Howard Zinn to North Vietnam to gain release of three U.S. prisoners of war. In October 1967 Dan's arrest at a Pentagon demonstration earned his status as the first U.S. priest arrested in civil protest just five days prior to Philip's arrest as one of four who poured blood on Baltimore draft records. The brothers were arrested together in May 1968 for burning draft records with seven others in Catonsville, Maryland. Their dramatic civil disobedience earned them wide national coverage, including an appearance on *Time* magazine's cover.

Daniel Berrigan's resistance did not end with the Vietnam War, of course. In 1980, at a nuclear weapons manufacturing plant in King of Prussia, Pennsylvania, he and Philip launched their Plowshares Movement to oppose nuclear proliferation. These actions typically involved breaking into restricted facilities and symbolically damaging nuclear weaponry to publicize their critique. Dan was arrested perhaps hundreds of times throughout his life in protest of U.S. military actions, wars, and weaponry.[4] He endorsed a

---

3. Later Clergy and Laity Concerned about Vietnam (CALCAV).

4. John Dear, "The Life and Death of Daniel Berrigan," *Waging Nonviolence*, May 2, 2016, https://wagingnonviolence.org/2016/05/the-life-and-death-of-daniel-berrigan/.

Catholic "consistent life" ethic that opposed abortion, and he cared for AIDS patients when others spurned them as pariahs. In so many ways Daniel Berrigan's remarkable and inspired life personified active nonviolent resistance to inhuman forces.

Thomas Merton's Relationship with Daniel Berrigan

Daniel Berrigan credited his brother Philip with his pivotal inspiration to resist, and the FOR's John Heidbrink also contributed to that. But as frustration mounted and temptations to break Church ties beckoned, he also drew upon Thomas Merton's stabilizing friendship. Berrigan was five years younger than the Trappist, but unlike the convert Merton, had been Catholic from birth. He joined the Jesuits two years before Merton entered Gethsemani Abbey and ended his novitiate three years sooner. But Merton's Trappist formation required only six years, far less than Berrigan's grueling fifteen-year Jesuit tutelage. And so, despite Berrigan's head start, Merton took final monastic vows seven years before Berrigan's formation was complete, and he was ordained to the priesthood three years in advance of Berrigan. Merton began his writing career even further ahead of Berrigan, since he published his first book of poetry in 1944, thirteen years before Berrigan's, and Merton's first major work of prose[5] in 1948 preceded Berrigan's by eleven years.

Getting Acquainted

Their shared writing talent led to their initial contact—a letter of appreciation Berrigan sent Merton following 1948 publication of *The Seven Storey Mountain.*[6] Apparently due to monastery restrictions on writing letters, Merton could not respond to readers' mail—if he even personally received Berrigan's letter. Despite this, and though Berrigan had not yet published any poetry volumes, Merton somehow learned of Berrigan as a fellow poet. Less than a month after *The Seven Storey Mountain* was published, he recommended

---

5. Merton's spiritual memoir, *Seven Storey Mountain*, was published in October 1948 but earlier he wrote several minor manuscripts on Cistercian spirituality, including a biography of Mother M. Berchmans, *Exile End in Glory* (Milwaukee: Bruce Publishing Company, 1948).

6. *To Dwell in Peace* indicates Berrigan contacted Merton "around the time of his ordination in 1947" (107), though Merton was ordained in 1949. *Disarmed and Dangerous* gives the unattributed account of Berrigan first writing "to praise his spiritual autobiography" (101).

Berrigan to his poetry publisher, James Laughlin, for inclusion in a proposed anthology of Catholic poetry Merton planned to edit.[7]

Dan quoted Merton when writing to Phil a couple years later,[8] though no direct communication surfaced for a decade. But when Berrigan responded to Merton's "The Root of War Is Fear" in the October 1961 *Catholic Worker*, Merton promptly acknowledged it and expressed appreciation for Berrigan's involvement in founding PAX. This late 1961 exchange launched regular communication that involved more than letters. Berrigan visited Gethsemani five times in the next six years and sent Merton at least seven tape-recorded messages, mostly during his 1963–64 year abroad. When the Vietnamese Buddhist monk Thich Nhat Hanh visited Merton in May 1966, they recorded a joint message to Berrigan.[9] The Jesuit's visits began in the summer of 1962 upon Merton's invitation, when Dan, Phil, and Dan's Canadian friend Tony Walsh all enjoyed a week of Abbey hospitality. While there Berrigan addressed Merton's novices (as did Walsh) plus a gathering of monks. The 1964 FOR peace activist retreat provided Berrigan's second occasion to visit, and he returned once in each of the next three years.

Common Bonds

Merton appreciated Berrigan as a fellow poet and identified him as such to others.[10] He told Pablo Antonio Cuadra, a Nicaraguan poet and editor of the Latin American literary magazine *El Pez y La Serpiente*, in 1964: "*El Pez* can have a very important mission, as being apart and independent of the big 'movements' whether progressive or conservative,...recognized and identified by the mass media....Fr. Daniel Berrigan, S.J. is one who would collaborate though he is not yet too well known."[11] In following years, Berrigan appears mostly in Merton's letters to activists such as Jim Forest, John Heidbrink, and others.

---

7. James Laughlin to D. Berrigan, November 8, 1948, Daniel Berrigan Correspondence, TMC/BU. The anthology was never published.

8. D. Berrigan to P. Berrigan, March 19, 1951, *The Berrigan Letters: Personal Correspondence between Daniel and Philip Berrigan*, ed. Daniel Cosacchi and Eric Martin (Maryknoll, NY: Orbis Books, 2016), 8.

9. Merton to Sister Therese Lentfoehr, June 7, 1966, *The Road to Joy: Letters to New and Old Friends*, ed. Robert E. Daggy (New York: Farrar, Straus and Giroux, 1989), 256. Cited hereafter as *RJ*.

10. Merton to Ernesto Cardenal, December 24, 1961, *CT* 130, and August 17, 1962, *CT* 134; Merton to Zalman Schachter, February 15, 1962, *HGL* 535; Merton to Sister Therese Lentfoehr, September 20, 1962, *RJ* 241; February 19, 1963, *RJ* 243; and April 1, 1964, *RJ* 248.

11. Merton to Cuadra, June 30, 1964, *CT* 191.

Merton also saw in Berrigan refreshing perspectives on the Catholic Church's role in the modern world and as a harbinger of creative liturgies to express that. Berrigan credited his experience of mentoring students at Le Moyne with sparking his interest in creative worship,[12] commenting to Merton in early 1962 that, "With all classes, one has courageously and in and out of season, to spell out social implications of the worship at our disposal."[13] Following Berrigan's first visit later that year, Merton noted in his journal:

> Fr. Dan Berrigan, an altogether convincing and warm intelligence, with a perfect zeal, compassion and understanding. This, certainly, is the spirit of the Church. This is a hope I can believe in, at least in its validity and its spirit. The dimensions of living charity come clear in such talks as he gave and that does much to exorcise the negativism in me.[14]

During the 1964 retreat of peace activists Merton recorded: "Dan Berrigan said a way-out Mass in the novitiate chapel yet it was beautiful too.... Dan's celebration of the sacrificial liturgy was simple and impressive. All in English and 'uncanonical' even to the extreme point not only of Communion in both kinds but Communion to the Protestants!!"[15] And two years after that:

> Dan Berrigan arrived by surprise Tuesday.... We concelebrated twice—once in the regular present rite, and today, with a new Mass he found somewhere which is very fine and simple. I don't know how legal we were. It was a very moving simple English text (Canon and all)... very open, simple, even casual, but very moving and real. Somehow I think the new is really better.[16]

They also shared frustration with Catholic inertia and superiors' reluctance to accommodate their vision. Merton planned to write the preface for Dan and Phil's joint book that censors prohibited. Phil later published his material

---

12. Berrigan, *To Dwell in Peace*, 151.

13. D. Berrigan to Merton, January 24, 1962, TMC/BU.

14. August 21, 1962, *Turning toward the World: The Pivotal Years. The Journals of Thomas Merton: Volume Four, 1960–1963*, ed. Victor A. Kramer (New York: HarperCollins, 1996), 238. Cited hereafter as *TTW*.

15. November 19, 1964, *DWL* 167.

16. October 13, 1966, *Learning to Love: Exploring Solitude and Freedom. The Journals of Thomas Merton: Volume Six, 1966–1967*, ed. Christine M. Bochen (New York: HarperCollins, 1997), 149. Cited hereafter as *LL*.

separately as *No More Strangers*,[17] for which Merton penned the introduction. Dan tried to separately publish his material, but censors again rejected it.[18]

Points of Difference

Despite these bonds, each recognized that the other held a different vocation. In an early 1962 exchange, Berrigan objected to "the Benedictine approach" of prayer as "open...to estheticism and human non-involvement."[19] Merton defended his order's Benedictine roots, suggesting that if viewed "in the Oriental context" Dan's objections would "vanish." Besides, "There is an absolute need for the solitary, bare, dark, beyond concept, beyond thought, beyond feeling type of prayer....Unless that dimension is there in the Church somewhere the whole caboodle lacks light and life and intelligence. It is a kind of hidden, secret, unknown stabilizer, and a compass too."[20]

Berrigan's impatience with non-engaged monastic withdrawal surfaced elsewhere in their letters, but each mostly accepted and affirmed their differences as complementary. As Merton moved toward hermit status Berrigan noted:

> I liked your ideas on continuing solitude. The first thing is, that is the form the Spirit is inviting you to; the second is, to be pragmatic and perhaps selfish, it is in solitude that you began to speak to all of us in a way that no noise, and not even the audible wisdom of good men, could have reached.[21]

A couple of years later, anticipating Dan's return from Latin America, Merton claimed the LaPorte affair convinced him to "renounce all illusions about a charism of leadership...however remote....[But] with you the case is entirely different because you are in the middle of things. In either case let us work for the Church and for people, not for ideas and programs."[22] As noted below, their most significant points of difference surfaced when resisting the Vietnam War.

---

17. New York: Macmillan, 1966.

18. Daniel's 1966 book, *They Call Us Dead Men: Reflections on Life and Conscience* (New York: Macmillan, 1966), may have incorporated material planned for their original joint venture.

19. D. Berrigan to Merton, January 24, 1962, TMC/BU.

20. Merton to D. Berrigan, March 10, 1962, *HGL* 73.

21. D. Berrigan to Merton, June 2, 1964, TMC/BU.

22. Merton to D. Berrigan, February 14, 1966, *HGL* 91.

Resistance in Letters

Their closest bonds of resistance centered on superiors' restrictions and Catholic reluctance to engage crucial issues. These concerns surface in their earliest exchanges, as in this 1961 letter from Merton:

> The great problem is the blindness and passivity of Christians, and the way they let themselves be used by crypto fascist elements who get stronger and stronger every day. I have just realized that, as Catholics, we are almost in the same position the Catholics were in before the last war in Hitler's Germany.... We are so far from reality. As if the Lord were bound to give us hundreds more years to get some sense in our heads.[23]

Over time, as they more directly addressed external forces of racial and military violence, the weight of their dialogue on resistance shifted from tensions of priestly obedience toward matters of public discourse. Berrigan's fierce sense of justice and his conviction that faith demands an active response often fed his frustration and discouragement. In such moments he sometimes vented to and sought counsel from his contemplative friend.

1963 Crossroads—Writing Straight on Crooked Lines

One of these occasions arose in a mid-1963 letter Berrigan wrote while on retreat, preceding a "day of prayer and discussion to ask where we go from here" with his brother Philip, John Heidbrink, and Catholic FOR staff member Brewster Kneen. He reflected on events of the past year: censorship of the brothers' manuscript, his impending departure from Le Moyne on a forced sabbatical, Phil's reassignment to Newburgh, New York, from his New Orleans segregation battles, a retreat speaker who dismissed his suggestion that monks address human need beyond their enclosures. Berrigan confessed a "sinking feeling sometimes of chucking it all over, the pseudo obedience cult that protects all the fences, and going to Birmingham," where Blacks campaigned against segregation. He speculated whether some bishop might then emerge to "protect a man who had gone in for civil disobedience and church disobedience, but who still wants to be a Catholic and a Priest." Berrigan lamented how "the whole Church is finding its peace in 'long term good' which is always just around the corner" and he chastised its "canonizing of a

---

23. Merton to D. Berrigan, November 10, 1961, *HGL* 71.

stasis of inaction." He longed for a religious community that could "break up their sacred housekeeping in the name of justice and social need—going to jail, freedom rides, etc, at call, and then would resume things afterward when the need was past, if such was God's will for them.... Should not a real contemplative life issue in and be allowed a freedom such as this? Or what is it for?"[24]

Merton's response as a "conscience-matter letter"[25] to avert prying abbatial eyes conceded that he asked similar questions. He suggested they must "grope our way with a great deal of prudence (the supernatural kind) and attention to grace." Without proposing an explicit path, he listed four observations. First, Berrigan should not consider the immediate circumstances in isolation, but rather in "the continuity of your work as a living unit." Only an "exceptionally grave reason" warranted a drastic break with superiors, because doing so would jeopardize the credibility of all he had accomplished, "turning adrift" those who followed his leadership. Second, though he conceded many good reasons to push for social concern within the Church, he cautioned that exposing the Church's apathy too starkly could backfire and lead to it being rejected rather than renewed. Third, he encouraged Berrigan to use his French sabbatical to seek fresh perspectives before acting. Finally, Merton sensed the civil rights movement was in flux toward a more revolutionary stage and that radical action now might soon lose its meaning and cut him off from future relevance. "At the present moment you can do more by talking and writing than by anything else."[26]

Merton concluded with his own venting. "If one reads the prophets with his ears and eyes open he cannot help recognizing his obligation to shout very loud about God's will, God's truth, and justice of man to man." But monastic restrictions had quieted his public voice lest he damage "the image of the contemplative vocation." In truth, "the monastic life is nothing if it does not open a man wide to the Holy Spirit.... What is the contemplative life if one becomes oblivious to the rights of men and the truth of God in the world and His Church?"[27]

Berrigan's direct response is lost, but he went on his sabbatical rather than "chuck it all." Yet he appreciated Merton's comments enough to share them with Phil, who then replied:

Merton's letter was marvelous—I guess he knows your dilemma and mine because it's also his own. It did a great deal to quiet some

---

24. D. Berrigan to Merton, June 21, 1963, TMC/BU.

25. Letters designated as such contained confessional material, confided to a priest, not to be read by others, including the abbot of a monk or superior of a priest.

26. Merton to D. Berrigan, June 25, 1963, *HGL* 77–78.

27. Merton to D. Berrigan, June 25, 1963, *HGL* 78–79.

of the unanswered questions, and I think, without the slightest exaggeration, that we can proceed with confidence.... But it is a very important point—in what context can you and I do the most good? I am of the opinion now that it is within the Church.[28]

While abroad Dan reported on his adventures. Once more he had encountered indifference and lack of vision among Church leadership. He saw a Church too captivated by Cold War politics to recognize its potential for a Catholic peace witness in Eastern Europe. Merton continued to encourage patience:

> Do not be discouraged. The Holy Spirit is not asleep. Nor let yourself get too frustrated. There is no use getting mad at the Church and her representatives. First there is the problem of communication, which is impossible. Then there is the fact that God writes straight on crooked lines anyway, all the time.... And we I suppose are what he is writing with, though we can't see what is being written.[29]

He later reassured the Jesuit that: "Really it is right to be in a kind of twilight area half indoors and half out of doors, ecclesial beats (not ecclesiastical). We have to be soaked in irony all the time." He compared their situation to a collapsing building masked by a "façade of smoothness." But he assured that "where it has fallen God will build and is building." And rather than worry over it, "when necessary, give it a good shove. Miters, crosiers, rings, slippers, baubles, documents, seals, bulls, rescripts, indults." He signed off, "In prayers and faith and mad hope."[30]

1966 Return from Exile—Charismatic Grace

Two years later, anticipating his return from brief exile in Latin America, Berrigan asked for Merton's perspective on how to navigate his homecoming. The Trappist's response laid out his vision for what would transpire, along with suggestions for how Berrigan might capitalize on the controversy his exile had created. Given his growing notoriety, Dan would be greeted by an array of both "hate types" and those seeking higher truth. In this milieu, Berrigan should state facts "quietly," tell the truth "patiently," and try to keep communication open with the hate people. "Don't needlessly get involved in big symbolic confrontations," he advised, although as questions of obedience and

---

28. P. Berrigan to D. Berrigan, July 1963, *Berrigan Letters*, 19.
29. Merton to D. Berrigan, February 23, 1964, *HGL* 81.
30. Merton to D. Berrigan, June 30, 1964, *HGL* 83, TMC/BU.

challenges to authority escalated, "there will indeed be symbolic confrontation and there will be a lot of chips down and a lot of people getting hurt. And maybe some institutions cracking wide open into the bargain. You are going to be one of the central figures in this.... So I would say go quietly and don't rush, you have a long road ahead of you and in any case nobody is going to stop the Vietnam war for a long time, it seems to me." Merton sensed much "emotional power pent up" that reflected real needs, yet which must find expression in "renewal and not just in a big bang and a lot of fallout." That "force is centering on someone like you" and perhaps to a lesser extent on Merton, though "you have a different job to do." For Berrigan, "the moment of truth will come when you will have to resist the arbitrary and reactionary use of authority in order to save the real concept of authority and obedience, in the line of renewal. This will take charismatic grace. And it is not easy to know when one is acting 'charismatically' when one is surrounded with a great deal of popular support on one side and nonsensical opposition on the other."[31]

With prescience Merton foresaw the escalation of frustrated activism to unfold following Berrigan's return as he urged patient communication over "symbolic" and "charismatic" acts. Berrigan in turn assured, "I will hope to be faithful to the spirit of your letter and to our friendship as the months go ahead.... So we will have to continue to run the gauntlet between the extremism of those who want nothing new, and those who want to blow up the Church overnight, for the sake of their own versions of the new Church."[32]

1966–1967 Intensifying Resistance—Risk for the Sake of Others

Merton's view from his hermitage grew even less clear as antiwar activity escalated that fall. Using a syntax that echoed this growing intensity, he shared with Berrigan:

> I don't know what to say about a peace movement: everything that anyone does anyway good bad or indifferent is just swallowed up and gone and in two days no one would ever know it was thought of. The sheer volume of things being done and said and shouted and pounded into people's heads is so terrific that in the end nothing remains but a pure flux of noise. Or that is the way it seems to me. That must be wrong because things do stick somewhere. But I wouldn't know where or how.[33]

---

31. Merton to D. Berrigan, February 14, 1966, *HGL* 89–91.

32. D. Berrigan to Merton, March 18, 1966, TMC/BU.

33. Merton to D. Berrigan, September 18, 1966, Department of Rare Books, Cornell University.

As Merton predicted, Berrigan's path led him deeper into tension with authority that strained his Jesuit obedience. By early 1967 Dan declared, "We have exhausted every legal means of protest against the war. That comes as the calm conclusion of almost three years of work and tears." He explained his plans to deliver Vietnamese medical aid despite threats of expulsion from his order if he did:

> Now, dear friend and bro. Tom, it is clear to me, in a dark sort of way, that on this occasion my superiors at last touched the Berrigan marrow.... My life has been building toward the gesture ... to risk great and good things, for the sake of others.... In a sense it seems inevitable, if I am not to destroy myself in a less visible but infinitely more spiritual way.[34]

Merton seemed resigned to Berrigan's resolve to move forward, counseling that, "sooner or later it is going to be a question of obeying God or obeying man.... Maybe this is the time." Still, he encouraged Berrigan to assure his action would clearly communicate the integrity of his intentions and to beware of others who might exploit his actions for their own ends. He released Berrigan to move forward: "If you think this is it, then go ahead. ... And don't worry about the consequences: but just watch yourself in the mushroom cloud that follows, be sure in all things you are really trying to do it in God's way as a real Jesuit."[35] But since visas were never granted for the trip, Berrigan never took that step.

1967 Violence to Property—An Important Choice of Direction

Their final exchange on resistance focused mostly on public, social dynamics as Phil Berrigan planned his inaugural Baltimore draft board raid for late October 1967, when he and three others poured blood on draft board records. Earlier that month, Phil had hinted to Dan of those plans as something "against military or gov[ernment] property," and sought his brother's input. Dan in turn reported to Merton on Phil's intent to challenge a governmental stance that elevated "property" above "persons." Phil anticipated "vindicating the truth of non-violence toward persons by working violence on idolatrous things, thus removing, at least by way of prophecy, all the garbage which expensively keeps persons from being human toward persons." Dan questioned: "Will such action communicate at all???" Nonviolent activists were encountering not only war-making violence but also Black Power rejec-

---

34. D. Berrigan to Merton, April 1967, TMC/BU.
35. Merton to D. Berrigan, April 15, 1967, *HGL* 94.

tion of nonviolence. "Do we have to be willing to lose socially—i.e., in bringing hope to the living [—] by refusing to take even such a chance as this step indicates?"[36]

Absent any specific context, Merton replied (reproduced below) with thinly disguised concern. He recognized that amid rising Black Power and Latin American calls for revolution, "We are all in a position now where some kind of important choice of direction is called for." He considered those revolutionary calls "irresponsible," "capricious," "pointless," "inviting disaster," and feared the Catholic peace movement might succumb to popular culture's "obsession with being 'with it' whatever 'it' may turn out to be...now non-violent, now flower power, now burn baby, all sweetness on Tuesday and all hellfire on Wednesday, [which] reflects sheer mindlessness and hopelessness." He would not "say violence against property is off limits ...[though] killing people *is*." Merton asked: "Politically: are we just getting involved in a fake revolution of badly mixed up disaster inviting people who are willing to do anything absurd and irrational simply to mess things up, and to mess them up especially for the well-meaning 'idealists' who want to run along proving that they are such real good hip people?"[37]

Merton suggested that "the CPF and Catholic left etc,...try to be less naïve" with "a kind of relative clarity and consistency and firmness that *stays with* a clearly recognizable Christian and Gospel position." He considered violence against property as "outside the Gandhian thing" and encouraged them to "stay with Gandhi's end of it until we have at least gone deep into it and seen what was there. (As King has.)" He concluded:

> In my opinion, the job of the Christian is to try to give an example of sanity, independence, human integrity, good sense, as well as Christian love and wisdom, against all the establishments and all mass movements and all current fashions which are mindless and hysterical....I don't say this comes anywhere near anything to the situation Phil speaks of...: I am just talking in terms of the whole situation judged by the smell of the smog that reaches me down here.[38]

Dan reproduced Merton's letter to distribute, but how widely it circulated is unclear. Neither do we know whether Merton influenced what tran-

---

36. D. Berrigan to Merton, October 6, 1967, TMC/BU.

37. Merton to D. Berrigan, October 10, 1967, *HGL* 96–98; emphasis in the original.

38. Merton to D. Berrigan, October 10, 1967, *HGL* 96–98.

spired as the Baltimore Four draft board raid. Berrigan later thanked Merton for the "marvelous letter you sent, when we were seeking light on Phil's activity,"[39] but that seems to be the last time he sought Merton's counsel before acting. He invited Merton to sign his appeal for Pope Paul VI to condemn the war, serve as symbolic recipient of draft cards from resisters, and visit his Cornell University campus to lecture on nonviolence. Merton agreed to the first but declined the others. Berrigan proceeded without asking Merton's input on both his February 1968 flight to Hanoi and Catonsville draft-board raid involvement that May. Both Berrigans asked Merton to testify at their trial, but Merton was by then on his Asian journey and declined to scuttle those plans for a court appearance. So, as Merton's final year unfolded, their paths of resistance diverged.

One Voyage Branching into Two

Prior to those questions of "violence toward property," Merton seemed in sync with Dan's path. He accepted Dan's accelerating public engagement, noting in early 1967: "It is foolish to pass judgment on a kind of life [conferences, jets, travel] that is simply not for me, or to seem to pass judgment.... I admire Dan Berrigan for his perfect acclimatization in all this."[40] After their final meeting in April 1967 he recorded: "Dan Berrigan looked like a French worker priest in beret and black turtleneck windbreaker. A good uniform for a priest."[41]

But as Merton's final year unfolded, they drifted more out of touch and less in tune. When his new abbot opened Merton's life to expanded travel options, Berrigan invited him to speak at Cornell against Vietnam. Merton made clear that only monastically related travel would be granted and explained that personally:

> If I...had to decide it myself, I would also be against any form of public appearance. It is not consistent with what my life has been and has become.... I don't think I can do what God and the Gospel demand of me personally unless I maintain the special kind of conditions I have been chosen for.... As regards peace movement etc.: my job continues to be putting it on paper as best I can, I think, and, by letter or otherwise, helping individual CO's with advice.[42]

---

39. D. Berrigan to Merton, n.d. [November 1967?], TMC/BU.
40. April 8, 1967, *LL* 215.
41. May 10, 1967, *LL* 233.
42. Merton to D. Berrigan, February 8, 1968, *HGL* 100.

Merton mostly focused instead on literary projects, travel in search of possible relocation sites, and his Asian journey, as Berrigan flew to Hanoi with Howard Zinn, joined the May 17 Catonsville draft board raid, and prepared for the showcase trial that followed. That raid occurred while Merton visited a monastery in New Mexico:

> Somewhere, when I was in some plane or in some canyon, Dan and Phil Berrigan and some others took A-1 draft files from a draft center in a Baltimore suburb and burned them in a parking lot. Somewhere I heard they were arrested but I've seen no paper and don't know anything, but an envelope came from Dan [describing the action]...and had scrawled on it, "Wish us luck."[43]

He was still processing this news a week later: "If in fact I basically agree with them, then how long will I myself be out of jail....One of these days I may find myself in a position where I will have to [break laws]."[44]

That journal entry coincided with hosting a retreat of contemplative nuns, with whom he reflected on Berrigan's activism. It was one of three such gatherings that last year at which his unfiltered comments to fellow contemplatives, captured on tape, show his struggle to comprehend the raids' objectives and his difficulty reconciling them with his own ideals. The first occurred in early December 1967 at Gethsemani Abbey, where he briefly discussed the Baltimore Four action. The second occurred in late May following Catonsville, and the third during his Alaskan sojourn in September, just after the Milwaukee Fourteen action. Those comments reflect a context of addressing contemplative nuns about their prophetic calling. They mirror the tensions and ambiguities he and the Berrigans had previously discussed regarding faithfulness within the institutional boundaries of religious vocations while also speaking to surrounding social realities. These challenges played out within a larger society he considered "totalitarian," one that "predetermined" human choices through economic structures rather than an authoritarian dictator.[45]

---

43. May 22, 1968, *The Other Side of the Mountain: The End of the Journey. The Journals of Thomas Merton: Volume Seven, 1967–1968*, ed. Lawrence E. Cunningham (New York: HarperCollins, 1998), 110. Cited hereafter as *OSM*.

44. May 28, 1968, *OSM* 124.

45. His December and May comments are preserved on recordings 181 Tr-1b, 203 Tr-1/2, TMC/BU. Edited versions were published in *The Springs of Contemplation: A Retreat at the Abbey of Gethsemani,* ed. Jane Marie Richardson (Notre Dame, IN: Ave Maria Press, 1992), though several specific references to the Berrigans were omitted.

Across these conversations, Merton shared his ideal of working within civic processes to the degree possible, such as seeking repeal of unjust draft laws, while also, like the biblical prophets, "stand[ing] on a different ground [to] make choices before God, not choices predetermined by society." This meant alternative stances to those of popular conservative, liberal, or revolutionary ideologies. It required being "radical enough to realize that we have to dissent" from them and sometimes make choices that "break with the establishment." But rather than just act symbolically, "we've got to really live" prophetically, which "might be a much less spectacular thing," perhaps "in a small group of a few people." When trying to influence the public, "if you want to [nonviolently] say the whole thing is unacceptable... you've got to make the other person see something that's true for him as well as for you. He has to be able to agree, from what you are doing, that there is a higher truth which is better than what he is committed to. And that's awful hard to do."[46]

Through the lens of these ideals, Merton felt the Baltimore and Catonsville raids fell short. Mainly, he thought they failed to clearly communicate, reflected in his own uncertainty about their intended message. He described pouring blood on draft files as the resisters saying, "These people are murderers" and "bad people," though it is not clear if he thought that message targeted draft board members or draftees. He saw burning draft files with napalm as a "desperate" symbolic act of "standing up and screaming" in a society that offered them no other viable political choices. He heard them saying that in a society where no one was truly free, one may as well be in jail because "what you get outside of jail isn't that different." He suspected that although Dan Berrigan was not himself Marxist, he perhaps modeled his actions after others, like French Franciscans and worker priests, who *did* seek Marxist revolution. To Merton, their actions only yielded shocked public incomprehension rather than concrete or constructive communication, and he cited monastery buzz as evidence: "They're all like, I can't understand it, what it means; what's happened to him, is he crazy?" He saw those measures as a "submission," an abdication of effort to "keep fighting" in the civic realm, that they had "put all their eggs in one basket" of political symbolism. Unfortunately, "society can absorb all the protest that they can give," and "in the long run [such protest] helps the system.... With all due respect to [Dan] and everything, he's not hurting the draft, he's helping the draft." Springing from the incomprehension and fear they elicited, "a lot of people who are undecided are gonna make up their minds now in favor of patriotism."[47]

---

46. Recordings 181 Tr-1b, 203 Tr-1/2, TMC/BU; *Springs of Contemplation.*
47. Recordings 181 Tr-1b, 203 Tr-1/2, TMC/BU; *Springs of Contemplation.*

At the same time, Merton respected the Berrigans' motives, affirmed their effort "to be heroic and prophetic," and encouraged his contemplative audiences to listen to them and other "people who are aware," like "hippies."[48] Yet his August journal betrayed a growing distance:

[Dan Berrigan] is a bit theatrical these days, now he's a malefactor —with a quasi-episcopal disarmament emblem strung around his neck like a pectoral cross. He wants me in N.Y. agitating for and with him in October or November, whenever the trial is. I definitely want to keep out of anything that savors of a public "appearance" or semi-public or *anything*, especially in America.[49]

And in the wake of September's Milwaukee Fourteen draft board raid, Merton let slip to nuns in Alaska his perplexed frustration with the turn Catholic peace activism had taken: "I am mad at my friends who are going around burning draft records. I think they are nuts. . . . They are ruining the whole thing they are trying to help. . . . You have to get to a sort of meeting point where everybody can more or less agree."[50] But despite private misgivings voiced to fellow contemplatives or in his journal, publicly Merton strove to follow the template he had laid out when negotiating with Jim Forest and the CPF more than two years earlier: personal support and friendship coupled with public clarification that he did not always align with their actions.[51]

Many years later, reflecting on this unsettling phase of their relationship, Dan Berrigan lamented that he never had a chance to personally discuss those choices with Merton during a time when he was unsure exactly where Merton stood. He saw it as a time of

one path or one voyage branching into two. When I think back with the rhythm of our friendship it has something to do with solitude that had become in many senses isolation as he became a hermit, and a consequent loss of context. . . . Part of the tragedy [of Merton's discomfort with Catonsville] was my inability to get down to Geth-

---

48. Recordings 181 Tr-1b, 203 Tr-1/2, TMC/BU; *Springs of Contemplation.*

49. August 5, 1968, *OSM* 150.

50. "Retreat (Day of Recollection) Given to the Sisters at Anchorage, Alaska," Recording 201-2-2, TMC/BU. Recorded September 29, 1968. The comment was omitted from *TMA*; thanks to Kathleen Tarr for sharing this unpublished excerpt.

51. Examples include: "Circular Letter to Friends," midsummer 1968, *RJ* 116; Merton to Mary Landon, June 24, 1968, *WF* 118; "Non-Violence Does Not . . . Cannot . . . Mean Passivity," *Ave Maria*, September 7, 1968.

semani after the action in May; the summer was just too crowded to be able to move out, and then he left, and then he died, so I was never able to offer a context for Catonsville: how many months of...spiritual preparation and strategic preparation...went into that action, which of course hit the headlines from nowhere, but it came from somewhere.

Berrigan remained confident that despite this, Merton in the end still grasped "something about the context that issued not out of despair but out of hope.... We were trying to convince people of the horror of that use, that misuse [of napalm] against innocent people."[52]

Concerning Resistance

That final year clearly suggests "one voyage branching into two." Berrigan had voiced similar thoughts less than three years after Merton's death. Alluding to Merton's classic "Rain and the Rhinoceros" essay, Dan wrote to Phil:

Stood by the window last night a whole hour as the rain started. ...It reminded me of Merton's meditation and at the same time was a stun reminder of things around + within. 1) I suppose an unprisoned rainfall will get to be rarer and rarer, and 2) I suppose it is one thing to be a monk with access to some hundreds of acres of unspoiled fields and forest—and another to be under (however mild) a turn of the screw.[53]

Yet in crucial ways, theirs remained a common voyage, though perhaps they began to sail in different vessels and navigate with different charts. They both grounded their voyage of resistance in common faith convictions, and their shared destination remained God's emerging Kingdom of love and peace, here and now. Berrigan plotted his course with an urgency to confront and obstruct sociopolitical mechanisms that impede God's Kingdom. His conscience led him directly into the gears of those mechanisms to slow their momentum

---

52. "Thomas Merton, Nonviolence, and Me: A Conversation with Daniel Berrigan, SJ," interview by Terry Taylor, April 16, 2004, published in *The Merton Seasonal* 41, no. 3 (Fall 2016): 13–14. Daniel Berrigan, *Portraits of Those I Love* (New York: Crossroad, 1982), 13–14, shares uncertainty about Merton's support in the absence of face-to-face interaction, though intuiting, "He trusted us, but his trust was tested hard."

53. D. Berrigan to P. Berrigan, September 12, 1971, *Berrigan Letters*, 68.

and expose the destructive forces they serve. Merton's vocation mapped a course of immersion into our common source of being that unites life and landscape. It positioned him to recognize the paradigms that construct and drive those same mechanisms and to deploy his public voice to expose and challenge them through literary communication rather than direct and symbolic confrontation. Perhaps their branching reflects a distinction decolonialist advocates sometimes make between "civil disobedience," behaviors to create space for civic reform, and "epistemic disobedience," refusal to adopt dominant ways of thinking/knowing to make space for broader social transformation.[54]

Still, each embraced both a consciousness-transforming "peace movement" and a strategically targeted "antiwar movement," though Merton's weight rested more with the former and Berrigan's with the latter. Both approaches aspired to unveil how structures and paradigms dominate, and Berrigan upheld Merton's witness long after his friend's death. In a 1979 tribute he derided "the church and the public" fixated on a "Merton in their image," someone who is "safe and cornered, contemplative in a terribly wrong sense, and therefore manageable." He described a Merton whose work "unmasked the spiritual forces which lie under the appearances of things. [He] was always digging beneath the varnished surface, telling the truth about the forces really at work in church and state."[55] Merton's counsel to Berrigan routinely advised caution and patience when considering dramatic action. But he also acknowledged that such action may be needed at certain times under certain circumstances. He offered no blueprint for when or how to act in radical public resistance—provided it communicated nonviolently and honored human personhood. Perhaps our best lesson from this branching of voyages could be that there is no one "right" way to resist.

As we discern resistance in our own time and setting, we risk more harm than good if we fail to consider Merton's cautions: Recognize the truth others hold, and value the personhood of those whose words and actions we resist. Try to maintain communication with those we consider "haters." Give the walls of entrenched structures a push when needed, but do so seeking renewal rather than sheer destruction "with a big bang and a lot of fallout." Do not conform to popular trends simply to appear "with it." Consider continuity

54. Malgorzata Poks, "Home on the Border in Ana Castillo's *The Guardians*: The Colonial Matrix of Power, Epistemic Disobedience, and Decolonial Love," *Revista de Estudios Norteamericanos* 21 (2017): 124–25.

55. Daniel Berrigan, "The Peacemaker," in *Thomas Merton/Monk: A Monastic Tribute*, enlarged edition, ed. Br. Patrick Hart (Kalamazoo, MI: Cistercian Publications, 1983), 219–20. Originally given at the Thomas Merton Center for Creative Exchange, Denver, CO, September 17, 1979, typescript, Daniel Berrigan Correspondence, TMC/BU.

with one's life of faith, not just the narrow urgency of the moment. Do not make radical breaks or take dramatic measures that may soon become irrelevant to the larger flow of social transformation.

Merton's approach to nonviolent resistance sought to open space that permits such transformation without trampling on the freedom and conscience of others. In doing so, he asks that we resist not only dominating structures, but also the demands of personal ego and movement scripts.

This letter responds to Daniel Berrigan's request for perspective on his brother Philip's plans for "violence to property" in the upcoming Baltimore Four draft board raid, without disclosing any specifics to Merton. It captures Merton's concern to retain a faith-based, person-centered, Gandhian niche within the larger peace movement. An abridged version appears in Hidden Ground of Love, *96–98.*

Oct. 10, 1967

Dear Dan:

Reaction to your airmail special about Phil and the group that wants to get violent. This will help me clarify my own ideas, too. We are all in a position now where some kind of important choice of direction is called for. What I am going to put down now is just my own way as it more or less appears to me at the moment.

1. First to size up the situation as I see it—dimly and at a distance. Perhaps I'd better formulate it in questions rather than statements.

a) To what extent is the new revolutionism, centered mostly on Black activism, simply irresponsible, capricious, idiotic, pointless, haphazard and inviting disaster? To what extent do these people realize they are so disoriented that at the moment all they can think of is systematic unreason and disaster—acceptable insofar as precipitated by themselves? And more acceptable if a bunch of docile whites come running behind, bleating friendship noises. And go over the cliff with them. Or even ahead of them.

b) A lot of talk about Che and Debray.[56] I think that in Latin America there may be something real behind all this, but in the USA I think it sounds so far

---

56. Che Guevara and Régis Debray, both Marxist figures in the Cuban revolution; both arrested that year in Bolivia for revolutionary activity. Guevara was killed the day before Merton wrote this letter.

like just noise. Hence I wonder if it makes sense to treat the thing as a serious revolutionary option in the first place? In Latin America I think a priest and a Christian might have a serious question to face. I don't think it is like that here—I mean in choosing for the Molotov cocktails.

c) The obsession with being "with it" whatever "it" may turn out to be. It seems to me that the indifference with which the radicals and some liberals are now non-violent, now flower power, now burn baby, all sweetness on Tuesday and all hellfire on Wednesday, reflects sheer mindlessness and hopelessness. Can it be that this is the surest and most disturbing sign of pre-fascist mental chaos, the kind of thing that makes some kind of fascist totalism, police state, etc., inevitable? Is it even the kind of reaction that unconsciously invites the support and security of a police state? Is radicalism asking to be put down? Looks like that to me. Then why get involved in that, especially as people are most certainly going to get killed. Needlessly, without meaning, and without message, in a way that will only confirm the squares in utter squareness. Is this a real view of it?

2. Should we then, CPF and the Catholic left, etc., try to be less naïve, try to go it more on our own, have a more or less firm and consistent position, is our best contribution to the whole mess a kind of relative clarity and consistency and firmness that stays with a clearly recognizable Christian and Gospel position? Have we ever even begun to explore what real non-violence is about? Is this just the testing that is essential before we even get sorted out enough to begin? Are we now ready for a novitiate? In my opinion the answer is to close ranks with people like King—insofar as non-violent: I don't know what his politics are right now. To become recognizable as committed to very clear limits on the violence thing? At least to take up enough of a basic position to be able to go on from there to decide whether yes or no we can be violent "against property." That is outside the Gandhian thing right away. My opinion would be some of us ought to stay with Gandhi's end of it until we have at least gone deep into it and seen what was there. (As King has.) (As maybe the SNCC[57] guys also have, I dunno. Here I talk and they were getting shot two and three years ago.)

Summarizing my feelings on this then:

a) Ethically and evangelically we are getting toward the place where we have to be able to define our limits. I don't say violence against property is off limits. It certainly seems to me that killing people is. But if it comes to burning buildings, then people are going to be in danger and whoever is involved is going to be partly responsible for people getting destroyed even on his own side in a way that the non-violent resister would not be responsible. (They—fuzz—have no right to kill a non-violent person but they certainly think they have a right to kill a violent one.)

b) Politically: are we just getting involved in a fake revolution of badly mixed-up disaster inviting people who are willing to do anything absurd and irra-

---

57. Student Non-Violent Coordinating Committee.

tional simply to mess things up, and to mess them up especially for the well-meaning "idealists" who want to run along proving that they are such real good hip people.

c) Psychologically: how nuts is the whole damn business?

In my opinion, the job of the Christian is to try to give an example of sanity, independence, human integrity, good sense, as well as Christian love and wisdom, against all establishments and all mass movements and all current fashions which are merely mindless and hysterical. But of course are they? And do we get hung up in merely futile moral posturing? Well, somewhere we have to choose. The most popular and exciting thing at the moment is not necessarily the best choice.

I don't say any of this comes anywhere near applying to the situation Phil speaks of, I have no idea whether that is sane or nutty: I am just talking in terms of the whole situation judged by the smell of the smog that reaches me down here.

Cornell[58] sounds good. Keep in there slugging. Pray!!

PS: I don't know about Groppi,[59] but Gordon Zahn[60] was in Milwaukee all summer and has very serious reservations about the whole thing.

---

58. Cornell University, where Berrigan taught.

59. James Groppi, a priest and civil rights activist in Milwaukee, Wisconsin, who in 1966–1967 organized picketing against local segregationist judges and lobbied for housing integration laws.

60. Catholic sociologist and Merton correspondent who wrote on peace issues, biographer of Franz Jaegerstaetter.

PART II

REACHING ACROSS THE RACIAL DIVIDE

Our modern era emerged not only through the Enlightenment and industrialization, but also through Europe's quest for ever more territory to extract resources, conscript cheap labor, and settle its populations. That quest proved catastrophic for the indigenous peoples of color who inhabited those territories. As it played out on the North American continent, Africans were torn from their native landscapes and pressed into the service of white advancement through Middle Passage across the Atlantic, enslavement, and Jim Crow segregation. Native Americans who survived European settlement endured a parallel process of removal to reserves, allotment of communal land into private parcels, and forced acculturation in residential schools. To rationalize this onslaught, Euro-Americans constructed a paradigm of whiteness that not only wrenched humanity from interconnection with landscapes and the life upon them, but deemed non-European people of color as subhuman. The enduring legacy of this alienation and debasement remained powerful in Merton's time, as it does today.

Merton showed sensitivity to this legacy early on. He supported India's right to self-determination during his British public-school years, and his memoir reflections on Black degradation in Harlem held such power that when in prison Eldridge Cleaver copied and carried the passage for inspiration. At Gethsemani, Merton's awareness of indigenous peoples across both Americas grew through contact with Latin American poets in the late 1950s.

He also interacted with two African American lay brothers at Gethsemani in the 1950s and early 1960s.[1]

But Merton began to more noticeably focus on Black experience in May 1960 after browsing through Robert Penn Warren's *Segregation: The Inner Conflict in the South*[2] at the Bellarmine College library. This small book recounts conversations that Warren, a novelist and poet, shared while traveling the South in the wake of the Supreme Court's *Brown v. Board of Education* decision against segregation. His vignettes capture the dissonance, angst, and resistance many white southerners felt as they grappled with the ruling's implications. Merton thought Warren's material offered a "good idea of the problems in its human aspect." It described "the reality of the south to which I belong—without ever thinking of it. You can be in a Trappist monastery and never become a Southerner. But I am becoming a Kentuckian and a conscious one. There is no point in trying to evade it. It means of course talking to people."[3]

The next year Merton logged a March 1961 entry about "Negroes and their struggle for integration into American society." He alluded favorably to Martin Luther King Jr. and commented that "one of the most difficult things is for them to admit completely in their hearts what they know intellectually: that they are in the right."[4] Three months later, E. Glenn Hinson confirmed Merton's growing awareness of race when he and two other Southern Baptist Seminary faculty members from Louisville visited Merton at his hermitage. Hinson recalls Merton as especially keen to discuss Baptist experience with race, and he told Merton of a Mississippi pastor fired by his congregation for promoting integration.[5] Two months later, Merton received the first letter discussed in this section, sent by Marlon D. Green, a Black pilot facing discrimination in the airline industry (chapter 5).

Merton's awareness of race in the United States expanded further in 1962 through letters and readings. These included Phil Berrigan's article on

---

1. Brother Josue (Thomas Glover), a former jazz saxophonist, present 1949–1962 (see chapter 7); Br. Martin de Porres (Matthew Deloach), present 1960–2016; Br. Paul Quenon email to Oyer, January 6, 2020. Merton noted of Br. Martin in December 1963, "he is now the only Negro in the community"; December 9, 1963, *DWL* 44.

2. New York: Random House, 1956.

3. May 18, 1960, *SS* 391.

4. March 8, 1961, *TTW* 99.

5. Oyer discussion with Hinson, August 20, 2019. Hinson visited Merton June 20, 1961.

segregation in the January 1962 *Catholic Worker*,[6] and his reading of John Howard Griffin's *Black Like Me*,[7] which shared Griffin's experience traveling the South as a white man with skin chemically darkened to appear Black. Merton met Griffin later that year and they began a steady correspondence. In May, Dan Berrigan reported on local Catholic concerns about integration's impact on parishioner property values and his work with Phil to send Le Moyne College students into the South.[8] Both Berrigans visited that August, offering the chance to learn from them firsthand. In December his friend "Ping" Ferry forwarded James Baldwin's "Letter from a Region of My Mind," published the previous month in the *New Yorker* magazine.[9]

By February 1963 Merton had also read Baldwin's *Nobody Knows My Name* and commented on it in several journal paragraphs. "He seems to know exactly what he is talking about, and his statements are terribly urgent. ... The liberation of the Negroes is necessary for the liberation of the whites." Baldwin exposed "the futility and helplessness of white liberals, who sympathize but never do anything."[10] A few weeks later, Jim Forest, as associate editor of *Liberation* magazine, offered Merton a chance to publicly comment on race by requesting his thoughts on a critique that likened Baldwin to the belligerent Shakespearian character, Caliban.[11] Merton responded in Baldwin's defense that April with his first published reflection on race, "Neither Caliban nor Uncle Tom," which appeared in *Liberation*'s June issue alongside the initial publication of King's iconic "Letter from a Birmingham Jail." Merton also crafted a letter to Baldwin, eventually published in *Seeds of Destruction*. In May Merton penned his poem, "And the Children of Birmingham," inspired by images of fire hoses and dogs turned upon that city's Black children who marched for integration. His correspondence with Louisiana priest August Thompson (chapter 6) began that October, the same month his best-known piece on the topic, "Letters to a White Liberal,"[12] appeared in print.

Merton's correspondence with African American classical singer Robert Lawrence Williams (chapter 7), which began in 1964, launched him into a unique project of collaboration with a Black person to address racial dynamics.

---

6. Merton to D. Berrigan, June 15, 1962, *HGL* 74.

7. Boston: Houghton Mifflin, 1961.

8. D. Berrigan to Merton, May 16, 1962, TMC/BU.

9. Merton to Ferry, December 31, 1962, *HGL* 213. Baldwin published the essay in his 1963 book, *The Fire Next Time*.

10. February 23, 1963, *TTW* 297.

11. Merton to Forest, April 23, 1963, TMC/BU.

12. *New Blackfriars* 2 (November 1963): 467–77; (December 1963): 503–16.

His January 1968 exchange with historian Vincent Harding (chapter 8) not only provided a singular engagement with a Protestant African American scholar and civil rights leader, but it also highlights his emerging voice on the Americas' indigenous legacy.

Certainly, no white person—Thomas Merton included—can fully appreciate all that the U.S. racial legacy imposes on its peoples of color. At times Merton himself may have presumed too much about his ability to identify with what they experience. Nonetheless, he displayed a profound capacity to listen carefully, grasp the enormity of the existential gulf, and reach across it. Perhaps remarkably, these correspondents sensed in Merton—as did Eldridge Cleaver —a rare white person who truly "got" much of what they experienced as African Americans.

With the exception of his letters to Robert Williams, these exchanges show Merton not in the role of collaborator, as with peace advocates, but rather as mainly a listener and encourager. Merton consistently encouraged these four men to continue their pursuits of the respect and dignity that white America denied them. He encouraged them not to accept an identity white society sought to construct and impose upon them, but to independently carve out their own; he encouraged their quest for self-liberation. As with his letters on peace, these also capture profound and incisive comments on this section's topic. But in contrast, themes chosen here as chapter titles emerge less from words Merton wrote than from his recipients' words and actions or from their relational dynamics.

Rather than lecturing Blacks on their response to racism, Merton recognized, as he wrote to Baldwin, "a duty to try to make my fellow whites stop doing the things they do and see the problem in a different light."[13] He held to this posture even as Black Power militancy later rejected the nonviolence he embraced. To address that duty, his published writings placed greater emphasis on themes shared with those on peace: meaningful communication, recognizing shared personhood, and unveiling the illusions and naming the myths that drive white supremacy.

Also, as with his conversations on peace, Merton addressed racial dynamics in letters to many others in addition to the four featured here. These include letters to white allies of African American civil rights, such as P. D. East, a Mississippi small-town editor who supported integration; Will Campbell, an outspoken Baptist pastor who led the Committee of Southern Churchmen and founded *Katallagete* magazine; and June and John Yungblut, Atlanta Quakers and personal friends of Martin Luther King Jr. William Apel

---

13. Merton, *Seeds of Destruction*, 306.

elsewhere demonstrates the influence of John Howard Griffin's letters on Merton's racial awareness.[14] Merton also learned of racism's harsh realities from other whites he encountered, like a Franciscan novice who entered Gethsemani in fall 1963 after the southern Louisiana school at which he taught was bombed to prevent its integration.[15]

But his letters to these four African Americans especially reveal Merton's capacity to reach across the U.S. racial divide—to shed popular assumptions about race and listen to, connect with, and relate to them as persons over the decade's course. By Merton's final year, Vincent Harding could sense that Merton owned "the scandal of [his] whiteness," and "knew, or intuited" Harding's own yearnings "as much as can be known by anyone outside of me." In presenting these letters, the following chapters especially seek to permit the voices of Merton's correspondents to speak for themselves. This is vital not only in order to grasp their significance in providing Merton with windows of insight into Black experiences that shaped his perception of race. Their words illuminate the work Merton encouraged, their insights often carry weight at least equal to his, and their undertold stories deserve to be heard and appreciated in their own right.

---

14. William Apel, "Out of Solitude: Thomas Merton, John Howard Griffin, and Racial Justice," *The Merton Seasonal* 36, no. 3 (Fall 2011): 17–22.

15. Merton to John Howard Griffin, October 28, 1963, *RJ* 132. Fr. Malakey Brogan entered Gethsemani October 21, 1963, using Trappist name "Patrick." Br. Paul Quenon email to Gordon Oyer, January 27, 2020.

5

RACIAL JUSTICE

THE MERTON-GREEN LETTERS

*It is just pitiful to what extent people will go in this country to avoid
facing the truth, and to evade the claims of justice and humanity in
this race issue. I am afraid the race issue is symptomatic of many
other weaknesses, and the efforts of those who are trying to bring
the injustice to light and to right the wrong in an orderly, reasonable
way, are of the greatest importance.*

*— Thomas Merton to Marlon Green
March 20, 1963*[1]

Peeling back the many layers of Western presumptions that for centuries de-
humanized people of color demands relentless persistence. That work consists of incremental victories and setbacks over time through both mass action and individual pioneering, reflected in multiple stories of multiple
people doing battle on multiple fronts at great personal cost. One such story
is that of Marlon Dewitt Green, who battled his way for seven years to a
United States Supreme Court victory before fulfilling his dream of piloting
commercial passenger jets. Green's was a frustrating and often lonely battle.
At one low point in that journey, he reached out for encouragement to Gethsemani Abbey's most famous monk. While Thomas Merton may not have
played a pivotal role in Green's legal efforts, he provided encouragement and
moral support at a critical juncture. Green's plea granted Merton perhaps his
earliest opportunity to interact with an African American engaged in the hard
work of seeking justice to break barriers of segregation and expand civil
rights for Black Americans.

---

1. TMC/BU.

Marlon Dewitt Green (1929–2009)[2]

Marlon Green and his four siblings were born in the oil boom city of El Do-rado, Arkansas, just north of the Louisiana border in Mississippi Delta cotton country. His father initially worked as a carpenter and mason but later managed the household of a wealthy dentist. Raised Southern Baptist, Green converted to Catholicism at age fifteen under the influence of a priest intent on winning converts in the local Black community. He was awarded a scholarship to complete his senior year of high school at an all-Black preparatory school attached to Xavier University in New Orleans, where he graduated as co-valedictorian.

Finding a Vocational Path

Green initially decided to become a priest in the Catholic Church, and in the fall of 1947 he enrolled at Epiphany Apostolic College in Newburgh, New York. This seminary for the Josephite order, to which Phil Berrigan would later belong, was also briefly attended by Phil's brother Jerome in the late 1940s; Phil himself was a novice at Epiphany in the early 1950s and taught at its prep school in the mid-sixties. Green's vocation proved short-lived, however, when the school clinic misdiagnosed him with gonorrhea, wrongly accused him of illicit sexual activity, and dismissed him that same December —a devastating personal blow. His local priest appealed the decision, but the college refused to readmit him. Green then chose a military career, hoping to learn a trade that would later provide a secure livelihood.

In 1949, following basic training as an aviation mechanic, Green transitioned to become a pilot. While stationed in Hawaii he began to correspond with Eleanor Gallagher, a white physical education instructor at Xavier University, whom he had briefly met during his senior year at Xavier's adjoining high school. Their correspondence led to marriage in December 1951 and with it came the hardship interracial marriage brought during those times. Since the marriage violated southern miscegenation laws, the Air Force relocated them from Louisiana to an Ohio air base. In the summer of 1956 the

---

2. Biographical details in opening paragraph and this section: Flint Whitlock, *Turbulence before Takeoff: The Life and Times of Aviation Pioneer Marlon Dewitt Green* (Brule, WI: Cable Publishing, 2009); "Robert Fikes, "Marlon Dewitt Green," Blackpast, September 24, 2017, https://www.blackpast.org/african-american-history/green-marlon-dewitt-1929-2009/; "Marlon D. Green—Biography," n.a., n.d., in TMC/BU; Thom I. Romero II, "Turbulence a Mile High: Equal Employment Opportunity in the Colorado Sky," *The Colorado Lawyer* 32, no. 9 (September 2003): 71.

Greens were transferred to Japan and, while there, Marlon read a news article stating that commercial airlines would begin hiring Black pilots. President Truman had desegregated the military in 1948, but Green nonetheless suffered his share of racially based indignities in the Air Force and was eager to find a well-paying civilian job. Based on hopes raised by the article, Green resigned from the military to become a commercial passenger airline pilot. Unfortunately, that decision met with even greater disappointment and indignity.

Battle for Employment Justice

Unknown to Green, the article he read mostly reflected political posturing for minority votes, not a firm commitment to hire African American pilots. He received no interviews after submitting dozens of applications. Some airlines explicitly told him they would not hire Blacks because they could not lodge them in the southern cities they served, or because some white passengers would not fly on planes piloted by a Black. Eventually, in frustration, Green left the "race" line blank on a Continental Airlines application and omitted personal photographs. He promptly received an interview and successfully performed a flight test, but he was not hired because of a stated lack of openings in the airline flight school. Green later learned that at the same time he had been rejected, the school had accepted five white men with only a third of his flight experience. He responded in August 1957 by filing a complaint with the Colorado Anti-Discrimination Commission.

The commission decided in favor of Green, but a series of appeals ensued that spanned six more years. When the commission upheld its decision, Continental turned to a Colorado district court, which reversed the commission's decision and ruled in favor of the airline. Green's attorney—T. Raber Taylor, a prominent Denver Catholic lawyer who waived his normal fees to argue the case—then appealed to the Colorado Supreme Court. Continental argued that hiring Green imposed an unconstitutional burden on interstate commerce and violated various regulations, court rulings, and federal laws. When the state Supreme Court also ruled for Continental on a 4-3 vote, Taylor filed with the United States Supreme Court. Robert Kennedy, as U.S. attorney general, plus the NAACP, ACLU, Anti-Defamation League of B'Nai Brith, American Jewish Congress, and an array of state attorneys general all signed onto the case in support of Green's petition. The Court's unanimous April 1963 decision favored Green, asserting that its *Brown v. Board of Education* decision outlawed segregation in all realms, including employment.

Green finished out his interim employment piloting a federal Bureau of Reclamation airplane as he negotiated for a job with Continental, which he began in January 1965. Though at times he nearly gave up in discouraged

frustration, Green's tena-
cious pursuit of employment
justice had opened doors
through which many would
follow. Under the weight of
Green's court victory, American Airlines had a month
earlier hired David Harris as
the nation's first African
American commercial air-
line pilot. Upon his own hiring, Green received employment tenure dating from his
1957 application forward,
and a year and a half later he
became the first Black pilot
to achieve captain status for
a commercial carrier. He occasionally encountered resentment among his fellow
pilots but was mostly well
received and flew fourteen
years for Continental before
retiring in 1978.

Marlon D. Green, 1965
(Courtesy of Green family)

Marlon Green received several awards for the barriers he had broken,
including a Lifetime Achievement Award from the Organization of Black
Airline pilots, and Continental posthumously christened a Boeing 737 air-
liner in his honor. But resentment over his frustrations took a heavy emotional toll, and though his professional life began to thrive, his personal life
did not. His divorce from Eleanor in 1970 was followed by three more mar-
riages, none of which lasted more than three years. Green's biographer, Flint
Whitlock, credited both the pressures of piloting and the accumulation of
racially based "slaps at self-respect" for his emotional decline. Among
these, Eleanor cited his expulsion from the Josephite seminary (which also
expelled two other Blacks shortly after Marlon), incidents in the Air Force,
and the stress of battling Continental Airlines. As she explained, "[Marlon]
saw himself discriminated against because of his color, and I believe in all
probability that he was."[3]

---

3. Whitlock, *Turbulence*, 307.

Thomas Merton's Relationship with Marlon Green

Marlon Green's religious faith faded in tandem with his emotional health during the later sixties, but in his earlier quest for employment justice he leaned heavily on that faith. As he waited in early 1961 for the Colorado Supreme Court to hear his case a second time, Green especially sought spiritual solace. That April he took his family on a short retreat to St. Meinrad Abbey in southern Indiana with which he and Eleanor affiliated as lay oblates. He felt the excursion offered some pleasure "in spite of the grave issues and the cruel effect of discrimination on its victims."[4] That cruel effect weighed even heavier in early August when Green wrote his attorney in a hostile tone, asserting that he would not pursue further action if the court ruled against him. To repair the breach, Eleanor explained to Taylor in an August 6 letter, "I fear that Marlon may be close to the breaking point. He is full of anger and frustration and it is bottled up inside him. We all attend daily Mass together and the grace of God keeps us going from day to day with some measure of peace, but I am afraid it cannot last much longer.... I think each plane [that flies overhead] is a knife in his heart as it goes over."[5] Taylor responded graciously to edify Marlon and predicted a favorable ruling. On the same day that Taylor wrote that exhortation, Green also penned a letter to seek relief from the despair that engulfed him. He addressed it to Thomas Merton.

An Extended Hand of Encouragement

Green's choice to contact Merton about racial justice seems a bit surprising. The Trappist's first publication on race would not appear for two years, and his first public words on Cold War nuclear madness had not yet appeared. But Green astutely noted hints of Merton's emerging social critique as he read *The Behavior of Titans*,[6] published five months earlier. In it, Merton's "Letter to an Innocent Bystander"[7] especially struck Green as "a beautiful expression of the right thinking which is essential to and produces right action in any given situation where morality is involved."[8]

---

4. Green to Stanley Gerwitz, June 8, 1961, TMC/BU.

5. Whitlock, *Turbulence*, 210.

6. New York: New Directions, 1961.

7. Published initially in French in *Informations Catholiques Internationale* (August 1958); first published in English in *The Behavior of Titans* (New York: New Directions, 1961).

8. Green to Merton, August 14, 1961, TMC/BU.

Merton's "Letter" included classic themes that would recur and be expanded upon in his social writings and correspondence during the coming years. He addressed his target audience of "intellectuals" in hope that communication remained possible and "that we are still sufficiently 'persons' to realize we have a common difficulty, and to try to solve it together." He suggested complicity in oppression when intellectuals presume innocence and "stand by" as those with modern technocratic power exert it over others. His readers must instead spurn support of the powerful and resist collaborating with or being used by them to "crush 'the others.'" He invoked

> hope for the impossible answer that lies beyond our earthly contradictions, and yet can burst into the world and solve them if only there are some who hope in spite of despair. The true solutions are not those which we force upon life in accordance with our theories, but those which life itself provides for those who dispose themselves to receive the truth. Consequently our task is . . . trusting life itself, and nature, and if you will permit me, God above all. . . . We can call ourselves innocent only if we refuse to forget this, and if we also do everything we can to make others realize it.[9]

Green sent his August 1961 letter to ask whether the essay's author would modify his thesis "in applying its principles to my plight as a Negro and airplane pilot," adding, "I believe you would not." Enclosures explained his situation, and he asked Merton's help "in bringing heroic Christian expression to this problem of adverse racial distinctions. (I am convinced that the opposition to racial equality is so malevolent and widespread that extreme heroism in Christ is the only solution.)" Green closed with humor to suggest founding "The Protagonists for Positive Precipitous Protest," whose only eligible members "without challenge" included his wife, his attorney, and "especially on the basis of your *Letter*, you."[10]

Merton's response shared his desire to help despite uncertainty as to how he might do so "in a more concrete way" given his monastic limitations. He offered to write a letter on Green's behalf and welcomed him to visit on retreat, but he cautioned that his abbot might limit personal access. Perceiving Green as "more or less alone," Merton encouraged him to persevere and noted that, beyond seeking employment, "isolated protest is not enough. . . . The man for you to follow, as you know, is Martin Luther King. His tac-

---

9. Merton, "Letter to an Innocent Bystander," *Behavior of Titans*, 51–52, 60–64.
10. Green to Merton, August 14, 1961, TMC/BU.

tics seem to me to be perfect and admirably Christian." It felt "good to see a Catholic getting into this," which made it "all the more important for you to think things out well and on deep Christian lines."[11] Green's biographer records that he was "heartened" and comforted by this reply, adding Marlon's recollection that "It was spiritually helpful to find a white person willing to say that racial justice is a thing to be sought and a thing to be worked for, and that injustice is a thing not to be tolerated. In those days, it was very meaningful to have it put in the name of God. So, yes, Father Merton was very meaningful to me."[12]

As things played out, Green met with Merton later that same month. To distract from his anxiety, he and his brother-in-law drove from their Michigan home to visit his parents in Arkansas with plans for Marlon to return by bus. The national press had publicized that summer's drama of aborted Freedom Rides through the South, and though Green avoided the violence Freedom Riders suffered, as he rode segregated buses he wore a "pinney" with "I am not a freedom rider..." printed on the front, plus "...and I am not free" on the back.[13] He later wrote the bus line to urge that they practice their "belief in the equality of your customers by ending the odious custom of racial segregation on busses, in waiting rooms, toilets and in all other terminal facilities."[14] Before he departed for home, Eleanor called to encourage him to return through Kentucky and visit Merton, which he did.

They met on August 31. As Merton had forewarned, they could not visit long, but Green appreciated their conversation. It lasted only twenty minutes, "but it did much to salve Marlon's emotional wounds." Whitlock shared Marlon's comment that, "I liked him and he seemed to be impressed by my history."[15] Merton's journal also logged this visit by "Marlon Green, a negro and a remarkable person. He is fighting for the right to be hired as a pilot by the passenger air-lines, which said they would hire negroes but in fact refuse to."[16]

Green's follow-up letter thanked Merton "for the privilege of discussing employment discrimination" and his "counsel and promise of continuing interest." Merton had arranged for him to consult another abbey visitor, Fr. Illtude Evans, a Welsh Dominican friar and editor of *Blackfriars* magazine. Green was "much impressed with [Evans's] cognizance of the problems of

---

11. Merton to Green, August 23, 1961, TMC/BU; Whitlock, *Turbulence*, 214–15.

12. Whitlock, *Turbulence*, 215.

13. Whitlock, *Turbulence*, 217.

14. Green to Continental Southern Lines, September 5, 1961, TMC/BU.

15. Whitlock, *Turbulence*, 218.

16. September 5, 1961, *TTW* 158.

race and his genuine efforts to overcome them." Merton also referred Green to his friends Robert Lax; Ed Rice, publisher of *Jubilee* magazine; and Fr. John Loftus, dean at Bellarmine College. He gave Green a copy of *Cross Currents* magazine that contained "The Negro in American Culture," an interview with five Black writers—James Baldwin and Langston Hughes among them—and a book excerpt by Emmanuel Mounier on "An Air of Greater Freedom." Marlon especially liked the latter piece and expressed gratitude for the contacts provided and conversations shared.[17]

Supreme Court Victory

Green's outlook improved following that mid-summer low point. But it would take another two months for the Colorado Supreme Court to hear Green's case, and another four to issue its February 1962 ruling in favor of Continental. The U.S. Supreme Court waited until October 1962 to decide that they would hear the case and then failed to schedule it until March 1963. Merton and Green apparently did not communicate throughout that year-and-a-half span, but once the date was set in March, Green reached out again for Merton's prayers. Merton assured Green of his "deep interest" and "whole hearted support"; he would "bring it to the attention of the [monastic] community and [an upcoming] Mass will be for your intentions." Merton was also pleased that the Jesuit magazine *America* had publicized the case, "as this is a rather conservative magazine, and hence it is all the better to have its support." But the meat of Merton's letter contained a paragraph that underscored his recognition of how slippery racial justice then was in the United States. "It is just pitiful to what extent people will go in this country" to evade dealing fairly with questions of race, he lamented. Merton assured Green that he was "not just working for yourself, or for the American negro, but for the whole country." Under separate cover he forwarded several pieces of his writing that he thought might edify Green.[18]

The pilot seems not to have directly informed Merton when the court ruled in his favor a month later on April 22. But the monk may have received a copy of Green's circular letter dated that day, in which he shared the good news he had heard on the radio that morning—"*a unanimous decision with*

---

17. Green to Merton, September 7, 1961, TMC/BU; *Cross Currents* (Summer 1961): 205–24, 225–39.

18. Merton to Green, March 20, 1963, TMC/BU. "The Marlon Green Case," *America* 108, no. 9 (March 3, 1963): 285.

no abstentions—WOW!" Green thanked all, friends and strangers, "who have 'hoped and prayed' us to this happy moment."[19] His first response from Gethsemani was sent by Abbot Dom James Fox. In his congratulatory letter to Green, drafted upon reading of the outcome in a newspaper, Fox assured him that "The hearts of all us monks here at Gethsemani go out to you.... Be assured, dear Marlon and Eleanor, that whenever you need prayers, just let us know. Meanwhile, realize that you are remembered in the daily round of our Trappist life of prayer and sacrifice here at Gethsemani."[20] Merton sent his own congratulations two weeks later (reproduced below).

Racial Justice

The sparse exchange of letters between Thomas Merton and Marlon Green, only three letters each, nonetheless displays several important aspects of Merton's commitment to reach across America's racial divisions. This appears to be his first direct interaction with an African American about racial discrimination in his adopted country, though he may have interacted personally with the Abbey's two Black monks.[21] More importantly, the letters reveal how from the early sixties Merton grasped the need to push boundaries in pursuit of racial justice, and the recognition that genuine reconciliation and relationship could never happen without doing so. He exhorted in his initial August 1961 letter: "You certainly should do all that you can to get the just treatment you deserve. There is no question that you should go ahead and employ all rightful means to secure employment and at the same time resist the unfair treatment meted out to you as a Negro. In this you can also help others."[22]

Merton consistently called for justice from the start of his published writings on race two years later. Written near the day of Green's Supreme Court ruling and close to Martin Luther King Jr.'s release from Birmingham's jail, Merton's first public commentary on race, "Neither Caliban nor Uncle Tom," stated:

---

19. Green to unnamed, April 22, 1963, TMC/BU.

20. Fox to Green, April 25, 1963; Whitlock, *Turbulence*, 254.

21. Dom James's letter to Green commented, "Here at Gethsemani we have given opportunity to many colored boys, but it seems our life is thus far a little too different for them to persevere. At present we have only one of the colored race." Fox to Green, April 25, 1963, Marlon Green Correspondence TMC/BU.

22. Merton to Green, August 23, 1961; Whitlock, *Turbulence*, 214.

No amount of sentiment, good will, public relations, and friendly images will serve to stem the tide of [racial] violence. The basic issue is one of rank, crass deeply rooted *injustice*. And the only thing that can right the wrong is justice in every sphere, in every level of society, in public and private affairs, in national and international relations, in everything, in every possible branch of social, political, economic, and personal life. Can we even begin to face this problem? It is on this, of course, that the survival of our society depends....

What is demanded is not that everybody *like* everybody else, or that everybody get together with smiles and bright maxims of optimism and mutual esteem. *What matters is that justice be done....* [This] is a matter of righting actual wrongs, paying definite debts, restoring very precise rights that have been ignored and violated.[23]

These sentiments echo his words sent to Green a month earlier: "It is just pitiful to what extent people will go in this country to avoid facing the truth, and to evade the claims of justice and humanity in this race issue," as he commended efforts to "bring the injustice to light and to right the wrong."[24]

Merton's final letter to Green (reproduced below) highlights another aspect of his racial justice critique: it is not simply a matter of legal mechanics but of transforming entrenched cultural patterns. After reflecting on the intense conflict unfolding 650 miles south of him in the streets of Birmingham, Merton asserted that not only did they live "in a time of crisis," but civilization in general embodied "a kind of sickness" and "the whole world is ill." Despite this, "God has placed a solid core of reality" in the world, and he hoped that "truth will eventually bring us to our senses."[25] As with his previous letter to Green, these reflections dovetailed with his concurrent "Caliban" essay, which asserted that "more than reason is involved here...[because] the race issue also involves deeply buried unconscious terrors and loves."[26] And as he stated later that year in "Letters to a White Liberal": "We live in a culture which seems to have reached the point of extreme hazard at which it may plunge to its own ruin, unless there is some renewal of life, some new direction, some providential reorganization of its forces for sur-

---

23. "Neither Caliban nor Uncle Tom," *Liberation* 8, no. 4 (June 1963): 22. Emphasis in the original. Merton forwarded this text to *Liberation* assistant editor Jim Forest in late April 1963.

24. Merton to Green, March 20, 1963, TMC/BU.

25. Merton to Green, May 8, 1963, TMC/BU; Whitlock, *Turbulence*, 255.

26. Merton, "Neither Caliban," 20.

vival." In other words, it required the same "examination of conscience" that he urged for the era's peace movement.[27]

Despite its brevity, Merton's exchange with Marlon Green clearly demonstrates his deep concern for racial justice well before his published commentary on it began. It displays his capacity to reach across America's racial divide and connect with African Americans as fully human persons.

In this letter, Thomas Merton responds to Marlon Green's Supreme Court victory that required his being hired by Continental Airlines as a commercial pilot. An abridged version appears in Turbulence before Takeoff, *254–55.*

May 8, 1963

Dear Marlon:

Great news. Congratulations. This is a very big step forward and you deserve a great deal of credit for the patient struggle you have gone though. I hope now that the decision will "take." God bless you for it. I am sure one day a lot of people will have reason to be very grateful to you.

The news from Alabama is nasty,[28] at least what gets through to me. But I think the spirit and courage of the non-violent demonstrators there is magnificent. At this moment the people that America can be most proud of are the Negroes: they are the only ones who are really living up to the ideal to which the whites, especially in the South, are more inclined to pay lip-service. I hope that gradually rights will finally get recognized and that the situation will change. But you know better than I do that it is not going to be easy.

We are living in a time of crisis, in which people do not want to change, and yet they are being forced to change in a million ways that nobody can control. I believe more and more that Freud was right when he said that civilization was a kind of sickness. It certainly proves to be that, in our day. The whole world is ill, and the worst of it is that they all think they are sane. If only more of us could realize how nuts we really are . . .[29] Fortunately God has placed a solid core of reality there which we cannot altogether ignore, and

---

27. Merton, *Seeds of Destruction*, 11, 12.

28. Three days earlier Birmingham police turned fire hoses and police dogs on marching children; demonstrators filled city jails to capacity.

29. Merton's ellipses.

maybe, who knows? His truth will eventually bring us to our senses. Let us hope so.

Meanwhile I keep you and your fine family in my prayers. I am sending you a copy of that book which Deasy reviewed.[30] I think his review was fair enough. The book was really written for monks in the first place, and then edited for laypeople, so in a sense he is right, it does not really fit. However, it may have some points of value. I don't attach much importance to this book myself. I stand more by the book of verse that is supposed to be coming out this fall, "Emblems for a Season of Fury."[31]

Again, all blessings.

Cordially yours in Christ,

30. Philip Deasy's review of Merton's *Life and Holiness* (New York: New Directions, 1963) in *Commonweal* 78 (April 19, 1963): 112–13. This suggests he received nonextant correspondence about it from Green.

31. New York: New Directions, 1963. It includes Merton's recently drafted "And the Children of Birmingham."

6

TELLING TRUTH

THE MERTON-THOMPSON LETTERS

*Far from dishonoring the Church, I think you have borne witness to
the fact that Catholics can think and speak out for the truth in these
matters.*

> — *Thomas Merton to August Thompson*
> *November 30, 1963*[1]

Two months after the Supreme Court unanimously granted Marlon Green's
bid for employment justice, a significant deliberation of a very different sort
unfolded far from Washington in the Deep South. In mid-1963, a controversial white author and an African American priest from Louisiana met to discuss how they would share the priest's experience of Blackness within the
Roman Catholic Church. Published in *Ramparts*, a Catholic cultural magazine, John Howard Griffin's interview of Father August Thompson would
jolt both Church and nation.

Thompson's bold statements of unvarnished truth exposed to many the
reality that Blacks routinely confronted in the South and in the Church he
served. African American Catholics represented a minority on three counts.
Not only were they part of a racial minority, as Catholics they comprised
only 5 percent of African Americans, and as Blacks a still smaller percent-
age of U.S. Catholics.[2] The comments of Black Catholic scholar Jamie T.
Phelps in 1997 applied even more to Thompson's era: "African American
Catholics experience a double invisibility, marginalization, and devaluation.

---

1. August Thompson Correspondence, TMC/BU.

2. Estimates for Black Catholics vary, but the article "25 Years in 'Integrated-
Segregated' Church" (Tom Haywood, *The Town Talk* [Alexandria, LA], June 5, 1982,
14) estimated 1.5 million in the early 1980s, or about 5 percent of U.S. Blacks and 3
percent of U.S. Catholics.

Fr. August Thomas, 1963
(Photo by John Howard Griffin)

In the Black world we are marginalized because of our religious identity as Catholics; and in the Catholic world we are marginalized because of our racial and cultural identity as African Americans." Regarding the latter, Phelps emphasized "the struggle of African American Catholics to be recognized as fully human children of God, disciples of Jesus Christ, and full and equal members of the Catholic Church in the United States."[3] Her words summarize August Thompson's own message broadcast through *Ramparts* thirty-four years earlier.

Throughout his career Fr. Thompson tirelessly labored on two fronts of this struggle. Locally he worked to empower, elevate, and expand economic and political access for his rural Black neighbors. At the same time, he persistently explained Black Catholic marginalization to Church leaders in hopes of chipping away at their blindness toward it. Thompson helped pioneer that message even before Black Catholics organized into caucuses and councils to amplify it, and he participated in that amplification during the decades that followed. His voice on race focused most on holding his Church accountable to their own words rather than seeking justice through secular courts, as Marlon Green had. But his community service lived out those truths in local economic and political relations. This required him to navigate an array of criticism, hostility, and threats using personal networks. In that, he relied heavily on his friend John Howard Griffin for support and occasional intervention. But when he faced significant decisions regarding his place within Catholic structures, Thompson turned to fellow priest Thomas Merton for counsel. Merton's replies did not articulate a theological framework for Thompson's truth telling, but they affirmed his passion to speak out and encouraged him to continue.

---

3. Jamie T. Phelps, "African American Catholics: The Struggles, Contributions and Gifts of a Marginalized Community," in *Black and Catholic: The Challenge and Gift of Black Folk*, ed. Jamie T. Phelps (Milwaukee: Marquette University Press, 1997), 21, 18.

Father August Louis Thompson (1926–2019)[4]

In a sense, Fr. August Thompson's personal history embodied the very presence of many Black Catholics within the United States. His family had been southern Louisiana Catholics as far back as their oral tradition reached. This suggests their affiliation descended from the eighteenth-century French and Spanish colonial legacy along the Gulf Coast. Those governments required baptism of slaves, and Jesuit, Capuchin, and Ursuline orders ministered to the colony's Africans, as well as Native Americans and white colonists.[5] This legacy made Louisiana home to the vast majority of American Black Catholics before twentieth-century migrations to northern urban centers.

Thompson's father, Louis, constructed their simple Louisiana home from scrap lumber on a small parcel forty miles southeast of Lafayette in the rural coastal community of Baldwin. Louis's wife, Eunice Barard Thompson, bore five sons and four daughters, with August as their second child. The family subsisted on food provided by their cow and a vegetable garden that featured corn, sweet potatoes, cucumbers, and string beans. Louis supplemented this through wages earned in menial labor in sugar mills, grocery stores, and elsewhere. As a young child, August also contributed by working in rice fields to earn twenty-five to fifty cents for a "long" half day of work.

---

4. Biographical details in this section compiled from: "Father August Thompson," *Avoyelles Today*, August 12, 2019, https://www.avoyellestoday.com/obituaries/father-august-louis-thompson; "August Thompson and John Howard Griffin: Dialogue with Father Thompson," in *Black, White, and Gray: 21 Points of View on the Race Question*, ed. Bradford Daniel (New York: Sheed and Ward, 1964), 148; Rita Joseph, "Student Nurse," *Jubilee* 3, no. 5 (September 1955): 32–37; Haywood, "25 Years"; Katrina M. Sanders, "Black Catholic Clergy and the Struggle for Civil Rights: Winds of Change," in *Uncommon Faithfulness: The Black Catholic Experience*, ed. M. Shawn Copeland (Maryknoll, NY: Orbis Books, 2009), 85–87, 89; "Rev. Thompson Cited at Convention," *The Town Talk* (Alexandria, LA), August 25, 1973, 13.

Additional studies of August Thompson and Merton: Gregory K. Hillis, "A Sign of Contradiction: Remembering Fr. August Thompson," *Commonweal* 146, no. 9 (October 2019), 29–31; Gregory K. Hillis, "Letters to a Black Catholic Priest," *Merton Annual* 32 (2020): 114–36; Paul R. Dekar, "God's Messenger: Thomas Merton on Racial Justice," *Merton Annual* 32 (2020): 137–54. I am especially indebted to Prof. Hillis for sharing research materials for this chapter, particularly these from the John Howard Griffin Papers, Rare Book and Manuscript Library, Columbia University: August Thompson/John Howard Griffin Correspondence (Box 11, Folders 380–83); Edward Keating/John Howard Griffin Correspondence (Box 11, Folder 386); Griffin journal on Griffin/Thompson and aftermath: December 1964–January 1966 (Box 8, Folder 266).

5. Cyprian Davis, OSB, *The History of Black Catholics in the United States* (New York: Crossroad, 1990), 72–77.

The Thompsons raised their children as devout Catholics. They said the rosary daily and regularly attended mass in their local segregated church, where Blacks sat opposite whites and were prohibited from receiving communion until all whites present had been served. August's penchant for observing and naming truth started early; at his First Communion he asked his mother, "Why are we always in back?"[6] He once joked to John Griffin that, "I cried out in protest the moment I got a lick on my back side when I was born. I have been crying ever since."[7]

The Thompson parents valued education and insisted their children attend local schools. August discerned a vocation for the priesthood early and entered seminary in 1941 at age fifteen. His white parish priest endorsed his application and encouraged him to seek ordination in their Lafayette diocese —a bold move considering only a hundred of the more than thirty-five thousand U.S. Catholic priests at the time were Black. He started his training at St. Augustine Seminary in Bay St. Louis, Mississippi, founded in 1920 by the missionary Society of the Divine Word as the first U.S. seminary to train Blacks for religious life. He also attended St. Paul and St. Mary's seminaries in the Midwest and finished his formation in 1957 at Notre Dame Seminary in New Orleans.

Upon Thompson's graduation and ordination at St. Louis Cathedral in New Orleans, the Lafayette bishop would not assign him to a parish, using the excuse that a missionary order had educated him. But the bishop of Alexandria Diocese in central Louisiana proved more accommodating and assigned him as vicar, or assistant pastor, at St. Anthony's Church in Cottonport. He was reassigned in 1962 as administrator and pastor of St. Charles Church in Ferriday, and in late 1969 he moved to pastor Our Lady of Succor Church in Mansura. Thompson held two more assignments before his 1997 retirement: rector of St. Francis Cathedral in Alexandria (1985–1991), and then simultaneously pastor of St. James Memorial Church and St. Juliana Church, also in Alexandria (1991–1997). He lived another twenty-two years before his death in Houston at age ninety-three.

Truth and Its Consequences

Telling truth amid systemic inertia and oppression occurs through acts as well as words, and Father Thompson "spoke" through both. His truth-telling elicited pushback from forces intent on maintaining the status quo, a status of

---

6. Haywood, "25 Years."

7. Thompson to Griffin, September 12, 1968, John Howard Griffin Papers.

diminished Black dignity. This dynamic played out most intently during Thompson's tenure at Ferriday, ten miles across the Mississippi River from Natchez, a center of Klan activity. In this time of regional tension, civil rights campaigns pursued integration in nearby Alabama and Mississippi, followed by passage of national Civil and Voting Rights Acts. Police and Klan alike violently resisted change with fire hoses, dogs, and bombs in Birmingham and guns in Mississippi, where Medgar Evers and "Freedom Summer" workers were murdered.

Truth in Deeds[8]

Amid these tensions, August Thompson's deeds of truth spilled beyond his parishioners into the Ferriday community. According to Gregory Hillis, who studied Thompson's ministry, he was remembered as a "much-loved priest in his own diocese, known for his ready smile and his willingness to pray with and bless anyone, no matter who they were."[9] Thompson nurtured his parishioners' self-respect and pride in their heritage. At Our Lady of Succor, he constructed its Uganda Center, named after nineteenth-century African martyrs, and painted the church's columns, baptistery, and other objects with the era's African liberation colors (black, green, red). He introduced Black spiritual music into the liturgy as "a people's response to God," and was one of the area's first priests to permit women as lectors.[10]

But Father Thompson's influence spread beyond local parishes as he entered national Catholic discussions on race from the early sixties on.[11] At a 1968 Catholic Clergy Caucus he joined sixty Black priests who informally convened amid the aftermath of Martin Luther King's assassination two weeks before. Sequestered without white attendees, they established the Black Clergy Caucus, a catalyst for later Black Catholic caucuses and organizations. Thompson had widespread informal relationships with seminary classmates, members of the Friendship House movement,[12] and friends in

---

8. Unless otherwise credited, information in this section relies on materials in the John Howard Griffin Papers.

9. Hillis, "Sign of Contradiction," 29.

10. Haywood, "25 Years."

11. Examples include meetings of the National Catholic Conference for Interracial Justice, Catholic Interracial Council, and Midwestern Clergy Conference on Negro Welfare.

12. Thompson probably connected with Chicago's Friendship House, a 1942 mission outpost of Harlem's house, while studying at St. Mary's Seminary in Mundelein, Illinois; possibly with a Friendship House briefly operated in Shreveport, Louisiana, during the 1950s. In 1941 before entering the monastery, Merton connected with the original Harlem Friendship House, founded by Catherine de Hueck Doherty.

Houston, Texas, where his parents had moved in 1954—Houston's bishop granted him full faculties to practice in the diocese. His involvements yielded far-flung speaking engagements, and his labors earned local, regional,[13] and national recognition.[14]

Locally, Thompson's influence extended beyond his church. In Ferriday, he served on the Southern Consumers Cooperative board, which empowered local Black farmers to bypass underpriced white-controlled markets, acquire property, and retain profits from the land they worked. His parish center provided a base to rally Black voters and "tell them they were people too," as he put it.[15] He became a notary so Blacks could file documents against discriminatory practices without alerting the broader community, as white notaries did. He established an integrated Head Start program and recruited northern white nuns to teach there during summers. At Mansura, he convinced the Southern Poverty Law Center to take a local case against discrimination by a funeral home that resulted in a class action victory with broad impact.

But such efforts won few friends among Ferriday's whites, who reacted with threats and violence. In October 1964 the house of a supportive local white was bombed, and in mid-December, the shop of Thompson's Black neighbor was also bombed before the assailants drenched him in gasoline and lit it. He died the following day, as the smell of burned flesh lingered in the neighborhood. In the spring of 1965 a visit from Dorothy Day, passing through Natchez to see a friend, undoubtedly boosted Thompson's spirits. But when two northern white nuns arrived that summer to teach at his new parish center, they were expelled from their apartment when their work with Black children became known. They then lived in Thompson's rectory and he in the church during their stay. His phone was tapped, he was harassed for ministering to whites, and rumors circulated that the Klan planned to bomb three local Blacks, including the "nigger priest." Two of those homes were bombed, though Thompson's rectory was not. Local violence bled into early 1966 before waning.

---

13. Regionally Thompson served his diocese as a Legion of Mary spiritual director, vicar for Black Catholics, member of its Presbyteral Council, College of Consulters, Liturgical Commission, and the first Black priest to be provincial representative on the Board of Directors of the National Federation of Priests' Councils ("Father August Thompson," *Avoyelles Today*).

14. In 1973 the National Black Catholic Convention awarded him as a priest of many years who "has been concerned for the betterment of people. His achievements have been accomplished after much struggle in which he still holds on to faith that results are possible" ("Rev. Thompson Cited," 13). In 1980 the Lewis University Black Students Union granted him its Outstanding Citizen Award ("Father August Thompson," *Avoyelles Today*).

15. Haywood, "25 Years."

During this period, John Howard Griffin pulled out all stops to seek federal protection for Thompson and his community. The FBI and Department of Justice made occasional appearances, though they made no arrests. But their visits, coupled with the frequent presence of Deacons for Defense and Justice —a Black self-defense group recently founded in Jonesboro, Louisiana, two hours away—may have saved Thompson's life. Throughout this time, no fellow white priests joined Thompson in solidarity to face the violence.

Truth in Words[16]

Louisiana's Catholic Church shared many southern white cultural biases, and it struggled to recognize how those traditions failed to align with its theology of universal inclusion. As a priest under vows of obedience to his bishop, Thompson needed to use special care when confronting decades of diocesan segregationist practice. These particular tensions came to a head following Thompson's most public telling of truth: his 1963 interview in *Ramparts*.

The opportunity sprang from serendipity. In late 1962 Thompson delayed his holiday visit to his parents in Houston, and that decision permitted him to attend a series of January 1963 lectures that John Howard Griffin gave in Houston on his book, *Black Like Me*. Griffin was drawn to Thompson's stories as a Louisiana priest, which aligned with his own experiences. They remained in contact, and Griffin visited Ferriday that May.

Meanwhile, *Ramparts* editor Edward Keating began plans for an issue on Black contributions to U.S. culture. But he later considered engaging Blacks on their cultural impact as akin to interrupting someone engaged in a mortal struggle to ask if they had read any good books. He next proposed an exchange of letters between James Baldwin and Thomas Merton on the topic of race, and both expressed interest. Merton later demurred, suspecting Blacks were losing interest in such dialogue, and proposed to instead craft his open "Letters to a White Liberal."[17] He submitted the essay in late July. As William Apel implies, the prescience of this piece—still remarkably relevant —surely fed off of Griffin,[18] whose own insights drew upon Thompson's. Griffin had recently written an article that derided assumptions about Black gratitude for moderate white appeals to compassion and justice when coupled with

---

16. Unless otherwise credited, information in this section relied on materials in the John Howard Griffin Papers.

17. There is no record that Baldwin received Merton's letter, published in *Seeds of Destruction*, 302–306. Merton may have drafted it in anticipation of the *Ramparts* exchange that he later declined.

18. William Apel, "Out of Solitude: Thomas Merton, John Howard Griffin, and Racial Justice," *The Merton Seasonal* 36, no. 3 (Fall 2011): 17–22.

requests that Blacks patiently wait for good whites to help.[19] Keating, having learned of Thompson through Griffin, also asked him for *Ramparts* material. The Louisiana priest preferred to be interviewed rather than write an article, and Keating asked Griffin to conduct it.

Keating assembled a blockbuster Christmas issue that hit the newsstands in late October 1963. Besides Merton's "The Black Revolution: Letters to a White Liberal" and Griffin's "Dialogue [with] Father August Thompson," it also featured Griffin's "Journal of a Trip South" (recounting racial tensions encountered on his visit to Ferriday) and two other articles on race. But the Thompson interview made national headlines: "Negro Priest Says Segregation Makes Second-Class Citizens" (*New York Times*), "Fear and Faith in Deep South" (*San Francisco Chronicle*), "Negro Priest Says Segregated Church Exists in the South" (*The Catholic Messenger*). The *National Catholic Reporter* printed the full interview, as did a Kansas diocesan paper, and it appeared in published anthologies.[20]

Examples Thompson gave starkly exposed the trials of southern Black Catholics. They could not receive nurse training at southern Catholic hospitals. Some dioceses prohibited access to retreat centers for retreats, days of recollection, or premarital Cana Conferences, even though non-Catholic whites were often welcomed. Blacks typically could not attend Mass with whites as long as segregated options remained. In one case, a white parish hired someone to drive a local Black to a distant Black parish rather than include her in their all-white Mass. Five of the South's twenty-five dioceses ignored official Church calls for school integration.[21]

Thompson also shared his personal frustration as a priest. He anguished over instructing young Black converts on Church beliefs of oneness in Christ only to see them "suffer the terrible shock of discovery" when prohibited from worship with whites. He recounted how white Catholics often refused to address him as "Father," how he was shunned from informal recreational activities with white fellow priests, how some churches prevented his attendance at confirmations and First Communions—and sometimes mere entry into the church building—let alone permit him to officiate. "The priesthood should take primacy over everything else," he lamented, "but with us it's a Negro first, a Negro second, and finally a priest." Rather than fill the tradi-

---

19. Griffin to Thompson, January 20, 1963, John Howard Griffin Papers.

20. Robert Bonazzi, *Man in the Mirror: John Howard Griffin and the Story of "Black Like Me"* (Maryknoll, NY: Orbis Books, 1997), 150–51. Daniel, *Black, White, and Gray*, 148–62, for example, published the interview.

21. John Howard Griffin, "Dialogue: Father August Thompson," *Ramparts* (Christmas 1963): 24–27, 30.

tional Catholic role as *alter Christus*, Thompson shocked even Griffin by describing southern Black priests as "second-class Christs." It seemed "almost impossible for non-Negroes, even in the Deep South where they think they know all about us, to realize how many doors that lead one to a love of the things of the spirit—education and religion particularly—are effectively closed to Negroes. Or how deeply we are scandalized to see Catholics helping to hold those doors closed to us by cooperating with the kind of segregation that Holy Mother Church has declared abominable."[22]

Local response to the interview initially seemed muted, but its most consequential fallout came from his own bishop, Charles P. Greco. This well-intended bishop supported integration in principle—he had, after all, ordained Thompson in his Alexandria Diocese when others would not. Yet he struggled to grasp the realities of Black experience within his fold. In early August 1963—no doubt with an eye on events in Birmingham that spring, Medgar Evers's July assassination, and Klan activity swarming through his diocese—Greco issued a nine-page pastoral letter on race. The document reflected local priorities that saw the Church's "primary and essential task" as "care of individual souls" and "administration of the sacraments." It invoked southern history and its enduring traditions, attributed to the South's "helpless and resourceless" condition following the Civil War "not imputable to the present generation of whites," which required patience to address. Though he admonished segregation, he also legitimized white concerns that "the Negro race as a whole" required more "advancement and progress toward cultural maturity and civic competence." These conditions called for the "special education" of both races and for Blacks to "elevate" themselves to "merit acceptance as did other peoples and nationalities" in American history and "work conscientiously to prepare themselves to exercise adequately, not only their rights, but the obligations and responsibilities... as loyal, respectable and law-abiding citizens."[23] This deference to local practice and perception elicited derision from elsewhere.[24]

---

22. Griffin, "Dialogue," *Ramparts*, 24–27, 30.

23. Most Reverend Charles P. Greco, D.D., "Pastoral on Race Relations" (Alexandria, LA: Alexandria Diocese, August 4, 1963). To his credit, Bishop Greco signed a July 4, 1964, statement of Louisiana bishops calling for compliance with the 1964 Civil Rights Act and issued another pastoral letter in 1965 that demanded integration of education, housing, voting, employment, and public accommodations, and announced desegregation of Catholic schools in his diocese starting with the 1965–1966 school year (Most Reverend Charles P. Greco, D.D., "Pastoral Letter on Race Relations" [Alexandria, LA: Alexandria Diocese, June 3, 1965]).

24. Griffin wrote to Thompson that Greco's pastoral was widely known, and he had been contacted about it by priests in four northern cities (Griffin to Thompson,

Bishop Greco was informed of Thompson's interview plans and told he could see the material before publication. But when he signaled that he might censor or even prohibit it, Keating balked at seeking his blessing; he considered the information vital for the broader Church. Without reading it, Greco consulted lawyers, threatened legal action, and tried to invoke canon law to block it. But since *Ramparts* paid Thompson for the interview prior to Greco's expressed concerns, it retained publication rights; because it was an interview rather than a written statement, canon law failed to apply. Griffin shared the interview with Greco, but too late for the bishop to respond prior to publication. Once published, it took a couple of weeks to catch up to Greco, who by then was participating in Second Vatican Council deliberations in Rome. But once he read it, Greco sent a scathing letter that chastised Thompson for what Greco considered exaggerated, distorted, and misleading statements that defamed the Church. He accused Thompson of plotting to undermine his authority and asserted that he had mistakenly trusted Thompson too much. Greco forbade Thompson to make further public statements on race, even in sermons.[25] Thompson, flabbergasted and at a loss as to how he might constructively respond, turned to his new acquaintance, Thomas Merton, for advice.

Thomas Merton's Relationship with August Thompson

The details of August Thompson's introduction to Thomas Merton remain unclear, but he was undoubtedly encouraged to contact Merton by John Howard Griffin, whose relationships with Merton and Thompson intertwined. Merton had been "moved and disturbed" when he first read *Black Like Me* in March 1962. It convinced him that race relations in the South reflected a "pathological" problem of whites rather than Blacks.[26] He considered responding to Griffin, but faced "a drawer full of unanswered letters" and opted not to "go looking for more trouble than I have already."[27] But they met later that year when Griffin visited Gethsemani on retreat, and their enduring friendship was launched.[28] The following August, eight

---

August 30, 1963, John Howard Griffin Papers). He also described how Greco's letter offended Black attendees at the Catholic Interracial Council when publicly quoted there (Griffin to Thompson, September 7, 1963, John Howard Griffin Papers).

25. Greco to Thompson, November 21, 1963, TMC/BU.

26. March 24, 1962, *TTW* 213.

27. Merton to Thomas McDonnell, March 28, 1962, *WF* 48.

28. John Howard Griffin, *Follow the Ecstasy: The Hermitage Years of Thomas Merton* (Maryknoll, NY: Orbis Books, 1993), 1.

months after he met Griffin, Thompson told Griffin of his intent to visit the monk. He did so in early October 1963 on his return from a Midwestern Clergy Conference on Negro Welfare in Cincinnati. In the following years, Merton wrote letters to counsel Thompson regarding three distinct Church matters.

A Letter of Clerical Counsel

Thompson's letter of thanks to Merton, penned a week later, reveals they discussed his soon-to-be-published *Ramparts* interview. Their talk gave Thompson "much confidence" in its legitimacy. "I have done only what I was asked to do, tell the truth as it was asked to me." He reflected on their conversation with Fr. Hubert, Gethsemani's guest master, who bantered over the need for "prudence" regarding race. Thompson hoped his preoccupation with prudence rather than other points they raised would not "give too much confidence to those priests who come for retreats and are trying to justify their prejudice stand." Regarding chagrin over discouraging high school students from attending white Masses lest they be rejected, he told Merton, "I myself just do until I am stopped. Yet, can I command others to do the same???"[29]

When Merton received his *Ramparts* issue a couple weeks later, he also reflected on their visit:

> *Ramparts* came with my *Black Revolution* and Griffin's very moving dialogue with Father August Thompson—Negro pastor in a small Louisiana town (I met him here late one evening coming in from Louisville). New light on the South, again, and how impossible the situation really is. Actually it is quite a unique one for which new formulas must be sought and are being sought. But what will it avail?[30]

Just a month later, Merton again heard from Thompson in an anguished three-page, single-spaced letter exploring his dilemma over Bishop Greco's condemnation. Thompson noted that he "certainly did enjoy your piece" in *Ramparts* but wondered if the bishop had read it. In contrast to several supportive responses, his bishop's invective presented a precarious situation where "the least slip of the typewriter may mean my head." Greco had issued a press release to Catholic media asserting that he had not given permission for the interview and Thompson's comments were naïve and misguided and

---

29. Thompson to Merton, October 16, 1963, TMC/BU.
30. October 29, 1963, *DWL* 30.

used extreme examples. Thompson laid out several points refuting Greco's claims and asked Merton to draft a response for him to consider.[31]

Merton did not provide a draft, but his two-page, single-spaced reply sympathetically outlined how Thompson might respond and suggested points to make. Merton wrote as one priest to another whose vocation within the Catholic Church was at risk, and he shared that, "I am in the same position as you are, in regard to writing about nuclear war." Merton's counsel echoes his response earlier that year to Daniel Berrigan as he considered ignoring Jesuit orders against joining protests in Birmingham. It also echoes his letter to Jim Forest regarding his own censure. In the case of all three priests, when truth and vowed obedience clashed, Merton saw the integrity of their vows of obedience as crucial. Thompson must reply to his ecclesial superior, not some passing critic. Merton advised, "the most important thing is the question of obedience, and I think this should be stressed more than the subject matter of the article." Thompson could then explain circumstances that complicated timing of publication prior to Greco's review, express regret for any misunderstanding, and assert the interview's value "for the Church to fulfill her mission adequately in saving all souls, not only white but also black people. For this it is necessary, many feel, for a fair hearing to be given the Negro's just grievances." He encouraged expressions of humility, personal sincerity in fulfilling his duty, and love of the Church.[32]

Merton also expressed genuine admiration for the interview's substance. He considered it "very frank and fair," "historic," "first rate," and "badly needed." He encouraged Thompson to simply let it "have its effect," where his obedient silence would "contribute to the force of the article," as "God will see that it has effects." Beyond that, Merton encouraged him "to have, if you can, some compassion for the Bishop" since "he can't handle it rightly." To refrain from further goading may help calm Greco and "be of some help to you and to the cause of the Negro."[33] As Gregory Hillis observes, in this regard Merton was encouraging Thompson to respond in a manner that might contribute to the bishop's own epiphany and conversion regarding race.[34]

Thompson took Merton's reply to heart and drafted a couple of versions of response that sought to address those many points. But in the end, his early December letter to the bishop mostly reflected the tone of Merton's encouragement to reply humbly and let the matter play out in God's hands,

31. Thompson to Merton, November 26, 1963, TMC/BU.

32. Merton to Thompson, November 30, 1963, TMC/BU.

33. Merton to Thompson, November 30, 1963, TMC/BU.

34. Hillis, "Sign of Contradiction."

rather than include Merton's specific suggestions. Thompson opened his brief, one-page response explaining that "If I could not present what I considered the truth in a few words then I would not be able to do it in many [which might] only confuse the issue more." He expressed sorrow over any pain the interview caused Greco and that "on my honor as a priest" he had no intent to deceive. He was "honestly convinced" that he had responded to interview questions with integrity and for the good of the Church, not just the good of African Americans. Thompson asked forgiveness for any harm done and signed it, "Humbly and obediently."[35]

Anticipating Protest and Violence

By his fourth letter to Merton, sent in late February 1964, Thompson's salutations had evolved from "Dear Fr. Louis" to "Dear Fr. Tom" to simply "Dear Tom." In that letter, Thompson reported the good news that Bishop Greco had said nothing more of the *Ramparts* interview after his initial outburst and now expressly supported Thompson's fundraising for a new parish center. But his main business item reported an invitation to participate in a Catholic Interracial Council discussion about joining Jewish and Protestant clergy in civil rights protests. Since it was an unpublicized, closed meeting, he felt the bishop's ban of public activity did not apply. He speculated they might conclude that bishops could not prohibit clergy from protest actions and again asked Merton for comments, suggestions, and any reflections to pass along on Merton's behalf.

Merton offered no specific suggestions or advice for either Thompson or the gathering. But on the eve of Freedom Summer in Mississippi and escalating racial violence in Ferriday, his reply was filled with prescient observations about where the Church and nation stood regarding race. He lamented how the Church too often depended on secular society, even while claiming freedom from it. "While talking down to the 'world' we are just completely tied up in it and dependent on money and prestige." He explored the dilemma of priestly obedience when "invoked constantly to frustrate the real work that ought to be done for genuine issues (war, race, etc.)....When the decision is constantly pushed back higher up and when no decision comes from higher up except to play safe and do nothing, there is a real problem." At the same time, Merton felt a burden similar to what Thompson felt toward his young parishioners—reluctance to encourage risky acts. Thompson was in a "very special and difficult position," and Merton discouraged simply challenging authority to be a "rebel." Make clear "just where you stand," he

35. Thompson to Greco, December 7, 1963, TMC/BU.

advised, but "do nothing needlessly to get your bishop on your neck." A fine line to walk indeed.[36]

Merton closed with one of his typical reflections on America's cultural brokenness, and he urged Thompson to embrace existential nonviolence:

> The evil of violence is very deep in this land, and there is a great sinfulness reaching down into the depth of this people, in spite of their pleasant exterior. It makes me very afraid to think of the consequences that will one day make themselves felt. The Kennedy affair[37] was just one little symptom of this sin that is everywhere and that people don't seem to be able to take seriously. On the contrary, they are fed with it more and more. How can this nation have the illusion that it is a nation of good people? It makes you shudder. All I can say is that I certainly hope God will protect you and your people, and that something can be done to change things. You still need an awful lot of courage and trust, and that is why you must see to it as far as you can that there is as little as possible of the same violence in your own heart. The courage that is without violence is the greatest of all, because it relies completely on God and not on man's strength.[38]

Letters on Vocational Discernment

The Kentucky monk and the Louisiana priest would not communicate again for three and a half years, a span during which Thompson saw to fruition his new parish center and significant community programs, even as he weathered his most dangerous threats of personal violence. He next reached out to Merton in late October 1967, briefly reporting that John Howard Griffin and Jacques Maritain had visited him in Ferriday with photos of their recent visit to Merton. Assuming the monk was "busy and not receiving newsy letters" Thompson quickly got to his point. An opportunity had arisen to work in Detroit, and he again sought counsel.[39]

This opportunity emerged from another of Thompson's pronouncements, this time pointed north and directed at the archbishop of Detroit, John F.

---

36. Merton to Thompson, February 27, 1964, TMC/BU.

37. In Thompson's region, police refused to fly flags half-mast and locals expressed joy over the assassination and regret that Kennedy's wife and brother were not also assassinated. Thompson to Merton, November 26, 1963, TMC/BU.

38. Merton to Thompson, February 27, 1964, TMC/BU.

39. Thompson to Merton, October 27, 1967, TMC/BU.

Dearden. In the wake of Detroit's summer race riots, Dearden publicly stated they showed the Catholic Church must invest funds and staff to serve Black non-Catholics. Thompson responded with a six-page letter to forcefully assert how the core issue lay not with Church resources for non-Catholics. "Until we have allocated a large amount of sincere, honest, unequivocal love first in the Catholic Church to Negro Catholics," its actions and words would remain ineffective and ambiguous. Although the Church had issued statements on race over the previous twenty years, they lacked prior consultation with Blacks, their concrete impact in local parishes was never assessed, and they seemed to reflect mere obligatory afterthoughts by Church hierarchy. Thompson shared personal examples, cited the dearth of Blacks in Church leadership, and quoted the likes of Martin Luther King Jr. and Muhammad Ali to drive home his points. "Federal Courts are accepting no nonsense. We should not accept any either. We should have been the first ones to accept no nonsense. People are marching, rioting, dying and our house is not in order. We have homework to do!... Shall we meet the challenge of love not in words, but finally in action...? We can only hope that love conquers before hate takes over completely!"[40]

Archbishop Dearden responded through his secretary with a one-sentence acknowledgment. But a month later his archdiocese urban parish apostolate director invited Thompson to serve in one of their parishes and assured him that both Detroit's local bishop and Archbishop Dearden were interested in his response.[41] That offer, which Thompson interpreted as Dearden's real reply to "put up or shut up," left him deeply torn and struggling with hard vocational discernment, which he relayed to Merton. He wondered whether the invitation might actually be God's request, yet feared that transfer entailed abandoning local responsibilities that still needed his leadership. Schools had become integrated thanks to the carrot of federal funding, though churches, retreat centers, and other areas of Church life remained segregated. Bishop Greco hinted at transitioning Thompson's small, underfunded parish to mission status served by a visiting priest and transferring him elsewhere. Thompson asked Merton, "Would I be running away from such 'fights' now by accepting this offer?... Would I be letting the people down here now?"[42]

Merton responded supportively, but lacking insight into consequences at stake, declined to decisively recommend a choice. He found Thompson's

---

40. Thompson to Dearden, September 1, 1967, TMC/BU.
41. Rev. Norman P. Thomas to Thompson, October 23, 1967, TMC/BU.
42. Thompson to Merton, October 27, 1967, TMC/BU.

original letter to Dearden "extremely powerful and right on the button" and suspected the archbishop took it seriously. Such leaders wanted to understand Black experience, "despite having so many blocks" they could not see the full picture. He reassured Thompson that "a Negro priest *any place* is beyond price for the Negro people." But although he affirmed either choice, the weight of his response tilted toward Detroit, where only one of the diocese's eleven hundred priests was Black. "The chips are down...[in] the bursting, rough revolutionary thing that the Northern ghetto is. Perhaps that is where the Spirit will really be pouring out the Flame. The spiritual Flame!" Hedging, he conceded that that view might really be "just a myth suggested by all the unrest and excitement." Yet he felt that "in some strange way God is calling you there." Merton would "pray that you may be guided by the Holy Spirit: many may depend on the choice you make, either way!"[43]

Thompson responded appreciatively: "Thank you! Thank you so much for your letter. It is a great help to me....I do need as much help and prayers as I can get at this time."[44] Four months later, in February 1968, Thompson finally traveled to Detroit and personally assessed the situation. In his last letter to Merton, sent that March, he shared that the visit had failed to bring clarity. Many besides Merton encouraged the move, but numerous factors clouded Thompson's decision. A friend from Minneapolis urged him to go but cautioned that in such a setting he could not successfully minister to young militants from a Christian stance because they viewed Christianity—especially Catholicism—as a white agenda irrelevant to their own. He had to engage them in their own language of Black Power militancy. Thompson fretted over whether he could therefore be terribly relevant in Detroit, whether his voice could be heard, since Christianity and Catholicism were all he had ever known. And despite assurances of good intent, Detroit's archdiocese had just installed two whites as bishops and no Blacks. Meanwhile in Ferriday, new white support suggested progress, and he had been appointed to a local board that funded African American health services. Thompson asked Merton to "Please pray very hard for me. I so want to do what God wants of me."[45] A month later, Merton's final letter to Thompson (reproduced below) continued to encourage careful discernment, this time leaning more strongly toward remaining where "concrete" bonds of "flesh and blood" held greater sway.[46] In the end, that is what Thompson chose.

---

43. Merton to Thompson, October 30, 1967, and November 9, 1967, TMC/BU.
44. Thompson to Merton, November 6, 1967, TMC/BU.
45. Thompson to Merton, March 20, 1968, TMC/BU.
46. Merton to Thompson, April 26, 1968, TMC/BU.

Friendship Remembered

As he had with Marlon Green, Thomas Merton served as listener and encourager for Thompson and, as Green had, Thompson greatly valued that support and friendship from a respected spiritual voice. He demonstrated his affectionate respect in traveling to Merton's funeral. The day after, when John Howard Griffin went to photograph his friend's grave, he found Thompson standing beside it in prayer.[47] Thompson also visited Merton's hermitage to say Mass using Merton's chalice. Later in life, Thompson commented that Merton had modeled how "those people who are great—they don't have to show you that. Instead, when you leave them they make you feel great."[48] Merton's letters demonstrate why.

Throughout their relationship, Merton reassured Thompson that the truths he spoke were "very badly needed" and "extremely powerful and right on the button."[49] He affirmed Thompson's voice as a "witness to the fact that Catholics can think and speak out for the truth," which helped counter "one of the great dishonors of the Church that Protestants can always taunt her with, silencing the opinions of the faithful."[50] And he reassured Thompson that "a Negro priest *any place* is beyond price," that he could "do immense good *anywhere*."[51]

Telling Truth

What comes through clearly from these letters is the priest's strong desire to name the truth of Black experience within the Catholic Church in hope of transforming it, and Merton's encouragement that he do so. Thompson challenged bishops and archbishops, and he addressed others from local churches and schools to national clergy conferences. But his voice surely echoed the farthest and strongest in his 1963 *Ramparts* interview:

> [The human spirit] hungers after dignity, freedom and love; and it never stops hungering after these things until it is finally crushed. ... The Negro has never become accustomed and he will never

---

47. Griffin, *Follow the Ecstasy*, 9.

48. Sidney Williams, "Local Priest Will Be Watching Merton Special with Interest," *The Town Talk* (Alexandria, LA), September 20, 1992, 32.

49. Merton to Thompson, November 30, 1963, and November 9, 1967, TMC/BU.

50. Merton to Thompson, November 30, 1963, TMC/BU.

51. Merton to Thompson, October 30, 1967, and April 26, 1968, TMC/BU.

become accustomed to being treated as less than fully a human being. The American Negro will never become accustomed to being treated as less than fully an American. The Catholic Negro will never become accustomed to being treated as less than a Catholic. ... Negroes and some percipient whites have for a long time tried to make these truths known—but they are too painful for most to face. And finally, you get tired of trying to bring forth the truth when no one listens. ... We are never right in suppressing any truth that could help bring about right. ... Many believe that we should keep our skeletons in the closet, but I am convinced that we simply cannot afford to have any skeletons—especially skeletons that disillusion souls and drive them from God. ... I doubt [the wisdom of keeping silent] when the silence serves to prolong the injustice. The longer we have this sort of scandal [of inequality] among Catholics, the more harm it does the Church.[52]

Thompson named another truth that Merton recognized but few whites of the era grasped: the racial disparity in U.S. society was mainly a white problem —white unwillingness to listen to Black experience, to see Blacks as fellow humans of equal capacity and value, to recognize—let alone acknowledge— the scope of daily degradation Blacks endured. Especially important for Thompson, most white U.S. Catholics of the era—like white Christians of any tradition—typically missed the disconnect between doctrinal assurance of God's "catholic" inclusion and routine realities of Church structures and member practices. Given that gap, Thompson bristled when leaders invoked "patience" and "prudence" to muzzle Black truth telling and balk at mean- ingful change. Throughout his life, August Thompson refused to remain silent about how those responses betray God's truth.

Merton's letters of support reminded Thompson to "live the truth that *in Christ* there is absolutely no distinction between Black and White," despite the "very real distinction" an "affluent society" had constructed through the "sins of history."[53] Their moment rested "on the verge of some earth shaking trouble which cannot be avoided or side-stepped," and "now is the time when it is more necessary than ever to believe and to respond to one's fellow human being in whatever predicament!"[54]

---

52. Griffin, "Dialogue," *Ramparts*, 27–29.

53. Merton to Thompson, April 26, 1968, TMC/BU.

54. Merton to Thompson, November 9, 1967, TMC/BU.

But Merton recognized the Louisiana priest's precarious posture and counseled Thompson differently than he had Marlon Green. Thompson lived in a southern community teeming with Klan hatred and filled a priestly Catholic role. This context led Merton to reply with greater nuance. In affirming the truths Thompson spoke, Merton also encouraged humility and obedience toward his Church superiors. He urged "compassion" for his fear-driven bishop, mired in white supremacist culture. Because Merton respected the sacredness of religious vows in tandem with truths that transcend ecclesial structures, he encouraged Thompson to navigate the tension between them with integrity. Merton's counsel for not "simply challenging his authority" or "just being a 'rebel'"[55] did not reflect fearful deference to white tradition or reluctance to name racist domination. His counsel sought to honor the integrity of those vows, maintain Thompson's vocation, and perhaps simply assure his physical safety.

Beyond his role of encourager and ecclesial counselor, Merton especially displayed throughout his letters with Thompson what Marjorie Corbman has named as an uncommon ability to listen to people of color and truly hear them.[56] He accepted what he heard from Thompson and other Blacks, that whites carried the burden to address their own ignorance and lack of love. His decision to abandon a dialogue with James Baldwin in favor of his "Letters to a White Liberal" speaks volumes in this regard. In Church matters he clarified options rather than confidently directed choices. Throughout their exchanges, Merton lacked a paternalism that assumed Thompson was misguided or failed to understand racial complexities, and he engaged him as a fellow priest rather than a more "knowing" white.

Half a century later, a glance at realities still faced by people of color confirms that the divide Merton breached with Thompson remains wide: household wealth disparity; mass incarceration; disenfranchisement through voter roll purges, poll closures, and gerrymandering; disproportionate numbers of missing and murdered native women; ethnically targeted deportations. As Thompson had struggled, diverse people of color still struggle—even within church structures—to tell of such truths and be heard. Those of us who are white must perpetually choose whether we will also listen and encourage, as Merton did. If so, we must also choose with him whether to

---

55. Merton to Thompson, February 27, 1964, TMC/BU.

56. Marjorie Corbman, "'Welcome Brother Merton': The Challenge of the Black Power Movement to Thomas Merton's Thought on Non-Violence," unpublished paper given at the Sixteenth General Meeting of the International Thomas Merton Society, Santa Clara University, June 29, 2019.

recognize and own and address the place of *our* entrenched whiteness in the truths they speak.

Rather than provide detailed counsel to specific situations, Merton's final letter to August Thompson, previously unpublished, mostly reflects on the question of race in that pivotal moment of history and on the role Thompson might play in it.[57]

April 26, 1968

Dear Thom:[58]

As usual, I got snowed under with letters and yours got lost in the pile. About Detroit or no Detroit[59]—maybe that's all decided by now. Actually, you can do immense good anywhere. It is for you to size up the situation, see where you think you can do best, all things considered, see where you think you are most needed . . . and decide on that.[60] One advantage of Ferriday[61] is that there you have individual flesh and blood people with whom you have bonds, and the work of charity has woven a mysterious unity there. In Detroit it is more a universal, ideological sort of question: the race in the abstract. In choices between abstract and concrete, ideology and personal bonds, perhaps a Christian instinct settles for flesh and blood. That is incarnation, no? Perhaps that is what makes you wonder. On the other hand, there may always be the fact of a call of the Church into an unknown, difficult, new area. As you see, I only amplify alternatives.

Since you wrote—the Memphis tragedy[62] has happened. And what followed. This country has not learned and probably cannot learn except the hard way. On both sides, senseless polarization. There is a great sickness, the sickness of decaying western civilization, a whited sepulcher, and yet there is still some health and energy: people still protest unjust wars, refuse to accept total

---

57. TMC/BU.

58. Thompson typically signed his letters, "Thom."

59. Thompson had previously written Merton about whether to transfer to that urban setting.

60. Merton's ellipsis.

61. Thompson then served as pastor of St. Charles Church in Ferriday, LA.

62. The assassination of Martin Luther King Jr., April 4, 1968.

blindness. But can it do anything against those in high places? We must try anyhow. The big thing for Christians is to live the truth that in Christ there is absolutely no distinction between Black and White, but the Adversary has made sure that a very real distinction exists (due to the sins of history). Neither can be ignored. We have to learn the reality of the difference, and emphasize Black and White identities and qualities and rights: and see beyond to the inner unity: but that unity is in Christ, not in the affluent society.

John Griffin is planning to come today, so I won't write more. He'll bring more if there is more to say. Peace, faith, courage and joy in the Lord. Let us pray for one another.

In Christ,

7

VULNERABILITY

THE MERTON-WILLIAMS LETTERS

*There will be a lot of us out in a kind of no-man's-land where we will
be misunderstood and rejected by both sides. Well, that's all right.
As you say very rightly, it constitutes a kind of monastic solitude.
So we all have to go on without the luxury of self-pity.*
— *Thomas Merton to Robert Williams*
September 5, 1967[1]

Thomas Merton's published words prompted a second African American relationship through letters, as well as one with Marlon Green. It began in
March 1964 when a young Black classical singer responded to Merton's
"Letters to a White Liberal" by asking that he write a series of poems about
Black experience. The singer, Robert Lawrence Williams, solicited them as
lyrics for songs he would perform to raise scholarship funds for Black students. When Merton agreed, he embarked on a role unique to these relationships: that of collaboration with an African American in a project to advance
Black inclusion.

Any collaboration requires connection, communication, and shared objectives, and these in turn depend on a capacity for vulnerability and trust. In
a culture that ranks worth by skin color, collaboration across racial lines in-
tensifies those risks, which grow even more complex when the players also
bring different life experiences, priorities, and personalities to their work.
Such was the case with Merton and Williams. Frustration and miscommunication at times raised barriers and emotions, which required that they bracket
their vulnerabilities to regain trust. Merton felt this sting more than once over
their four-year relationship. But his stings paled in comparison to the disap-

---

1. *HGL* 602; TMC/BU.

pointments the young Black singer felt as his initial dream for the poems became sidetracked and then derailed. Yet despite the hurdles, Williams and Merton remained in relationship. That it lacks a clear and satisfying resolution only enhances the value of their story for reflection on the inherent vulnerability of collaborating across racial lines.

Robert Lawrence Williams (19?? – ??)

Our knowledge of Robert Williams begins and ends mostly with what he shared in letters to Merton, and those scattered threads fail to disclose the full story of his origin and fate. He was born in Louisville, Kentucky, orphaned at an early age, and raised Catholic, apparently in an orphanage. He left no solid clue as to when he was born, likely the late 1930s or early 1940s,[2] but he shared a childhood memory of visiting Merton's Gethsemani Abbey:

> I remember too, so vividly again, as I read your book [*A Thomas Merton Reader*], that as a younger fellow, my Confessor there in Kentucky, Louisville, where I was born, hoping to foster a vocation brought me to Gethsemani. Due to several other stops we arrived there after the gates had closed and the sun was going down. We stood there in the beautiful warm evening listening to the Monks chant the Vespers, and the beauty of it all was nearly more than my young soul could contain as the tears rolled down my cheeks and I surrendered my young heart to its Creator.[3]

Williams linked his orphan status to his sense of vocation: "I do so very much want to use the talent he has given me for His Glory, for I am aware that this is why He took my whole family while I was a babe and left only me."[4] A brief *Boston Globe* account suggests he attended Xavier University of Louisiana and the New England Conservatory of Music, followed by voice training in Rome, though the archives of neither institution can confirm this.[5]

---

2. The index of Louisville birth records shows six "Robert L. Williams" and three additional "Robert Williams" born during this span; inquiries to archdiocesan baptismal archives failed to yield a match.

3. Williams to Merton, June 9, 1964, TMC/BU.

4. Williams to Merton, October 27, 1964, TMC/BU.

5. Brendan Malin, "Green Patch," *Boston Globe*, October 21, 1965, 50.

Boston Singer

Williams was still young when he contacted Merton in the spring of 1964—his photo in a 1963 flier[6] he sent to Merton suggests someone under thirty. By that time he was based in Boston as a singer of classical music. He named no other livelihood, but he mentions studies "financed by" Cardinal Cushing,[7] then archbishop of Boston's archdiocese, and "the Millionairess here who paid for all of my lessons with the help of Cardinal Cushing,"[8] and that, "here in Boston, the Cardinal has Catholic Scholarships For Negroes, Inc., which at the present has 200 Negroes in Colleges throughout the nation."[9] He does not name that resource as his own underwriter, but it seems likely that it, coupled with the patronage of a wealthy local, paved his path from Louisville, perhaps via New Orleans, to Boston.

Williams enjoyed an active performance schedule, often tied to Catholic entities. The 1963 publicity flier recaps his 1961–62 schedule and boasts of three performances in New York City, three in Fullerton Hall of the Chicago Art Institute, another at "McCormick Place" (presumably Chicago's), and a tour abroad that included performances in Canada, France, Switzerland, Spain, and Rome. Williams also wrote of several New England concerts booked for the fall of 1964, and he spent the latter half of 1965 in Europe, mostly in Ireland, where he performed benefit concerts for orders of missionary nuns and sang in a show titled *Gaels of Laughter*. He toured U.S. Catholic colleges in 1966, returned to Ireland the next year, and remained based in Boston until late 1967 and 1968, when he wrote from a Harlem YMCA apartment and planned a Carnegie Hall appearance.

Williams was apparently still maturing as a singer during those years. In mid-1964 he wrote to Merton, "My voice is still in the opening process and gets bigger and stronger by the month....I work for four hours daily on this technique...to perfect my instrument."[10] The music critic of the *Boston Pilot*, the archdiocesan newspaper, agreed that Williams held potential. His review of a spring 1965 concert suggested that Williams did "not yet fully realize how good his voice is," as he "showed a diffidence which is

---

6. "Boston Group Plans Jordon Hall Benefit Concert to Aid Massachusett's [*sic*] African Students," n.d., n.p., Robert Williams correspondence file, TCM/BU.

7. Williams to Merton, May 14, 1964, TMC/BU.

8. Williams to Merton, August 19, 1964, TMC/BU. The *Boston Globe* account names as his benefactors Richard Murphy, vice-president of "Newmont Mining Co., Montreal," and his wife, residing in the Boston suburb of Charlestown. Malin, "Green Patch."

9. Williams to Merton, September 29, 1966, TMC/BU.

10. Williams to Merton, August 19, 1964, TMC/BU.

personally commendable but may severely handicap a performing musician. His voice did not seem fully warmed up until shortly before the intermission, perhaps partly as a result of his recent illness. In the program's second half... he showed a voice of great potential, though he kept it rather severely reined in... I look forward ... to hearing him sing with the freedom and confidence that his abilities obviously deserve."[11]

Robert Williams, ca. 1966
(Courtesy of Thomas Merton Center,
Bellarmine University)

The review described Williams's audience as "very enthusiastic," and Williams concurred that the audience "loved" it: "After 21 songs, they kept calling for more, more, more. They wouldn't allow me to leave the stage even to catch my breath."[12] He mentioned that a 1963 audience called for seven encores, and the *Boston Globe* account described his 1965 Irish musical performances before "overjoyed audiences" as "winning the hearts of Dubliners."[13]

Quest for Purpose

Beyond these hints of his origin and early career, Williams expressed to Merton his desire to integrate aspects of his identity—Black, Catholic, a singer with the good fortune to overcome disadvantage—into a life of elevated purpose. Williams especially yearned to enhance the lives of Blacks, both American and African, and he creatively gathered an array of relationships to help advance a career that would inspire others. His pursuits sometimes seem naïve and unrealistic, bordering on grandiose, but they drew on strong faith commitments and social ideals. That quest naturally bumped against racial barriers and institutional inertia, and he often changed course when navigating those realities. Impassioned plans voiced in one letter

---

11. Joseph MsClellon, "Music," *Boston Pilot* 136, no. 20 (May 15, 1965): 16.
12. Williams to Merton, May 22, 1965, TMC/BU.
13. Malin, "Green Patch."

evaporated by the next, replaced with a new opportunity that dangled more immediate promise before him.

Toward these goals, Williams established "The Foundation for African Students" in 1962 to fund scholarships for Catholic African student exchanges and lay educational programs of "the Catholic Bishops of Africa."[14] He assembled a board of thirteen directors, chaired by the president of Boston's National Shawmut Bank, with the Boston College Law School dean, Jesuit Robert Drinan, as both "Honorary Advisor" and board member. Thomas Merton served as its sole "Honorary Sponsor."[15] During his 1965 European tour he wooed an unnamed "very powerful and influential Catholic person" in Paris as an "International Sponsor" to help him open "all doors of the world."[16]

Williams worked closely with the Franciscan Missionary Sisters of Africa, founded by Irish nuns under the leadership of Teresa Kearney, or "Mother Kevin." They had established a house in the Boston suburb of Brighton a decade earlier, and Williams used their address for his foundation. They introduced him to Kenyan bishop Caesar Gatimu, who stayed with them on Boston visits, attended Williams's 1963 concert, and became his foundation's official patron. Williams mentioned the sisters often and apparently related to their Franciscan mendicant ideals.[17] He dedicated a U.S. concert to them for their benefit and another, when he was in Ireland, for the benefit of their motherhouse.

Williams mentioned other relationships within his network, such as "Italian friends" in New York and Rome and correspondence with "William Dawson," probably the long-standing U.S. representative from Chicago, then one of only five Black congressmen. Williams also hoped to support African missions through the Boston Archdiocese Propagation of the Faith society, and in the fall of 1966 he established the "Robert Lawrence Foundation," modeled on the National Conference of Christians and Jews,[18] whose

---

14. "Constitution of the Foundation for African Students," n.d., accompanying Williams to Merton, October 24, 1964, TMC/BU. Williams to Merton, March 14, 1964, TMC/BU indicates it would support the "African and Colored Mission Board of the Propagation of the Faith" for "African and Negro Missions" and give "African and Negro youngsters a chance to educate themselves so that they may later help in educating their people."

15. Per letterhead of Williams to Merton, February 12, 1965.

16. Williams to Merton, May 22, 1965, TMC/BU.

17. Malin, "Green Patch."

18. Established in 1927 to promote interfaith activism, renamed to National Conference for Community and Justice in 1998, disbanded in 2005, with local chapters continuing as the National Federation for Just Communities. https://en.wikipedia.org/wiki/National_Conference_for_Community_and_Justice

Catholic executive director had befriended him. This second foundation's program "teaches youth of all races [and religious groups] to work, play and live together as Americans, helping them to get to know and understand one another." It would also benefit "African and Negro Mission" scholarship funds in each diocese where he performed.[19] Despite his structures and connections, Williams lacked staff and performed all foundation work: "When the people find that we are just getting the foundation started and that we are not rich or powerful, they lose interest."[20]

"Freedom Songs"—Catalyst for Collaboration

Merton's relationship with Robert Williams revolved around the eight "Freedom Songs"[21] that Williams commissioned. Over time the poems drew others into their orbit and took on a life of their own, which diluted the influence either man had over their objective.

Dreams Pursued: 1964–1965

Robert Williams opened his March 1964 letter announcing that: "The National Foundation For African Students would like to commission you to write for us a series of poems on Brotherhood and Faith, which will be set to music for Tenor Soloist and presented in a formal concert this coming November 1964 as a salute and tribute to our late beloved friend, President John Kennedy." The project could "do something constructive to aid our [Black] people, keeping within The Holy Dignity of Holy Mother The Church."[22]

When Merton promptly agreed to write them, Williams assured creative latitude, but hoped the poems would reflect the insight of Merton's "Letters to a White Liberal" and offered suggestions. They might portray Blacks as equal players in U.S. society, "proud of [their] American Heritage and very determined to stand up now and be counted along with [their] American Brothers of other races and nationalities"—a "Patriotic Dedication" possibly titled "Songs For Americans." They might be reminders of how Blacks fought and died for this country, where God dwelt as father to all races, how in death all stand before a God who asks each "what he has used the color of

---

19. Williams to Merton, September 29, 1966, TMC/BU.

20. Williams to Merton, March 21, 1965, TMC/BU.

21. See also William H. Shannon, *Silent Lamp*, 234–37, and Shannon, "Freedom Songs," in *ME*, 167.

22. Williams to Merton, March 14, 1964, TMC/BU.

his skin to accomplish for the betterment of his brothers and God's universe." They might also channel King's dream of integration and contrast it with realities like Harlem, where those "frightened like me...because of their color have lost hope and faith in everything except their God."[23]

Merton offered his own vision for "an authentic expression of the Negro's struggle for his rights, and not just a friendly expression of concern by someone who lives comfortably looking on." It warranted music in the "Negro tradition...between spirituals and the blues," where "the jazz element is essential."[24] Merton downplayed Williams's patriotic exuberance while affirming his wish to show Blacks as fully American. Though he might address that theme in an article, as "more of a European" at heart he lacked Williams's "deep feeling for the land and the continent," and could not "poetically" express those feelings. But he liked Williams's Harlem imagery.[25] A month later Merton forwarded his first poem: "Sundown," based on chapter 3 of the prophet Micah, and by early June he had forwarded all eight "Freedom Songs."[26] They drew on the psalms and biblical prophets, since "the Prophets were the voice of the oppressed and the Psalms are the prayer of the Anawim, the poor of Israel." Having written them "in connection with the Christian non-violent movement for Civil Rights," these biblical voices, with which Christ also identified, held "special truth and relevance [for] ...oppression and the struggle for human rights in every age."[27]

To others, Merton downplayed their poetic quality as "rather poor," "second rate," and "lousy,"[28] though friends felt otherwise. Hervé Chaigne, a French Franciscan colleague, translated and published them in his periodical, *Frère du Monde*. Zalman Schachter, a Jewish rabbi, praised them as "tremendous" and "wonderfully delightful," as they "caught so many of the Hebrew puns inherent in the text" and "the rhythm, and the way in which the prophet

---

23. Williams to Merton, March 31, 1964, TMC/BU.

24. Merton to Williams, March 21, 1964, *HGL* 588.

25. Merton to Williams, April 23, 1964, *HGL* 588–89.

26. The other seven songs and their derivation are: "Evening Prayer" (Psalm 140, 141); "All the Way Down" (Jonas 2); "I Have Called You" (Isaiah 43:1); "Be My Defender" (Psalm 4); "The Lord Is Good" (Psalm 71); "There Is a Way" (Isaiah 35:8–10); "Earthquake" (Isaiah 52). All eight are published scattered in Appendix II of *The Collected Poems of Thomas Merton* (New York: New Directions 1977); see page 668 to locate page numbers for each.

27. Merton, "Eight Freedom Songs," n.d., typescript, Robert Williams Correspondence, TMC/BU.

28. Merton to W. H. Ferry, July 1, 1964, *HGL* 218; Merton to Vera Zorina, July 10, 1964, TMC/BU; Merton to Thomas Glover, August 16, 1964, TMC/BU.

would repeat certain phrases." He liked how Merton "kept things more on earth" rather than emphasizing the heavenly.[29] Schachter's praise moved Merton, and he tended to mute his criticism for a time, though never lauded the poems either. But he hoped they might somehow help the nation's racial climate. Despite the new Civil Rights Act, there remained "a deep, deep wound. ...Let us hope that truth and song may begin to bring a little healing."[30]

Williams responded enthusiastically and set sights on a composer, hopefully a Jew and specifically Aaron Copland, to assemble a diverse trio of Catholic priest lyricist, Jewish composer, and Black singer. Williams dreamed of using the songs to promote his foundation with "terrific events," including their New York City debut in early 1965 to launch a national, then world, tour.[31] He also planned a "$3.98 album of the eight songs [to] be sold through every Church, Organization, School, Fraternity, etc. throughout America and eventually Europe."[32]

As one might expect, Copland wished them luck but declined, and Merton then aided Williams in his search for a composer. He sought advice from Tommy Glover, an African American jazz saxophonist and former Trappist brother at Gethsemani, who liked the poems but felt they needed more "rhyme and simple rhythm" for this purpose. Echoing Williams, he reminded Merton that Black Americans were "proud" and "spiritual and patriotic, insisting that our contribution to culture be accepted."[33] Merton contacted at least five others,[34] but no composer surfaced, and Williams grew impatient. At one point he considered writing his own music and hiring a "professional tunesmith" to arrange it, but three days later conceded that would "ruin your beautiful songs."[35] Finally in March 1965, Williams approached liturgical composer Alexander Peloquin of Boston College, who consented. Though not schooled in spirituals or other Black music, Peloquin was inspired by Vatican II reforms to compose the first High Mass in English, which premiered at a 1964 liturgical conference in St. Louis.

---

29. Rabbi Zalman M. Schachter to Merton, November 19, 1964, TMC/BU.

30. Merton to Williams, July 30, 1964, *HGL* 589.

31. Williams to Merton, June 9, 1964, TMC/BU.

32. Williams to Merton, August 19, 1964, TMC/BU.

33. Thomas Glover to Merton, August 24, 1964, TMC/BU.

34. These included: Vera Zorina, a ballerina, actress, and choreographer, married to the president of Columbia Records; "sister Jeremy" at the nearby Sisters of Loretto convent; John Howard Griffin (for suggestions); Denis Fitzgerald, composer of a recent "vernacular mass," in Chicago; an unnamed Detroit composer.

35. Williams to Merton, October 24 and 27, 1964, TMC/BU.

As Williams embarked on his European tour later that spring, Merton shared his hope "with all my heart" that the songs would come to "say something for the Negroes everywhere and to join my voice to theirs. It is one of the few honorable things I can think of at the present time."[36] In June, Peloquin visited Merton to discuss the music, and Merton wrote Williams that Peloquin planned to study his performance tapes "to make sure that his settings are right for your voice," predicting "a most unique concert."[37]

Dreams Deferred: 1966–1967

But it was not to be. Adding a third creative force to the mix opened wider the door for miscommunication that began the end of Williams's dreams for these songs, though details of how that transpired remain unclear. Some letters between Merton and the others are missing, we have none between Williams and Peloquin, and it appears all parties failed to copy each other when corresponding. Beyond this, Peloquin preferred telephone calls over letters—problematic for a cloistered hermit with limited phone access and a singer traveling overseas. Such dynamics conjured a perfect storm of triangulated communication, and Williams returned that December to discover in shocked anger that, "Mr. Peloquin has turned our Freedom Songs into a symphony and has engaged Eileen Farrell, the Metropolitan Opera Soprana to introduce them."[38]

Missteps by all three contributed to this painful juncture. Williams had written to Merton in the "early fall" that he was "tied up in Dublin, and would not be able to come back," having landed his part in *Gaels of Laughter*. This preempted preparation for a fall Freedom Songs debut, and we don't know if he informed Peloquin or expected Merton to do so. But he failed to tell Merton he still intended to debut them whenever he returned, and the monk then presumed it was "understood" that Williams's new plans overrode his commitment to debut them. Merton therefore told the composer he "was free, if he wished, to consider composing the songs for another singer." He heard nothing more from Peloquin after their June meeting and assumed Williams had meanwhile contacted him.[39] But without contacting Williams, Peloquin instead ran with Merton's news, perhaps reinforced by the October *Boston Globe* blurb that mentioned Williams's Dublin run, and planned the songs for a wholly different project.

---

36. Merton to Williams, May 27, 1965, *HGL* 594.
37. Merton to Williams, June 30, 1965, *HGL* 595.
38. Williams to Merton, December 12, 1965, TMC/BU.
39. Merton to Williams, December 17, 1965, *HGL* 596.

Merton explained the misunderstandings to his collaborators and made certain they both knew he had given Williams rights to the poems. He urged Williams to now find an African American composer since "I think you will find few white composers that are ready to say [what you want] effectively."[40] But, though things at one point became "rather heated" with Peloquin, Williams retained him as composer, telling Merton he remained "determined not to make an enemy" of Peloquin, had "stopped pressing so hard," and gave him until November 1966 to complete them.[41] Peloquin meanwhile suggested that Williams premiere one song at an upcoming liturgical conference, but Williams insisted on waiting to introduce them until all were complete.

Merton next heard from Williams in April 1967, when he reported that in the two years since Peloquin had agreed to the project, he had composed music for just one song. When contacted by Williams's lawyer, Peloquin then required a fee to continue the work, though Williams felt they had agreed to set financial arrangements once the music was completed. Williams considered renouncing his claim on the songs, but Merton discouraged that.

Dreams Denied: 1968

When communication resumed in February 1968, the composer wrote to Merton that a national liturgical conference that summer had scheduled Martin Luther King Jr. as keynote speaker and showed interest in Peloquin's pitch to perform Merton's song "Earthquake" following King's message. For this prestigious venue, Peloquin now proposed a Black *baritone* (not tenor) soloist. He conceded to Merton that following "problems with Bob" over "'OUR' Freedom Songs" he had ceased composing for them and asked if Merton thought he could now proceed.[42] Though Merton guardedly affirmed the possibility, he insisted that Williams retained formal rights to the poems and, given Williams's feelings, perhaps they were best left unsung.

Peloquin quickly replied that he had now begun writing music for three additional songs[43] and Williams had released the poems to him, which prompted Merton to consent to the composer's plans. Williams reacted to this news with a not-so-veiled threat to publicize that the songs had been

---

40. Merton to Williams, January 15, 1966, *HGL* 597.

41. Williams to Merton, May 31, 1966, TMC/BU.

42. C. Alexander Peloquin to Merton, February 22, 1968, TMC/BU.

43. "Sundown!," "All the Way Down," "The Lord Is Good"; C. Alexander Peloquin to Merton, n.d., TMC/BU.

stolen from him. When Merton again asked Peloquin to drop the project as unworkable, Peloquin phoned Williams to chide him for this major disservice to Merton, his "Christian friend," and Williams then assured Merton he would cooperate.

Merton assigned much of the responsibility for this tension to Peloquin as "a bit high handed and independent," his search for another singer as "the source of the trouble." But he also saw Williams as ambiguous, prone to comments "heavily laden with emotion or fantasy," "confused and unrealistic ... and very masochistic"—maybe even "a little bit nuts." But he conceded, "I suppose that is easy to say!"[44]

The April 4 assassination of Martin Luther King Jr. further altered the songs' course. With a King keynote now off the table, Peloquin next proposed a televised memorial to King. He revisited Merton on April 8 to share his music and asserted that Williams's voice was not "baritone enough" for the music—unsurprising, since he had written it for a baritone though Williams sang tenor. Merton shared Peloquin's proposal with his friend June Yungblut, a King family neighbor and friend. Mrs. King agreed to it, and Yungblut began to facilitate the arrangements.

Merton still lobbied for a Black singer, though he now relied on Yungblut to move things along. Coretta King insisted the tribute retain a spiritual rather than commercial tone, and the television and liturgical conference options merged. The songs would be performed at the liturgical event in August and recorded for a broadcast sponsored by the National Council of Catholic Men. Merton asked that they "reopen the question (with A. Peloquin) of fitting in somewhere the tenor Robert Williams who suggested writing the songs in the first place and who owns them,"[45] but this request went unheeded. Merton had also delegated the legalities of literary rights to his legacy trust lawyer, John Ford, and though Ford now wrote directly to Williams, Merton followed those letters with his own to soften their formality.

At the songs' August 19 performance, Merton's wish for an African American singer[46] was fulfilled in Matthew Fraling, cantor and musician at

---

44. Merton to Robert M. MacGregor (editor at New Directions publishers), March 28, 1968, TMC/BU; March 28, 1968, *OSM* 73.

45. Merton to Richard J. Walsh, June 27, 1968, TMC/BU.

46. Peloquin earlier proposed two others to replace Williams: Harry Belafonte and "Father Rivers." It is unclear if Belafonte, a friend of the Kings, was asked. Father Clarence Rivers, an acclaimed vocalist and pioneer African American liturgical music composer, merged Gregorian chant and African American spiritual styles. He gained national attention performing his song "God Is Love" at the 1964 National Liturgy Week in St. Louis. http://liturgicalleaders.blogspot.com/2008/09/alexander-

Baltimore's St. Gregory Catholic Church. Another Catholic, "Sister Laetitia, RJM," also soloed, and they were accompanied by the choir from King's Ebenezer Baptist Church, which included King's sister. Peloquin's choir also performed, along with an orchestra. The audience received the songs well. Dorothy Day attended and penned a note to Merton before retiring that same night: "The songs were enough to break down the walls of Jericho. People wept with joy. What beautiful music! Magnificent! . . . I have been so entranced by the music and the words. Thank you, thank you."[47] The next day Yungblut's telegram on behalf of herself and Peloquin described the concert as "powerful and moving." Following Merton's death that December, Coretta King's words of condolence to Gethsemani Abbey also mentioned the songs, now a tribute to her late husband rather than a vehicle to promote Williams's vision. She suggested they might eventually be considered a classic, a prophecy that has not come to pass.

Thomas Merton's Relationship with Robert Williams

Despite challenges to come, Williams and Merton developed good rapport over the first sixteen months of their exchanges. The singer expressed his desire to visit Merton throughout 1964, but prior to each of the four arrival times he targeted, some newly emerged plan arose to defer it. After his intent to visit in January 1965 dissipated, he no longer raised the possibility, and the two never met. Their correspondence extended from March 1964 through August 1968, with occasional gaps of a few months. The archival collection holds twenty-seven letters by Williams and thirty-one by Merton, but up to nine from Williams and a couple from Merton have not survived. Encouraged by the monk's empathetic listening and responses, Williams opened up to Merton and shared many impressions and concerns. In his responses, Merton sought to moderate Williams's expectations as he assured him of his support and addressed the complexities of America's racial landscape.

---

peloquin.html. Merton seemed unaware of Rivers and assumed he was white (Merton to Peloquin, March 2, 1968, Peloquin Correspondence/TMC/BU; Merton to Yungblut, April 9, 1968, *HGL* 695).

47. Day to Merton, August 19, 1968, *American Catholic Pacifism: The Influence of Dorothy Day and the Catholic Worker Movement*, ed. Anne Klejment and Nancy L. Roberts (Westport, CT: Praeger, 1996), 119.

Vulnerability through Letters—Robert Williams

Because Robert Williams shared freely, his letters offer a candid window into his experience as a Black man in 1960s America. His commitment to his Church complicated that terrain. Even as he entrusted outcomes to God, he engaged a church administered by flawed humans living in a flawed white supremacist culture. This lived tension adds nuance to the emotional volatility sometimes palpable in Williams's letters. At least three aspects of his vulnerability emerge in them.

Black and Catholic

The first aspect echoes the marginalization August Thompson also felt in being simultaneously "Black" and "Catholic." Tension as a Catholic among Blacks emerged in Williams's very first letter:

> As you probably know, Father Louis, the greatest amount of work in winning first class citizenship for the Negro people is being done by the Protestant Negro. But for a number of reasons, we Negroes who have embraced The True Faith, have no effective instrument with which we can properly work, since we must at all times keep in mind the Great Dignity of our Mother, The Church, and since we desire to shield Her from all harm.[48]

A year later, following Selma, Alabama's "Bloody Sunday" and march to Montgomery, Williams raised the flip side of this dynamic: being Black among Catholics:

> Just now everyone is taking a second look at The Catholic Church, for the Nuns and Priests are joining the Demonstrators and the Sit-Ins, as never before.... But my being Negro has rather hindered the work a bit, as the ones I should receive the help from are only willing to share in that which is already started by the Protestants, rather than help bring something new into being.... Feeling that we should wait on God is all well and good, but God's time is now.... I have been shown that a black man can't do what I had in mind, alone. Not in the Catholic Church. It seems we are willing to follow the Protestants in whatever they start in the Civil Rights Movement. It has not yet reached the time when we start creating our own little nitch [*sic*] within the movement.[49]

---

48. Williams to Merton, March 14, 1964, TMC/BU.
49. Williams to Merton, March 21, 1965, TMC/BU. "Boston Clergy, Laymen

He lamented a lack of Church support for its Black members: "Everyone seems so very busy and no one really wants to get involved. I find this to be especially true among our white Catholic brothers. They just don't seem to care. I must really do something publicly to wake them up."[50]

As this last comment implies, Williams bore great personal responsibility to correct that dynamic on behalf of both races. He once found notes on a discarded concert program that described his performance as "very beautiful" but had also added, "plenty niggers present." He explained his burden for those whites:

> I don't desire just to give a beautiful concert, Father Louis. . . . I desire to make my audience think: . . . to ask themselves if they, too, are on God's side and if they truly are members of that band . . . of whom [Christ] asked nothing else, other than that they love God with all of their hearts, souls, and minds and all men as themselves. I desire that they know when they leave our concert that unless they do this as He commanded, no matter what Church they attend, they are not following Christ.[51]

Writing from Paris in the spring of 1965, his complementary burden for Blacks weighed heavily when observing impoverished Africans:

> Would that my heart were big enough to place a wall of protection around them all, and care for them and nurse their poor wounded spirits, more so than their bodies, for seemingly the spirit dies a bit too, each day, when it is born into a black body in our lily white world-wide society. But God will give me the strength to do all that I desire for them; this has been revealed unto me, and it is He Who has brought me unto this hour. . . . All [the concert applause] seems to me so shallow, for my poor brothers are still suffering because of their black faces, and I know that there will never be any joy for me in singing merely for singing alone, for singing makes my heart ache with (for) something that . . . *is never there*, even with all its glamour, cheers, and gaiety. Something I can only find when I am aware that my efforts from singing have aided another black face [to] tolerate its earthly purgatory a few years longer.[52]

Join Selma Protest," *Boston Pilot* 136, no. 11 (March 13, 1965): 1. An estimated eighty priests from sixteen dioceses participated.

50. Williams to Merton, July 8, 1964, TMC/BU.
51. Williams to Merton, March 31, 1964, TMC/BU.
52. Williams to Merton, May 22, 1965, TMC/BU.

But by spring 1967, loss of control over the Freedom Songs' destiny, exacerbated by the rise of Black Power's social critique, overwhelmed him. In dejection, Williams told Merton he would leave the Catholic Church: "To me a black man, it is just an organization determined to keep us in the place our white brothers have made for us. They are not interested in me or any other black person, and I am so very sick of hypocrisy while my poor people are suffering for no other reason than being born black." He had trusted Peloquin "as one of my fellow Catholics," but now considered relinquishing any claim to the songs since "after all, they are for Catholics." He thanked Merton for trying to help, but now saw that "as black men we can only free ourselves from the Devil, and we know too, now, that he is far from being [just] a Spirit."[53] Merton's response, reproduced below, graciously accepted and supported his choice.

Williams later reversed that decision and remained Catholic. The harder he tried to leave the Church, he conceded, "the more I seem to love Her," even though "she hasn't been a Mother to her black children." His postscript added a poetic meditation on Blackness: "I have just found out a wonderful secret. I too am in a Monastery / Its walls are the color of my black skin / The hurt inflicted upon this body because of it, are the penances I offer Our Blessed Lord."[54] To Merton, Williams's choice "shows once again that the Spirit and the Church are far beyond any lines of division that humans can think up for themselves," and that God could not let the Church "continue to be a 'white' Church." For "Christians and men of mature thought, the hard way is the only way left.... As you very rightly say, it constitutes a kind of monastic solitude."[55]

Hesitance to Trust
A second aspect of Williams's vulnerability captured in his letters highlights the difficulty for Blacks to trust that a white, even one who wrote as forcefully on race as Merton, could truly "get" the challenges and implications of Blackness. Williams's letters reveal the fragility of that trust, the readiness to believe it had been misplaced. Merton's "Letters to a White Liberal" seeded enough trust for Williams to request the poems, and when he encountered the essay again seven months later, he enthused: "Thank you, Father Louis, for seeing God in black faces and hearts also; for loving us, and for caring about us. The more I read about you, the more I see that this wonderful love for our people was established in your heart by God, long before

---

53. Williams to Merton, April 20, 1967, TMC/BU.
54. Williams to Merton, August 29, 1967, TMC/BU.
55. Merton to Williams, September 5, 1967, *HGL* 601–602.

he lead [*sic*] you to Gethsemani. Thus I know you understand so well."[56] But only after Merton sent a copy of *Seeds of Destruction* in December 1964 did that trust solidify:

> Blessed Be Our Great God, Who has revealed so very much to you. . . . I know now that we are of the same heart. *Before I wasn't sure,* because I feel so strongly on the issues of today, and I am so used to getting carried away in talking to our Priests, for they haven't been blessed with the foresight that you have, and they can't understand how a black Catholic feels. It seems to be impossible. Now, when God does will our meeting, the fear of just talking to and insulting another white priest will have left me, for you, too, are God's messenger, for only He could have revealed such things to you, when others with your same calling . . . have closed their hearts to The Lamb's gentle voice. I fear no longer, for I see now that the same gentle voice speaks to us both. . . . My prayers are to become the man you already are.[57]

But even this powerful trust was quickly shattered a year later when Williams learned a white opera star planned to sing the Freedom Songs: "They are your songs, and you and Mr. Peloquin must have decided when he was there just what you wanted done. . . . I am very use[d] to stepping out of the white man's way when he decides he wants something." With words that surely stung, he continued:

> I felt when I asked your help and that of Mr. Peloquin that you both loved the Africans as much as I do and were concerned most about their welfare. When has the white man ever really been concerned about his black so-called brother? . . . Father, you wanted to add your voice to the voice of the struggling Negro people. . . . With Mr. Peloquin's help you've merely added your voice to the voices of our enemies, who seek to keep us suppressed, All In The Name Of Christ.[58]

This torn trust was repaired following Merton's restrained response, which focused on moving forward to resolve the snafu rather than defend the

---

56. Williams to Merton, October 11, 1964, TMC/BU.
57. Williams to Merton, January 15, 1965, TMC/BU. Emphasis in the original.
58. Williams to Merton, December 12, 1965, TMC/BU.

past. But the patch failed to hold. Two years later, after Peloquin told Merton that Williams had relinquished his song rights, Merton lamented the end of their plans to Williams but assured him that it must be "God's will." Williams chafed at the idea God willed that, though he conceded God may have permitted it, "just has he has allowed, or rather suffered, all of the white man's wrongs to be." Williams saw Peloquin's and Merton's posture as "typical of the Catholic Church today and yesterday, its nuns and its priests. You are not our friends. Nor are you friends of God," for they ignore God's commands to treat others well "and then try to appease yourselves by saying it is God's Will."[59] Williams again restored their relationship and regained faith in Merton's good intent, but it remains unclear whether he ever regained the level of trust he once felt.

Barriers of Blackness

A third vulnerability that Williams's letters reveal involves his frustration, sometimes rage, over setbacks stemming from his skin color. From our distance it remains hard to tease out the complex traits that converged to thwart his dreams. Williams was young. He lacked experience in what makes for institutional and social success. He possessed talent, but exactly how much remains unclear, and even the most talented performers need serendipity and breaks to gain recognition. Such factors may have played into the collapse of what he had hoped for. But surely his race did too. Even the best-intended white allies rarely grasp how opportunities in *their* hands usually play out much differently when held by Blacks.

Williams poignantly expressed this reality in early 1968 upon realizing he would never debut the Freedom Songs. Merton's assurance that he had written the poems for Williams felt "rather like the white man setting the Negro free from slavery" without providing means to navigate that freedom:

> You see, Father, the white man has tried to make himself God, through his stolen goods and power that he has killed and raped to secure all through the world. He has built his churches, monasteries, and convents, which are really anti-Christ to begin with, hoping to appease God by offering his stolen power and wealth to him on his terms. He has even dared to try and speak for God to all nations, but is beginning to realize now that God is about to speak for Himself, at long last.... I believe not in you or your Christianity any more,

---

59. Williams to Merton, March 23, 1968, TMC/BU.

but I do believe in the sweet, kind, little humble Jesus, who came to earth nearly 2000 years ago to teach us how to live.[60]

Intrinsic Good Will

Despite these vulnerabilities and Williams's human tendencies toward reaction and vacillation, his capacity for good will and desire for reconciliation repeatedly won out to restore their relationship. Five days after his spring 1968 condemnation of white supremacy, as he accepted that others would perform the songs in tribute to Dr. King, he resolved, "With the love I profess for The Christ Child, I embrace Mr. Peloquin, you, Father, and the songs, and shall pray for their great success when he presents them this summer."[61] Williams's last preserved letter suggests that his affection for Merton endured:

> It seems that it is so very easy to hate today, for it is all around me, and in some circles here in Harlem it has even become the right and natural thing to do, and I do feel things so very strongly, and always have, but I don't want to ever hurt you Father, for you are good and kind.... There is a chance there is still a bit of God within me, also. ...I hate no one and never will, regardless.[62]

Vulnerability through Letters—Thomas Merton

Thomas Merton responded to the requests, reflections, and laments of Robert Williams with different voices of his own as their circumstances shifted. To his credit, he mostly offered patience and encouragement, and he added his tabgible support to Williams's project when compatible with his sequestered vocation. Beyond aiding the search for a composer, he sought to link a Spalding College scholarship program to Williams's foundation, and he made sure that Williams received royalty payment for a published Italian translation of the Freedom Songs. Merton embraced his own vulnerability by readily relinquishing the songs' control to Williams and by permitting the singer to govern their path. But he also sought to mitigate vulnerabilities by moderating expectations or advocating for interests of Williams, himself, or both. When Williams vented about his Catholic African American experience, Merton mostly sought connection, showed empathy, and encouraged.

---

60. Williams to Merton, March 23, 1968, TMC/BU.
61. Williams to Merton, March 28, 1968, TMC/BU.
62. Williams to Merton, July 14, 1968, TMC/BU.

Moderating Expectations

From the outset, Williams expected quick results. He wanted lyrics written, music composed, facilities and musicians scheduled, and an initial performance completed within eight months of initiating contact. Merton promptly supplied the poems, and Williams presumed Aaron Copland would provide music equally fast. When he did not, Merton reminded him of their limited control and counseled patience: "The best thing is to wait patiently. The Lord's time for these songs is perhaps not yet. But it will come, and they will be all the better for the waiting."[63] "I am sure that if we are patient something good will come up. You must realize it is the ordinary way of God's dealings with us that our ideas do not work out speedily and efficiently as we would like them to."[64]

But Merton distanced his counsel for patience from that of the "white liberals" he had critiqued; waiting on God "obviously does not justify complete passivity in political affairs, such as the civil rights struggle."[65] He agreed with Williams that some composers may be "frightened of the civil rights cause," but reminded him that "anyone who is not committed [to civil rights] would hardly be able to do a good job in writing the music." Speaking from "long experience," Merton assured him that "when God wills to bring fruit from a work, [God]... puts all sorts of obstructions in the way... to really bring the thing to maturity," and added, "Do not worry, Freedoms Songs will be needed for a long time to come."[66] Late in their search, Merton presciently cautioned how costly patience might become:

> You may in fact even be deprived of tasting the full fruit of success. But if you simply forget about the results and do the work with all your heart because it is pleasing to God and for the benefit of your brothers, and if you take that as reward enough in this life, you will achieve far more than you could ever hope.... The work will then take care of itself.[67]

Merton returned to this perspective on success in 1968, when it was clear the songs would debut without Williams:

---

63. Merton to Williams, October 28, 1964, TMC/BU.
64. Merton to Williams, October 30, 1964, *HGL* 591.
65. Merton to Williams, October 30, 1964, *HGL* 591.
66. Merton to Williams, December 21, 1964, *HGL* 592.
67. Merton to Williams, March 10, 1965, *HGL* 594; TMC/BU.

In the end, a successful person is no better off than anybody else, as far as real gains are concerned.... Of course, I admit, some people are satisfied with success, a good image, and a fair amount of money. You would not be any more than I am. You are a different kind of person. For that very reason you cannot do the mean and ruthless things that have to be done in the jungle of contemporary life.... But that is the kind of person who is a success and goes places.... [I]f your dream of fame did not suddenly come true, you are perhaps a very lucky man. You will do it in some better way, and it will mean more. In the end what really matters is not race, or good breaks, or bad breaks (though these are certainly important) but who you are as a person. And if you have real quality as a person (which you do, let me tell you), it does not matter whether the market is interested. The market... just guesses sales value.... So don't dream dreams that are dictated by the man and his Madison Avenue philosophy. It is when you are relatively indifferent to success that you will be able to make your way freely in the jungle.[68]

Although this stance toward success, offered by a highly successful middle-aged writer, may seem easier said than done to a frustrated young Black man striving to carve out a career, Williams surely valued Merton's affirmation of his personal value.

Managing Interests
Many friends encouraged Williams, but few could supply the savvy advice needed to publish and perform classical music, which left him to find his own way. Merton sometimes lent such counsel. In mid-1966, Williams decided to print the poems in a pamphlet rather than wait to sing them. Betraying an inflated sense of their economic value, he considered printing a million copies to sell for $2.00 apiece. At Williams's request, Merton supplied his photo for the pamphlet, but advised that he downscale sales expectations —a million copies would never sell at that price. To safeguard Merton's publishing contracts, he asked Williams not to bind them as a book.

When Williams forwarded the pamphlet four weeks later, Merton's eyebrows no doubt rose. Williams's photo, not his, graced its second page, and the eight-page, fifty-cent booklet was titled, "'Reflections on Love': Eight Sacred Poems by Thomas Merton, The Little Monk of Our Lady of Gethsemani Abbey, Trappist, Ky." It stated they were "written for, and are dedicated

---

68. Merton to Williams, July 16, 1968, *HGL* 605–606; TMC/BU.

to Robert Lawrence Williams, 'Little Singer Of The Destitute'" and would soon be "set to music" and available on an "LPD, sung by America's newest young tenor, Robert Lawrence Williams."[69]

Merton seemed at peace with the pamphlet but reacted with alarm at Williams's leaflet to promote an upcoming concert, which took considerable liberties with Merton's gift. It indicated Merton's "sacred writings," valued at $30,000, had been "awarded" to Williams and would be sold for that amount as requested by the "Little Trappist Monk" in support of Catholic African and Negro missions.[70] Merton feared this leaflet implicated him in fundraising beyond donating the lyrics and felt vulnerable from having empowered Williams to proceed on his own. He anticipated conflict with his publisher and perhaps violation of canon law, which prohibited unapproved fundraising. Merton alerted his agent and abbot and asked Williams to not attribute words to him without checking. Williams apologized, asked forgiveness, and assured him that he would publish no more commentary on Merton or the poems.

Merton's most frequent technical counsel pertained to literary rights. In donating the poems he had relinquished those rights, though without seeking legal counsel or consulting his agent, publisher, or abbot. As control of the poems slipped from his grasp, Williams announced multiple times that he was either returning rights to Merton or transferring them to Peloquin. Merton consistently declined to accept their return and urged Williams to formalize his literary rights with legal aid. When accusations of theft surfaced, Merton pushed that they be abandoned: "It would be ultimate foolishness if they came out with melodies of [Peloquin], and were sung by pious white Catholics."[71] As their letters ended in mid-1968, Merton enlisted his Legacy Trust lawyer to help Williams secure financial benefit from the poems.

Profound but Imperfect Reflections on Race

In response to the singer's many laments over racial obstacles, Merton's letters affirmed his observations, encouraged his perseverance, and captured many insights on race. Merton sometimes owned his complicity in U.S. racism: "Every day I am ashamed of being a white man, and I suppose that is only just, since the white people have contrived, for generations to make Negroes ashamed of their gift from God, their own skin."[72] King's Nobel Peace

---

69. Quoted from pamphlet accompanying Williams to Merton, August 9, 1966, TMC/BU.

70. Naomi Burton Stone Papers, St. Bonaventure University. Special thanks to Fr. Daniel P. Horan, OSM, for sharing this leaflet.

71. Merton to Williams, May 1, 1967, *HGL* 601.

72. Merton to Williams, May 27, 1965, *HGL* 594–95.

Prize had shown how "much more depends on the courage and resourceful-
ness of the Negro than on the initiative of the white people, unfortunately.
How sad it is to have to continue to admit this."[73]

But in seeking to cultivate solidarity and camaraderie, he sometimes implied "they" rather "we" carried that burden: "Christ in the world today is not
white, nor black, either," but is "present and suffering in the black people and
colored people of the earth. The white world is purely and simply under judgment. And they don't know it."[74] In this aspect, his critique could sound detached from his own whiteness, even as it captures perceptive nuances on it:

> The big problem you run into in dealing with white people is that...
> no doubt they are sympathetic, but they aren't black, and because
> they aren't, they don't know what it feels like and they are not able to
> enter into the experience except abstractly. Hence they may have
> good intentions, but these will lead nowhere or will easily peter out.[75]

Then in response to an issue of *Ebony* magazine Williams had forwarded, Merton reflected:

> The first thing that occurs to me on seeing this magazine is that a re-
> ally integrated American culture would be much more lively and in-
> teresting than the present "lily-white" variety... at least as it is re-
> flected in the mass media. I wish the American white people were
> capable of realizing how much the Negro can and does contribute to
> making American culture an authentic reality in its own right. Fail-
> ure to realize this is not only an added injustice, but it deprives
> America of advantages it would otherwise enjoy.[76]

Merton also noted economic aspects of race. Whites proved "more cal-
culating" in their search of a "good deal, a return on [their] investment," and
showed a "refusal to be human with one's fellow man, and the insistence on
treating him as an object to be used for profit and pleasure, covering this up
with superficial friendliness." This was tragic, not simply due to whiteness,
but because "all rich people, irrespective of color, tend to get that way."[77]

---

73. Merton to Williams, November 21, 1964, *HGL* 592.
74. Merton to Williams, September 5, 1967, *HGL* 602.
75. Merton to Williams, August 16, 1964, *HGL* 590.
76. Merton to Williams, November 21, 1964, *HGL* 592.
77. Merton to Williams, January 29, 1965, *HGL* 593.

Though usually patient, Merton reacted at least once. When Williams denounced invoking "God's will" for the poems' fate, Merton let slip: "I agree, it is awfully easy to make vague statements about God's will. They might mean anything or nothing.... [But] if it gives you personal satisfaction to kick me in the teeth about all this, then go ahead, it's been done before."[78] Here Williams pushed back at Merton's taking offense, implicitly reminding him that Merton was after all part of that same white society: "I merely cried out to you for help and in so doing repeated in my letters what you have so often written me about our society in yours. Why is it that all of a sudden I am kicking you in the teeth[?]"[79]

As Williams's loss of the songs became clear and his tone grew more radicalized after relocating to Harlem, Merton's May 1968 attempt to empathize sounds a bit forced, even as he urged Black self-liberation:

> Few of us really realize what effect the brainwashing of the black people by the white has had in this country. Now at last it is surfacing, and the black people are fighting for their *identity* first of all. I can only encourage everyone to resist the kind of mental domination exercised subtly by our affluent society: it means freedom for us as well as for you. Few white people know this.... Whitey isn't in a position to know how mixed up he is. But it is for you to get yourselves un-mixed-up, fighting the white man's values within your own soul. The only reason why I can claim partly to understand is that I have to fight the same battle in myself, and know how sickening and discouraging it can be.[80]

Compounding the ambiguity of his claims to understand Black experience, Merton implied that his monastic life—with its abbatial and Trappist restrictions, demands for obedience, and censorship—approximated the alienation of Williams's Blackness. After Williams vented over plans for a white opera singer to sing the Freedom Songs, Merton wrote to him:

> I would certainly feel the same way if I were in your position. I know how it is to be in the dark about what is going on and then suddenly discover that all one's plans have collapsed through the intervention of others. The monastic life is full of that kind of thing,

---

78. Merton to Williams, March 27, 1968, *HGL* 602–603.

79. Williams to Merton, March 30, 1968, TMC/BU.

80. Merton to Williams, May 5, 1968, *HGL* 604–605; TMC/BU.

unfortunately.... It is a miserable feeling, and it is far worse when one's whole life is condemned to that kind of frustration.[81]

Even when confirming that whites cannot fully grasp Black experience, his confidence in personally transcending that weakness comes through:

> You are of course right to say that the failure of your plans, which were so beautiful and idealistic at the start, is partly because you are black. You are right also in saying that no white man can really understand all that a black man has to go through in a racist society. I don't deny that. On the other hand, you must not think that white people have it all the way they like just because they are white. I happen to be able to understand something of the rejection and frustration of black people because I am first of all an orphan and second a Trappist.[82]

Merton elaborated further on his own personal and monastic parallels with Blackness, but he would better have simply ended this with, "I don't deny that." Here and elsewhere his instinct to avoid one-sided absolutes and stress our shared humanity perhaps too readily equates experience across racial lines. Granted, his monastic restrictions and frustrations were instructive and surely facilitated his capacity to sympathize with those who lacked autonomy and access to power. But that was after all his choice, one that carried its own credibility and recognition. It remains distantly removed from the intrinsic barriers that accompany birth into an existential status of racial marginalization.

Risking Cross-Racial Collaboration

The story of Robert Lawrence Williams and his dreams of collaborating with Thomas Merton to provide a Catholic voice for civil rights fascinates on many levels. His pilgrimage from a Louisville orphan to a classical singer on stages in Boston, Chicago, New York, and Europe of itself deserves attention, and hopefully more of it will surface. His story further illuminates Merton's calling to listen and encourage the hard work of dismantling racial barriers. But this correspondence especially highlights vulnerabilities that arise with collaboration in that work.

---

81. Merton to Williams, January 15, 1966, *HGL* 597; TMC/BU.
82. Merton to Williams, July 16, 1968, *HGL* 605.

African Americans have always lived with vulnerability, especially within a culture driven more by pragmatic self-interest than benign goodwill. Williams's unique origins and circumstances—coupled with his sensitivity, naiveté, and faith in divine guidance—surely deepened his vulnerability. As he tried to "gift back" his good fortune, he sought support from others who intended well but remained vested in their own careers and interests and had limited ability to accompany him. Williams also miscalculated how far Merton and his poems might lift him over practical obstacles that he seemed poorly equipped to surmount, obstacles a cloistered hermit monk was likewise neither prepared nor positioned to fully navigate on his behalf.

Merton also encountered vulnerabilities in their project, though chosen, not innate. The trust nurtured by even the best-intended collaborators across America's racial divide remains ever fragile. Verbal assurances alone cannot repair generations of trauma or dissolve encoded habits of whiteness. It took nine months, eight letters, and reading *Seeds of Destruction* before Williams could confidently say he considered Merton "of the same heart," conceding that "*before I wasn't sure.*" But even that certainty was too weak to prevent him from later assuming that Merton had abandoned him as his own control over the Freedom Songs withered.

For Merton, Williams's accusation of broken trust followed on the heels of peace activist blowback from Merton's reaction to Roger LaPorte's self-immolation. Both encounters merged to heighten his sense of vulnerability, as noted in his journal:

> I seem to be living in a shower of boomerangs which I thoughtlessly threw out into space one, two, three years ago not knowing what they were. All of them have something to do with my writing about "the world" and my desire for witness and "engagement." Purpose of the boomerangs—to convince me of the large part of illusion and myth there was in all this. For example now—the Eight Freedom Songs. Bad poems, written at the request of a young Negro singer, for a fittingly idealistic project which was more or less improvised and without order.... Now Robert Williams is (rightly) disgusted at what has happened to his songs (which no longer have much to do with Negroes!) and blames me for betrayal, for cynically treating the sorrows of the Negro as something to exploit, etc.[83]

---

83. December 18, 1965, *DWL* 325.

These letters also suggest another, more subtle vulnerability that comes with differing views on modern affluence and power as seen from opposite sides of our racial divide. This divide's dominant white side sets the conditions for economic success and social acceptability on its own terms. The divide's underside sees those terms of racially skewed access and acceptance as our society's fundamental flaw, and equalizing that access as our fundamental social mission. But for Merton, American criteria for power and economic success *of themselves* manifest an inherently flawed, unsustainable illusion, something more to be deconstructed and transformed than equally accessed. This dissonance arose when Williams encouraged Merton to write songs of "patriotic dedication" and pride of Black participation in a shared "American Heritage," as Merton's former fellow Trappist Tommy Glover would also encourage. Merton wisely declined to challenge that aspiration and deflected it as something a foreign-born person could not "poetically" express. But these dissonant critiques beg questions of how Merton's later encouragement to spurn accepted social criteria for "success" resonates with peoples of color deterred from it by racial and ethnic barriers.[84] His letters leave unanswered how to broach these divergent priorities without adding to the frustration of those excluded.

Given such vulnerabilities, Williams's occasional suspicion that Merton enabled the forces of whiteness should not surprise. Merton mostly fielded those outbursts with admirable sensitivity. But Williams was not wrong to turn Merton's critique of "other" whites back upon him. Sympathetic intentions, desires, and actions cannot erase culpability or inoculate against all benefits of whiteness. As Merton wrote, "The tragedy is when people have warm and generous hearts, and reach out impulsively to what ought normally to be a warm human response, and then meet with incomprehension"[85]—a dynamic experienced on both sides of the racial divide. But the interactions of Thomas Merton and Robert Williams still offer a model worth emulating, despite—or perhaps even because of—their vulnerabilities. They model the willingness to risk and remain in sometimes strained relationships to sustain, however imperfectly, the hope of social transformation.

---

84. Reparations to remedy past racial oppression did not receive sustained attention during most of the sixties, though the idea surfaced late in the decade.

85. Merton to Williams, January 29, 1965, *HGL* 593.

This letter responds to Robert Williams's bitter announcement that he was leaving the Catholic Church. Williams asserted that white Catholics had let him down, and Blacks generally, but closed affirming love for Merton and his "beautiful Kentucky." Merton's gracious reply demonstrates willingness to relinquish control over Williams's choices and embrace his own vulnerabilities. An abridged version of this letter appears in The Hidden Ground of Love, *pages 600–601.*

May 1, 1967

Dear Robert:

I do not want to delay any longer in answering your deeply moving letter. First of all, I realize to some extent how much I am involved in the same problem you are. The behavior of so many white Catholics has effectively silenced me and deprived me of any possibility of giving you advice about the Church. All I can honestly say is that the decision[86] is yours, and that the Church has to some extent forfeited the right to demand loyalty of her black children since she has not lived up to her role of mother in their regard. I speak now of the Church as institution. Invisibly, the union of believers who really obey God is another matter. The one thing that is essential is obedience to God in all sincerity, even when it may cut across the apparent obligation to obey men. At times there are differences. On the other hand, while the white man has behaved in all truth like a devil, he is not the only one who has demons. They are everywhere, so be on your guard. The demon of power and hate corrupts everyone. The answer is true faith in God and a really obedient heart that hears and follows His voice, careful not to be deceived. Let us pray for each other that we may always follow that voice: we will remain in a secret, underground way, united.

Robert, I have no illusions about the future. Many chickens are coming home to roost in the white man's parlor.[87] Some of them are going to be pretty large chickens, and some of them are going to have the manners of vultures. Too bad. The white man thinks himself sincere and honest, but he will gradually begin to find out what a con man he has been. It is a pity that you have run into such things: people who think themselves disinterested and idealistic can be in reality the crassest kind of operators, and never realize it. That is the pity of so many Catholics: in the name of God

---

86. This refers to Williams's decision to leave the Catholic Church.

87. Though a common cliché, Merton may be alluding to Malcolm X's comment that President Kennedy's assassination reflected "chickens coming home to roost," which led to his silencing within the Nation of Islam. Merton began reading *The Autobiography of Malcolm X* three days before writing this letter (*LL* 226).

and the Church they are ruthlessly ambitious, aggressive, arrogant, self-seeking characters. They cannot see it. But these traits are universal, unfortunately, and if we imagine that they belong only to this or that group, then we never get out of confusion. However, I admit that for the time being the white man is the one who is getting all the prizes in the contest.

My own part is to accept things as God gives them to me, and to enter into the confusion without too many illusions and too many hopes of making sense out of it all. I will try to diminish the evil and the hatred where I can, and I will try to bring light into the confusion when I am capable of doing so. It is true that being here I cannot do much. But I think if I were out there I would be able to do even less, because I would inevitably get caught in the political and institutional net.

The only thing I regret is that you gave away the songs: but I hope he won't use them. It would be ultimate foolishness if they came out with melodies of his, and were sung by pious white Catholics. That is indeed a rueful ending. But I preserve the ability to laugh even at that too—with you. I don't care about any supposed achievement of my own. I know too well that it is all wind. So good luck, man. Pray for me once in a while, if you remember. And God bless you wherever you go and whatever you do.

All my friendship,

8

WHITENESS

THE MERTON-HARDING LETTERS

*The idea of a history that is lily white is just monstrous. And I am
with you in wanting to see it all through the eyes of the black and
the red. What myths we have to contend with! The chief of them is
of course that this is a peaceful place to live in—for anyone.*
— Thomas Merton to Vincent Harding
January 16, 1968[1]

The final set of letters in Part 2 of this book consists of a brief yet significant
exchange. In contrast to the previous three correspondents, Vincent Harding
was Protestant and an academic. He provided leadership in the era's civil
rights movement as an associate of Martin Luther King Jr.; as a historian, he
played an important role in establishing the academic discipline of Black
studies. By the time Harding and Merton interacted, Harding's pilgrimage
had led him to rethink his personal sense of Blackness and Black experience
generally. He questioned his relationship with the Mennonite denomination
that had nurtured his embrace of nonviolence, yet—as the Catholic Church
had for August Thompson and Robert Williams—failed to fully grasp the
challenges he faced as a Black person in a white world. Harding remained
committed to nonviolence, but he also grappled with the call of Black Power
for distance from—rather than simply access to—white social and economic
power. His academic, historical perspectives on colonialism and the legacy
of whiteness it constructed carried with it cultural insight that few could
match and dovetailed with Merton's concurrent immersion in anthropological readings and reflection (chapter 9). On all counts, Vincent Harding offered Merton a unique window into racial dynamics. And in Thomas Merton,

---

1. *WF* 243.

Harding encountered one of the era's few whites who seemed to comprehend those dynamics with an awareness of how pervasively and stubbornly the legacy of white dominance remained entrenched within U.S. culture.

Vincent Gordon Harding (1931–2014)[2]

Vincent Harding was raised in Harlem as the only child of a single mother of Barbadian descent. Together they attended a small, close-knit congregation, a Seventh-day Adventist off-shoot that embraced Marcus Garvey's pan-African nationalist movement. This church became Harding's extended family and offered him early leadership opportunities among its youth. Following high school, he obtained a bachelor's degree in history and a master's in journalism, and near the close of the Korean War, he was drafted into the army. His Church of the Nazarene girlfriend urged him to look beyond his Adventist focus on the Old Testament and more closely examine New Testament teachings. In taking up her challenge, Harding found that the Gospels he studied clashed with his weapons training objectives and raised doubts about his aspirations for a military career.

Pastor, Historian, Movement Leader

When his term of service ended, Harding decided to leave the army and set sights on a history PhD. He attended the University of Chicago rather than one of his Ivy League options, mostly because his congregation asked him to serve as part-time minister for a fledgling mission outpost in the Chicago area. By happenstance, Harding crossed paths in 1958 with a Mennonite fellow graduate student who introduced him to his congregation near campus, one that sought a racially integrated fellowship. The denomination's New Testament focus on the teachings of Jesus appealed to Harding, and that same year he joined the bi-racial pastoral team of Lawndale Mennonite Church. This transition led to his decade-long Mennonite affiliation, which fostered theological and relational grounding for his emergence as a civil rights figure.

Later in 1958, Harding and four other congregational leaders—a team of three whites and two Blacks—embarked on a car trip through the South to personally witness the realities of Jim Crow segregation. When traveling in Alabama, they spontaneously telephoned Martin Luther King Jr.'s home in

---

2. Unless otherwise noted, biographical information is from *The Movement Makes Us Human: An Interview with Dr. Vincent Harding on Mennonites, Vietnam, and MLK*, ed. Joanna Shenk (Eugene, OR: Wipf and Stock, 2018).

Vincent and Rosemarie Freeney Harding, early 1960s (Courtesy of Rachel Harding)

Montgomery to request a visit. King welcomed them from his bed, where he lay recovering from a knife wound by a would-be assassin. In conversation, he challenged Harding and his Black companion to return south and invest their nonviolent theology in the civil rights movement.

In the fall of 1961, Harding and his new wife, Rosemarie Freeney, moved to Atlanta to found and direct Mennonite House under the auspices of the Mennonite Central Committee. The house provided space for young whites to live and work in a segregated southern community—the region's first integrated service unit of its kind. Locally, the facility made an especially deep impact as one that featured whites working under Black direction.[3] As it happened, the only available site in the chosen neighborhood large enough to house the project stood around the corner from Martin and Coretta Scott King, then living in Atlanta. The families became friends, and the Hardings spent considerable time with King, both informally and in movement venues; they worked with civil rights groups such as the Southern Christian Leadership Conference (SCLC), the Student Non-violent Coordinating Committee, and the Congress of Racial Equality. They also became friends with John and June Yungblut, who had founded nearby Quaker House in 1960[4] and were friends of the Kings and later of Merton.

---

3. *Remnants: A Memoir of Spirit, Activism, and Mothering*, by Rosemarie Freeney Harding with Rachel Elizabeth Harding (Durham, NC: Duke University Press, 2015), xiii, 127.

4. John Yungblut, "Triple Revolution in Atlanta," *Friends Journal* 10, no. 13 (July 1, 1964): 293–94.

Engaging Blackness

In 1964 the Hardings returned to Chicago for Vincent to complete his PhD dissertation. Once this was accomplished, they moved back to Atlanta in 1965, and Vincent joined the Spelman College history department as professor and chair. Harding remembers the following years of 1966–1970 as a period when:

> All over the black community lots of people were exploring and discovering their own deepest cultural rootages. And that was the case for me. And that whole period of Black Power, Black Consciousness, Black Culture, was a period of deepening introspection and discovery. I remember . . . a kind of hesitation that I had about moving too deeply into the world of blackness, and wondering how that would affect my life and the world of Christian faith. . . . It was a time when a lot of my Mennonite friends weren't quite sure how to read where I was and where I was going. . . . There was a period in this time of blackness when I felt that where I needed to stand was in the heart of the black community—partly because I had been given the gift of learning and knowing and receiving many things that many people in the black community had not been able to experience.[5]

His connections with Mennonite structures would fade as his quest to better grasp his Black identity intensified, and the years 1967 and 1968 proved especially consequential in that pilgrimage. Early in 1967, King asked Harding to draft a speech that would announce King's opposition to the Vietnam War, which he delivered April 4, 1967, at New York's Riverside Church. To construct the speech, Harding relied on reports by Mennonite Central Committee service workers in Vietnam who witnessed and experienced the war's impact on the country's peasantry. During the last week of July, Harding himself delivered two forceful messages to the Mennonite World Conference assembled in Amsterdam, The Netherlands. He called upon this international body to focus not just on U.S. happenings, but on anti-colonial revolutions rising around the globe. Noting those upheavals, he challenged the denomination not to remain "huddled behind the barricades of the status quo, praying the storm will soon be over so that life can continue undisturbed." He urged them to instead put their centuries-old peace theology into practice, "associate ourselves with Jesus of the beggars," and "find

---

5. Harding, *The Movement Makes Us Human*, 48–49.

our way among" those beggars who are "rising and marching and demanding a right to live as men."[6]

Martin Luther King's assassination followed just months later on April 4, 1968, one year to the day after he delivered the Riverside Vietnam speech that Harding had developed. In the wake of King's death, Coretta King asked Harding to establish and direct the King Center for Nonviolent Social Change, and later in 1968, Harding also became founding director of the Institute of the Black World, a think tank devoted to connecting diverse disciplines with contemporary Black issues. Over the years that followed, Harding became a respected elder in and interpreter of the "Southern Freedom Movement," or the "black-led movement for the deepening and broadening of democracy in the United States," terms Harding preferred over the "civil rights movement."[7] Throughout his life Harding mentored many—white and Black—in nonviolent resistance to forces of social domination. His academic career took him from Spelman College to Temple University, Swarthmore College, and finally Iliff School of Theology. Harding also published books on Black history and Martin Luther King Jr., and he served as a senior consultant for the PBS documentary *Eyes on the Prize*. In 1997 he and Rosemarie founded the Veterans of Hope Project designed to "gather and share wisdom from elder activists about the role of spirituality and creativity in their work."[8] He also delivered the First Annual Thomas Merton Black History Month Lecture at Bellarmine University in 2007.

Thomas Merton's Relationship with Vincent Harding

Most of what we know about this brief relationship resides in the two letters they exchanged: the first from Harding to Merton, handwritten in the early morning of New Year's Day 1968, and Merton's response, dated January 16 of that year. Harding's letter refers to their having first met in person at Merton's hermitage during his "all too brief encounter with you and the monastery."[9] Harding suggested returning with Rosemarie, who "long envied me even for my few hectic hours of this past summer," an encounter with Merton that had taken place in early July 1967, before he departed to address the Mennonite World Conference in Amsterdam. Merton mentioned in a July 10

---

6. Harding, "The Beggars Are Marching... Where Are the Saints?" in *The Movement Makes Us Human*, Appendix B, 95, 94.

7. Shenk, "Introduction," *The Movement Makes Us Human*, xvii.

8. "About Veterans of Hope," http://www.veteransofhope.org/about-us/.

9. Harding to Merton, January 1, 1968, TMC/BU.

letter to Jim Forest that "Vincent Harding the Negro Mennonite" had been there "a few days ago" and described him to Forest as a "fine guy."[10] Coincidently, about the same time that Harding visited Gethsemani, Jim Douglass forwarded to Merton "a fine article" by Harding. Douglass described him as "a Negro Mennonite who, judging from this piece, is really with it!" and added, "I had never heard of Harding...[though] you may know him well."[11]

How Harding and Merton first made contact remains unknown. During his 2007 lecture at Bellarmine University he mentioned their meeting as a "long, long story," but failed to elaborate.[12] They may have connected through the Yungbluts, by then their mutual friends,[13] though the couple's 1967 letters to Merton do not mention Harding. But in early 1968 Harding did converse with the Yungbluts about a different visit to Gethsemani, one never realized— a retreat at the Abbey to include himself, King, and others. It would have focused on preparation for the Poor People's Campaign march on Washington that King and the SCLC were planning for the spring. Merton was receptive and suggested dates but cautioned that in order to secure his abbot's support it must be informal, unpublicized, and not explicitly tied to the politicized march. King meanwhile turned his attention toward the Memphis sanitation workers' strike and was assassinated before the retreat could be scheduled.

Harding's Letter to Merton

Harding's New Year's Day letter recalls the powerful impact of his visit with Merton the previous summer and opens with: "My dear Brother." It hints at the personal questions and challenges he confronted during that time of trying to reconcile his place as a Black person in a world dominated by whites. Harding was prompted to write it upon reading Merton's essay on Native Americans, "The Shoshoneans," published in the *Catholic Worker* the previous June.[14] It reminded Harding of how "immensely glad"

---

10. Merton to James H. Forest, July 10, 1967, TMC/BU.

11. James W. Douglass to Merton, July 5, 1967, TMC/BU; he did not mention the article title.

12. "Vincent Harding: First Annual Thomas Merton Black History Month Lecture. February 22, 2007." Recording CD-0220, TMC/BU.

13. The Yungbluts also knew Dan and Phil Berrigan and Will Campbell (Committee of Southern Churchmen founder), friends of both Merton and Harding. See also William Apel's treatment of the Merton-Yungblut correspondence in *Signs of Peace*, 143–60.

14. Review of Edward Dorn and Leroy Lucas, *The Shoshoneans: The People of the Basin-Plateau* (New York: William Morrow, 1966) in *The Catholic Worker* (June 1967): 5–6. Merton wrote the review mid-May 1967.

he felt when they visited to learn Merton was reading Vittorio Lanternari's *Religions of the Oppressed: A Study of Modern Messianic Cults*,[15] and it brought to mind his own essay, "The Afro-American Past," which Harding enclosed.

Harding surely referred to his "Uses of the Afro-American Past," crafted in 1967.[16] He described it as a "progress report on the specific bag of a scholar of the black experience in America." Its incisive reflections on that experience fit as presciently within today's milieu as they did in that of the sixties, and it displays a critical understanding of the sway white colonialism still holds over Western culture. Harding demanded incorporation of Black history into the U.S. historical narrative as a corrective and foundation for America's future. Like Merton, he denounced American myths and illusions that hinder clear-eyed self-assessment and impair their nation's moral health. Americans thought their nation "incapable of failure, powerful and pure enough to succeed at anything it chose," with a history that moved "on a straight line upward from perfection to perfection, from goodness to betterness, from being better than other nations to being the best and most complete nation God had ever stood over." Its corollary myth: "American failure at home or overseas had to be explained by subversion or conspiracies, or—at worst—a mistake in well-intentioned American judgment." Squarely facing its Black history would help lift the veil of illusion and myth that blinded Americans to the destruction they wreaked in Vietnam and cloaked the reasons other nations opposed them.

In words that resonate with Merton's own concurrent anthropological studies (chapter 9), Harding noted how Black history could also illuminate American complicity in Western colonialism: "The world experience of the last 500 years has meant that the vast majority of the earth's humiliated people have been non-white, and their humiliation has come at the hands of the white, western world." America's history of "unbroken success" and immersion in the "strange joys of advanced corporate capitalism" rendered it one of the era's "least comprehending national states," isolated from much of global reality and subject to its great blind spot: "the realm of understanding the oppressed, the wretched of the earth." Embracing Black history would also illuminate America's domestic dilemmas: "It is only as America faces a Den-

---

15. N.p.: MW Books, 1963.

16. Vincent Harding, "Uses of the Afro-American Past," typescript, Spelman College, 1967, Stuart A. Rose Archives and Rare Book Library, Emory University, Vincent Harding Collection #868, Box 42, Folder 16. Later published in *Negro Digest* 17, no. 4 (February 1968): 4–9, 81–84; *The Religious Situation*, ed. D. R. Cutler (Boston: Beacon Press, 1969), 829–40.

mark Vesey, a Nat Turner, a WEB Dubois, a Paul Robeson and a Malcolm X, that the nation will begin to be ready to understand a Stokely Carmichael, a Rap Brown and the host of black radicals yet to come."[17]

For Harding, Blacks' integration was not absorption into whiteness, but the injection of wisdom and insight from Black experience. He invoked W. E. B. Du Bois's caution from a decade before that "most American Negroes ...do not fully realize that they are being bribed to trade equal status in the United States for slavery of the majority of men." Harding insisted that African Americans must instead "stand in solidarity with the black and anguished people of the earth." They must "be so aware of their black fathers and the wealth of their spiritual and intellectual heritage that they will sharply illuminate the disadvantages in an isolated, beleaguered middle-class white world." They must become "more than black Anglo-Saxons," as "God knows we have enough white ones without adding carbon copies." Though Americans saw themselves as God's "chosen," they had forgotten that being chosen by God demands suffering, or maybe they simply relegated the required suffering to their Black co-citizens. "Perhaps," Harding suggested, "We are chosen together, and we cannot move towards a new beginning until we have faced all the horror and agony of the past with absolute honesty. Perhaps integration is indeed irrelevant until the assessment of a long, unpaid debt has been made and significant payments begun. Perhaps atonement, not integration is the issue at hand." As the Americans "open enough and sensitive enough and scarred enough as a group to lead this nation into true community with the non-white humiliated world," perhaps "only the black branch will be allowed to shape the future of the nation and determine its calling in the world."[18]

Early in his essay Harding named the "rising tide of brutality against blacks and Indians" as poisoning U.S. relations abroad. But after that, he omitted Native Americans from his analysis of its colonial legacy, once naming Black experience as "perhaps the only true epic poem that America has ever known."[19] In his letter to Merton, however, Harding conceded that reading Merton's "The Shoshoneans" had suggested his essay might remain incomplete without "putting the red and black experience together into some coherent outline of a philosophy of American history," despite his scanter knowledge about "the history of my brothers in pain." Merton's article prompted him to consider how "America's two classic minorities" might

---

17. Harding, "Uses of the Afro-American Past."

18. Harding, "Uses of the Afro-American Past."

19. Harding, "Uses of the Afro-American Past."

relate, and he now questioned whether there could be "any epic black poem without its red part."[20]

Harding's resonance with "The Shoshoneans," Merton's review of Edward Dorn's book by the same title, does not surprise. Merton linked Black and red experience in several of its passages. He noted, for example, that indigenous dances like the "Ghost Dance" could hold a "deeper meaning" similar to "the innocent sounding songs of Negro slaves." When praising the book's photos of Native American faces, Merton observed how they were

> marked with suffering, irony, courage, sometimes desperation: always with a human beauty which defeats sometimes obvious degradation. Perhaps the explanation for this clear vision is the fact that [photographer Leroy] Lucas is a Negro and knows what he is seeing when he looks at people who have been systematically excluded from life, and who yet manage to remain very much alive, at once present and lost, accusingly separate and outside. Yet very much "there."[21]

Merton spared little in his critique of a white mentality that wantonly degraded others to further its agenda of power:

> The ultimate violence which the American white man, like the European white man, has exerted in all unconscious "good faith" upon the colored races of the earth (and above all on the Negro) has been to impose on them *invented identities*, to place them in positions of subservience and helplessness in which they themselves came to believe only in the identities which had thus been conferred upon them.[22]

In the review's only sentence where Merton used all capital letters as emphasis, he named this mentality as one where "THE INDIAN (LIKE THE NEGRO, THE ASIAN, ETC.) IS PERMITTED TO HAVE A HUMAN IDENTITY IN SO FAR AS HE CONFORMS TO OURSELVES AND TAKES UPON HIMSELF OUR IDENTITY."[23] This focus on identity echoed his encouragement to Robert Williams for self-liberation and resonates with Harding's own call for African Americans to draw on their heritage and become "more than black Anglo Saxons."

---

20. Harding to Merton, January 1, 1968, TMC/BU.

21. Thomas Merton, "The Shoshoneans," in *Ishi Means Man: Essays on Native Americans* (Greensboro, NC: Unicorn Press, 1976). 11, 7.

22. Merton, "The Shoshoneans," 11.

23. Merton, "The Shoshoneans," 10.

Beyond mentioning admiration for "The Shoshoneans," Harding also offered heartfelt testimony to how Merton had moved him during their personal encounter. His words illuminate the monk's capacity to connect with another's personal struggle:

> I feel myself much in need of you and your spirit. As you have surely guessed, these past two years or so have been times of difficult pilgrimage concerning my blackness and its relationship to the essence of my being and the relationship of whoever I was to those who had not ever known the experience of being black in America. I sensed you knew—or intuited—what I am trying to say, to write, to become—at least as much as it can be known by anyone outside of me. I sensed that you ... were enough at peace with the scandal of your whiteness and all of its implications that you could be at peace with me and my searchings. And I felt you loved the world, and that its ragged, surging madness pained you deeply but did not totally disorient you. At times I feel most disoriented and torn apart. I do not come looking for peace, only for friendship, and whatever it means to be brothers in this strange age. I am at times more fearful than I should be about things like the capacity of this nation to do to black people what it did to the Indians. (Thus the process would be reversed, and our physical destruction would come *after* our spiritual degradation.)

Harding requested that Merton respond to both the letter and his essay, and closed by addressing him as "my brother" and asking that "peace be with you and with all our wild and raging brothers."[24]

Merton's Letter to Harding

Merton typed his response two weeks later, on a day of packed letter-writing that also included one to the Yungbluts about his qualified support for a retreat with King. He also told them of his "very fine letter from Vincent Harding" with hopes to respond "as soon as I can get in the clear to answer a bunch more mail." Merton added, "Our new abbot needs to meet Vincent H. and the community needs to hear him."[25] He apparently managed to work though his "bunch more mail" that same day to squeeze in his response to Harding (reproduced below). Merton opened this letter by noting the greater difficulty

---

24. Harding to Merton, January 1, 1968, TMC/BU.
25. Merton to John and June Yungblut, January 16, 1968, TMC/BU.

responding to "letters as good as the one" Harding had written, rather than just "dash[ing] off an answer to a business letter."[26] The comment offers a glimpse at how Merton approached his correspondence workload and implies that he rationed his energy and attention depending on how much he needed to personally invest in crafting his letters. He resisted "dashing off" letters of personal connection simply to cut into his workload, but approached them with respect and forethought. Harding concurred in his lecture forty years later, suggesting that Merton's prompt, pre-internet turnaround demonstrated he "was serious about his correspondence," and "had to engage himself in it, not put it into a machine, but put himself into the process."[27]

Merton's response affirmed Harding's "fine piece on the Afro-American past" and assured him that he agreed with its premise and his desire to incorporate Native American experience. He noted that his own work engaged similar themes and shared his interest in cargo cults[28] and their apocalyptic meaning. Merton concurred with Harding's essay that "white America is right up a blind alley, and under judgment," which elicited his personal discomfort, since he did not "take happily to wrath." He also affirmed Harding's vulnerable personal disclosures and underscored the importance of Harding's work as a Black historian by lamenting the "monstrous" legacy of history viewed though "lily white" eyes. He seconded Harding's observation that white society mistakenly assumed it might sidestep the consequences of its own history and gain "peace by bypassing the holiness of suffering and sacrifice and of love in which conflict is resolved."[29] His letter personally affirmed Harding and it encouraged his choice to venture ever deeper into his own Black identity.

Merton also strongly encouraged Harding's return visit with his wife, which regrettably never occurred. Rosemarie Freeney Harding was a Southern Freedom Movement force in her own right, sharing in the work of Atlanta's Mennonite House and their movement organizing. As their daughter Rachel recalled, "When my parents were able to work together they were an absolutely amazing pair. Both intellectually sharp and full of imagination,

---

26. Merton to Harding, January 16, 1968, *WF* 242.

27. Harding, "Black History Month Lecture."

28. The term "cargo cult," now out of favor, originated as a pejorative term. Current terms include: "nativist movements, revitalization movements, messianic movements, millenarian movements, crisis cults, Holy spirit movements, culture contact movements," Malgorzata Poks, "Borderlands of Cultures, Borderlands of Discourse: Cargo Cults and Their Reflection in Thomas Merton's Poetry," in *Representing and (De)Constructing Borderlands*, ed. Weronika Laszkiewicz, Gregorz Moroz, and Jacek Partyka (Newcastle upon Tyne, UK: Cambridge Scholars Publishing, 2016), 167–83.

29. Merton to Harding, January 16, 1968, *WF* 242–43.

Mama and Daddy were capable of deeply inspired thinking and, at their best, each generously fed the other's genius."[30] Harding's letter had noted Rosemarie's "envy" of his time with Merton, undoubtedly due to her own strong mystical bent, as attested in her memoir. Rachel also recalled that their home's book collection included, among others, "people like Gerald Heard and Thomas Merton, and of course, Howard Thurman."[31] Without question, Rosemarie Harding and Merton would have enjoyed each other's company and conversation.

Relationship Coda

When given the opportunity late in life to reflect once more on their brief encounter, Harding again shared his deep respect of Merton with his Black History Month audience:

> He was one of those blessed children of God who really tried to believe that God loved the world, all the world, especially the world in pain, the world in limbo, the world separated from its own best self. And he loved his country, not as a patriot, but as a healer.... Living the way that he did, writing the way that he did, condemning America's dependence on military power the way that he did, loving black folks and all suffering folks the way that he did, he was censored by the church that he loved because he loved the world too much! Loving it so much that he could not remain silent in the presence of its self-destructive tendencies. Like [Martin Luther] King he loved his country so much that he could not resist the call to prophesy. [32]

Unmasking Literary "Blackface": Parallel Critiques of William Styron's *Nat Turner*

One more reference in Merton's letter exposes still another intersection with Harding's work. In mentioning his review of William Styron's *The Confessions of Nat Turner*,[33] Merton touched on a controversial subject that both men addressed, though without discussing it together. Styron, a white author, had published the novel in the fall of 1967 as a narration of Nat Turner's role in

---

30. Rachel Elizabeth Harding, *Remnants*, xv.
31. Harding, *Remnants*, xii.
32. Harding, "Black History Month Lecture."
33. New York: Random House, 1967.

the 1831 slave revolt he led, written in Turner's voice. Initial reviews praised the novel, and it was awarded a Pulitzer Prize. But for both Merton and Harding, the novel constituted, as Merton phrased it in both his journal and his letter to Harding, "an affront."

"Who Is Nat Turner?"

Solicited in November 1967 by James Holloway,[34] editor of *Katallagete* magazine, Merton's review, titled "Who Is Nat Turner?"[35] was published in the magazine's spring 1968 issue. "Styron has gone far beyond legitimate bounds in his artistic 'transformation' of historic fact," Merton asserted:

> What we have in this novel is not an authentic portrayal of a black rebel but simply a meditation of a sophisticated white Southerner, projecting upon a Negro character some of his own ambivalences about the culture based on slavery.... But apparently people are reading the book with a misplaced conviction that they are learning some of the deep reasons behind Black Power and ghetto rebellion today. They are merely tuning in on another closed-circuit all-white program.[36]

Merton criticized Styron's playing with historical fact in order to pigeonhole events into fictional white perceptions of both historic slave and modern Black experience. For example, Styron omitted Turner's marriage to a slave and his later separation from her by her sale to another master, and Merton framed Styron's portrayal of Turner's inner dialogue as 1960s "Black Power" rhetoric, which failed to explain how "suddenly he has a Bible and is quoting it."[37]

Styron also portrayed sexual desire toward a white woman as Turner's key motivation, though that circumstance appears nowhere in historical documentation: "Evading the more difficult task of creating the character of a prophet, he substitutes a frustrated masochist." Rather than acknowledge

---

34. Merton to James Holloway, November 28, 1967, TMC/BU.

35. "Who Is Nat Turner," *Katallagete* (Spring 1968): 20–23. See also *The Literary Essays of Thomas Merton* (New York: New Directions, 1981), 152–58. Merton sent the review to June Youngblut to share with King: "I heard Martin L. King went to jail some time back with the Styron book under his arm: he (and you) might be interested in the enclosed"; Merton to June Yungblut (February 1968, *HGL* 640). She indicated she would give King the "Turner article"; June Yungblut to Merton (March 2, 1968, TMC/BU).

36. "Who Is Nat Turner?" *The Literary Essays*, 152–53.

37. "Who Is Nat Turner?" *The Literary Essays*, 156.

Turner's prophetic credibility, Styron "tries to account for his religious impulses in terms of sexual frustration," not a "sense of religious terror in the presence of the 'totally Other.'"

> [That Turner's] religious drive is unreal, arbitrary, imposed from the outside, worn like a costume...is a great shame[, since]...all over the world...there are scores if not hundreds of Nat Turners... discovering themselves to be messengers of the apocalypse, appointed to announce the doom of the white world and the beginning of a new creation....[T]hey are to be taken seriously as manifestations of a "religious" drive that is not without deep significance. And some anthropologists are beginning to see the importance of understanding them in these terms....[Styron's] Turner offers us no such understanding.[38]

"You've Taken My Nat and Gone"

Merton was not alone in his concern over the acclaimed novel. Though James Baldwin, a personal friend of Styron, supported the book, the younger radicalized Black community of the time echoed Merton rather than the Pulitzer committee. That contingent forcefully voiced its objections in the July 1968 publication, *William Styron's Nat Turner: Ten Black Writers Respond*.[39] The debate it launched became a pivotal point in American literary criticism. Though the *New York Times Review of Books* mostly panned the publication, its reviewer included this assessment:

> Except for occasional entertainment, we need deal only with the essays of two young and gifted writers, Mike Thelwell, who teaches English at the University of Massachusetts, and Vincent Harding, who teaches history at Spelman College. Virtually all the serious points made in the book may be found, skillfully presented, in Thelwell's essay, but for some suggestive material on slave religion we must turn to Harding's.[40]

---

38. "Who Is Nat Turner?" *The Literary Essays*, 155–57.

39. *Williams Styron's Nat Turner: Ten Black Writers Respond*, ed. John Henrik Clarke (Boston: Beacon Press, 1968); Introduction dated March 1968.

40. Eugene D. Genovese, "The Nat Turner Case," *New York Review of Books* 12 (September 1968), http://www.nybooks.com/ articles/1968/09/12/the-nat-turner-case/.

Titled "You've Taken My Nat and Gone,"[41] Harding's contribution to the anthology strongly resonates with Merton's *Katallagete* review. Harding described Styron as "without comprehension of either the meaning of the [Turner] drama, or the profound and bitter depths through which America continually moves towards the creation of a thousand Nat Turners more real than his could ever be." Styron's novel was inspired by an 1831 oral history based in turn on a prison interview of Turner prior to his execution. That interview was then published as *The Confessions of Nat Turner*—the same title Styron gave his novel, a choice that implies its allegiance to the historical document. Based on his readings of both, Harding suggested as more appropriate titles for the novel, "The Annihilation of Nat Turner" or "The Emasculation of Nat Turner," since "no other conclusion seems sensible if one takes the basic historical document . . . with the same seriousness claimed by Styron," a document from which Turner "leaps forth as a religious mystic, a single-minded black believer with a powerful sense of messianic vocation."[42]

Like Merton, Harding accused Styron of failing to "perceive Turner's role as a tragic-triumphant hero in the biblical genre." He lauded Styron's choice of Ezekiel as a model prophet, since "Turner surely lived in the world of those divinely obsessed spokesmen, including one Jesus of Nazareth." Ezekiel "was driven to enter personally and without reserve into the very words and judgments he spoke," "to fill his stomach with the terrible oracles of God," to live out his words in his own specific context. But that was "precisely what William Styron fails to do with the world and words of Nat Turner. He has been unable to eat and digest the blackness, the fierce religious conviction, the power of the man." He had "distorted and broken each major truth of Old Prophet Nat" to the "strange accompaniment of [white] critical applause for his 'total integration' into Turner's world."[43]

Harding's historical reading also called out Styron's attribution of Turner's religious training to his white owners, though Turner credited it to his own Black parents and "especially his grandmother." Further, Styron portrayed Turner's baptism as an individual response to guilt over an undocumented, therefore fictitious, sexual encounter with another Black man, whereas the historical record "referred to only one joint baptism" that involved "himself and a white convert." Styron also mentioned that biracial baptism, but (without historical grounding) portrayed the white man as a mentally deficient child-molester. The sexual obsessions toward white women

---

41. Vincent Harding, "You've Taken My Nat and Gone," in *William Styron's Nat Turner*, 23–33.

42. Harding, "You've Taken My Nat," 23–24.

43. Harding, "You've Taken My Nat," 25–26.

of "Styron-Turner" and the novel's other Black males also lack documentary support, and Harding asked, "Is it only sex and insanity which can motivate a black man to such a large-scale attack on white lives?"[44]

"But it is the loss of religious center with which I am most concerned," Harding argued. "There is in Styron's work no black messiah, no true lover of Ezekiel, not even a superior religious exhorter," because

> the "divine fury" of Old Testament experience is almost totally absent. Though Nat Turner is a preacher, only one major attempt at a sermon is made . . . , and it fails to catch any of the peculiar rhythmic and thematic strengths of this black folk art form. Equally striking is the fact that the religious music of Afro-Americans never enters as a major structural element.[45]

The novel "snatched Nat Turner out of the nineteenth century, out of a community of black religious rebels, and placed him totally into our own age of nothingness and fear." Styron portrayed Turner's ultimate salvation and reception by God as hinging on his gallows-inspired repentance of murdering the white woman after whom he lusted.[46] Harding bemoaned the implications of white America's praise for the book, which disclosed its "eager acceptance of this uninspired offering of homosexuality, pseudo-religion, and dreams . . . of black-white grapplings in the dust as an authentic view from under the black skin" and their acceptance that "entrance into black skin is achieved as easily as Styron-Turner's penetration of invisible white flesh."[47]

Resonant Insight

Merton's review and Harding's critique contain significant parallels. They both denounce Styron's lack of religious motivation for Turner's quest and its replacement with "Black" sexual frustration. Both caution how modern white domination cultivated "scores if not hundreds" (Merton) or even "a thousand" (Harding) contemporary Nat Turners. Merton's letter had referred Harding to the upcoming publication of his review without actually sharing it. But

---

44. Harding, "You've Taken My Nat," 26–28.

45. Harding, "You've Taken My Nat," 28–29.

46. Here Styron echoes claims of rape as justification for Jim Crow–era lynchings. See, for example, Henry Louis Gates Jr., *Stony the Road: Reconstruction, White Supremacy, and the Rise of Jim Crow* (New York: Penguin Press, 2019), 141–48.

47. Harding, "You've Taken My Nat," 30–32.

since he described it as "in line" with "The Afro-American Past," that essay perhaps cued Merton to Harding's own sensitivities on the topic. Their discussion of *Religions of the Oppressed* that summer may also suggest conversation that helped dovetail later output, though the book fails to address U.S. slave religion. But despite temptations to speculate on cross-fertilization, no evidence of direct influence exists. They met in July 1967, and given the novel's September 1967 release could not have discussed its content.

Merton had promised his review to *Katallagete* in early January,[48] so Harding's January letter may at least have nudged Merton to embark on it. Merton's journal documents his reflections on the novel beginning with an entry on January 4, about when he would have received Harding's New Year's letter. Merton noted he was "getting down to work on Nat Turner for *Katallagete*—a clever but false book I think,"[49] and he added the next day, "Nat Turner is nothing but Styron's own complex loneliness as a Southern writer. A well-fashioned book, but little or nothing to do with the real Turner—I have no sense that this fastidious and analytical mind is that of a prophet."[50] He last mentioned it on January 10, noting he had just "finished *Nat Turner* and wrote my article." Reflecting on the impression it made, Merton first quoted Dietrich Bonhoeffer: "It is only when one sees the anger and wrath of God hanging like grim realities over the heads of one's enemies that one can know something of what it means to love and forgive them." He continued:

> This is the key to the dishonesty of Styron's treatment of Nat Turner. Styron "enjoys" wrath as an indulgence which is not seen as having anything serious to do with religion whatever. Religion suddenly appears on the last page as a suggested preposterous reconciliation (in purely sentimental terms). To treat a prophet of wrath while having no idea of the meaning of wrath, and reduce that wrath to the same level as masturbation fantasies! The whole thing is an affront to the Negro—though it is well-meant, even "sympathetic." It reduces me finally to desperation! How can white people do anything but cheat and delude the Negro, when that is only part of their own crass self-delusion and bad faith![51]

---

48. Merton to James Holloway, November 28, 1967, TMC/BU.
49. January 4, 1968, *OSM* 33.
50. January 5, 1968, *OSM* 34.
51. January 10, 1968, *OSM* 37.

His journal comments therefore tend to confirm that Merton mostly built his opinion of Styron's novel on his own reading of it, sandwiched between reading and responding to Harding's letter. And although we don't know when Harding drafted his critique, *Katallagete* published Merton's review in its spring issue and the anthology's introduction was dated March 1968, so it seems unlikely that Harding read Merton's assessment prior to writing his own. Regardless of any speculated mutual influence, both commentaries reinforce, and in fact illustrate, Merton's pointed observation in "The Shoshoneans" that the "American white man, like the European white man, has [imposed] upon the colored races of the earth . . . invented identities."

The Scandal of Whiteness

Reading the Merton-Harding letters alongside "Uses of the Afro-American Past" and their reviews of Styron's *Nat Turner* reinforces a sense of how deeply Merton grasped the nuances of what Blacks experienced in the United States. It illuminates his perceptiveness of the imprint left by a Western colonial legacy, his sensitivity toward the incomprehension with which whiteness gazes upon Blackness in U.S. society, and his awareness of the violence it impresses onto U.S. Black experience. This reading also suggests how crucial it is for whites to squarely face U.S. Black history, to come to terms with ways white identity has fed off its own denial as it constructed Black identities that privilege white experience. Doing so can remind us all how that denial of history and of existential Black reality remains a barrier to unveiling white illusions that impede attaining a just and fair society—to unmasking the scandal of whiteness.

On an interpersonal level, this exchange of letters again reveals Merton's skill at compassionately connecting with another person through face-to-face interaction and in correspondence, this time with a young Black Protestant scholar who grappled with his racial identity. In this regard, Harding's words from his 2007 lecture offer a fitting close:

> Here is what I valued about Tom. . . . [He was] willing to look at whiteness in America and look hard at it. [He was] willing to stop talking about, "Oh, I am colorblind." Because I say to anybody who says that she is colorblind, "Stop now! I want you to see me!" . . . And that was Tom. Refusing to be blind. Refusing not to see.
>
> What I found in Thomas Merton . . . was a man called "white" who had determined not to let his whiteness become a shield against the pain of the world. Nor to let his whiteness become an instrument

of overcoming other people, but instead to let his whiteness become a bridge over which people could walk in either direction.[52]

The only known letter from Thomas Merton to Vincent Harding was first published in Witness to Freedom: Letters in Times of Crisis, *pages 242–43.*

Jan. 16, 1968

Dear Vincent:

Letters as good as the one you wrote New Year's night are hard to reply to: much easier to just dash off an answer to a business letter. Meanwhile, after John and June [Yungblut] left, we have been preparing for and then having an abbatial election. That's over and things are getting back to normal.

Also one thing I have done in the meantime is a review of Styron's Nat Turner, which strikes me as an affront. The review says why: I don't have a copy to spare at the moment but it is supposed to come out in *Katallagete*, so you will see it. Anyway, that's in line with your fine piece on the Afro-American past. Of course I agree entirely with you about that and about the Indians. More and more my work seems to be tending in that same sort of direction, though the new Abbot wants me to concentrate on mystical theology, etc. (He isn't at all aware what these things mean.) I'll dig around and see if I have any other Indian pieces. Eventually they should add up to a book.[53] And also I am very involved in the Cargo Cults and their apocalyptic meaning. It certainly seems to me that white America is right up a blind alley, and under judgment. It is not a situation in which I for one can be comfortable. I don't take happily to wrath.

John [Yungblut]—yes, the complete liberal—has probably spoken to you of his idea about a retreat here, Martin King, etc., before a big march this spring. I have been thinking about that and I have another idea. Because our new Abbot is young and doesn't understand what's going on or the import of it, I think it would be too ambiguous to have a retreat more or less overtly hooked up with some public act of that size. He wouldn't be able to cope with the consequences. I think it would be much better to have simply a private and quiet retreat in which the Abbot himself could participate and learn what

---

52. Harding, "Black History Month Lecture."

53. Eventually published as *Ishi Means Man: Essays on Native Americans*.

it is more or less all about by contact with Martin Luther King and you and so on. This would be at some other time and not publicized. Also I think it would be better that way from the retreat point of view itself, to have it unhooked from any other event: and we could just be people in our contemporary predicament.

But anyhow that doesn't have to affect the possibility of a visit of you and Rosemarie. When? Any time, though Lent is bad for me, I want to keep it visit-less if possible. Later in the spring? Let's certainly plan something when convenient for you. I'd like very much to have you here for a couple of days.

In any case, to go back to your talk on the Afro-American past: the idea of a history that is lily white is just monstrous. And I am with you in wanting to see it all through the eyes of the black and the red. What myths we have to contend with! The chief of them is of course that this is a peaceful place to live in—for anyone. Newman's saying, "holiness rather than peace,"[54] takes on a new meaning in this torn-up place where everyone's idea is to obtain peace by bypassing the holiness of suffering and sacrifice and of love in which conflict is resolved (because conflict is first realistically accepted).

Peace in [remainder illegible]

---

54. John Henry Newman (1801–1890), an English Anglican philosopher of religion who converted to Catholicism and became a ardinal and leader in Catholic higher education. "Holiness rather than peace" was a personal motto that reflected his commitment to pursuing truth at the cost of harmony when needed.

Part III

RE-VISIONING A FRAGMENTED WORLD

As the first two parts of this book demonstrate, Thomas Merton personally invested in the two broadest social movements of his day: opposition to war (whether cold/nuclear or hot/Vietnam) and support of civil rights for African Americans. But as those two parts also capture, Merton felt that healing the dysfunctions they addressed demands more than superficial resistance to their symptoms. Meaningful transformation also requires confronting cultural dynamics that fuel them and veil them in illusions to obscure their scrutiny. As he sought clarity of vision into those dynamics, he set his sights on at least three key realms of modern human experience: the decreasing capacity of language to effectively communicate; misguided hope in modern industrial technology; and an anthropology, a human self-perception, that alienates us from the natural world on which we depend. He felt that real solutions to war and racism require grappling with these realms.

Merton did not explore these questions in sustained exchanges with specific correspondents over time as he did regarding the two movements just addressed. He approached letter writing differently depending on his objective. In their most intimate and profound form, Merton's letters sought to relate to and connect with their recipient in deeply personal and meaningful ways. The letters explored in chapters 1 though 8 reflect this cultivation of personal relationships and the themes they featured. In their most superficial form, Merton's letters might simply "dash off an answer to a business letter," as he noted to Vincent Harding, or acknowledge/cover transmission of some article or poem. Between these two levels, Merton also wrote letters that mainly explored ideas of mutual interest without seeking deeper intimacy. Although he still pursued genuine connection and resonance in such letters, a shared interest in ideas more than a personal relationship anchored them.

This final section of the book relies more on this last form of Merton's letter writing, coupled with fragments from assorted correspondence and published works. It explores those three realms of modern human experience as vital to Merton's re-visioning a transformed society, a vision that anchored all letters addressed in this book. Chapter 9 briefly explores these three themes, relying mostly on published writings supported by selected letter excerpts. Chapter 10 closes the book with three sets of letters that express Merton's call for a refocused vision of society that draws upon a shared, holistic consciousness in harmony with our planet's rhythms of life.

CONFRONTING MODERN CULTURAL DYNAMICS

The situation of man today . . . is a far-reaching, uncontrolled, and largely unconscious revolution pervading every sphere of his existence and often developing new critical tendencies before anyone realizes what is happening.

—Thomas Merton to Lord Northbourne
August 30, 1966[1]

Undergirding Thomas Merton's signs of hope for social transformation lay his evolving concern with at least three pivotal and intersecting dynamics of modernity. Merton's quest for personal insight relied upon contemplation, a practice he encouraged for all persons of faith, not just monks and hermits. But in his pursuit of healthy human experience, engagement with three touchstones of modern life—communication, technology, and the place of humans in the natural world—stand out.

Language and Communication[2]

Merton saw effective communication across difference as foundational for any hope of advancing a gospel of peace or reaching across the racial divide. But he sensed our diminishing capacity for this as shared meanings seemed

---

1. *WF* 316.

2. See also Christine M. Bochen, "Language and Propaganda," *ME* 242–44; Robert E. Daggy, "Thomas Merton's Critique of Language," *The Merton Seasonal* 27, no. 1 (Spring 2002): 11–15; Ross Labrie, "Thomas Merton on the Unspeakable," *The Merton Seasonal* 36, no. 4 (Winter 2011): 3–12.

to break down in our use of modern language. Merton showed glimmers of this concern in his early social commentary, "Letter to an Innocent Bystander," the 1958 essay that led Marlon Green to contact Merton about racial justice. Here Merton expressed "hope that a civil exchange of ideas can take place between two persons—that we have not yet reached the stage where we are all hermetically sealed, each one in the collective arrogance and despair of his own herd," a situation he feared "may not continue to exist much longer."[3] Merton's concern did not focus on literacy or grammar. It focused on our innate need to freely express Truth and Love rather than seek Power and Control. As he wrote in *Conjectures of a Guilty Bystander*: "We are afflicted, hesitant, dubious in our speech... [because] our inborn natural sense of the *logos*, our love for reasonable expression... shames us with a false sense of guilt" over our tendency for "playing with words, manipulating them." In response, we must "take courage and speak [and]... dare to think what we mean, and simply make clear statements of what we intend."[4]

Merton pointed to advertising[5] and propaganda as prime examples of manipulating words to avoid truth in search of power. In *Conjectures* he devoted eight pages to propaganda,[6] much of it inspired by reading Jacques Ellul on the topic. He recounted how genuine "facts" get strung together to intentionally express "untrue" ideas, and he especially lamented euphemisms that sanitize concrete realities to justify war and violence. His 1967 essay, "Auschwitz: A Family Camp," noted this in Nazi references to the extermination gas Zyklon B as "disinfectants," "materials for resettlement of Jews," and "ovaltine substitute from Swiss Red Cross." His 1968 essay "War and the Crisis of Language," observed the same in U.S. language about the Vietnam War. The military created "free fire zones" by leveling everything to clear them of "hostile civilians." "Acceptable levels" of enemy deaths for "pacification" could "save American lives." Today we use "enhanced interrogation techniques" (rather than torture) to hold "terror" at bay. For Merton, such "language of escalation" mixed "banality and apocalypse, science and unreason." Such "officialese has a talent for discussing reality while denying it and calling truth itself into question." It relies on "circumlocution" and "doubletalk and doublethink" that "encircles reality as a doughnut encircles

---

3. Merton, "Letter to an Innocent Bystander," *The Behavior of Titans* (New York: New Directions, 1961), 51.

4. Merton, *Conjectures of a Guilty Bystander*, 92–93.

5. For example, Merton, "War and the Crisis of Language," *The Nonviolent Alternative*, 237–38.

6. Merton, *Conjectures of a Guilty Bystander*, 235–43.

its hole." As a result, Merton felt "language itself has fallen victim to total war, genocide, and systematic tyranny."[7]

Merton expressed similar concerns in his 1965 essay "Events and Pseudo-Events: Letter to a Southern Churchman." There he addressed our construction of "images" to support collective "illusion" and "myths" that think for us and make us unable to "separate the truth from the half-truth, the event from the pseudo-event, reality from the manufactured image." He lamented our obsession with making "newsworthy" (or perhaps "like-worthy" or "tweet-worthy") public expressions. This pandering to media marketability can make our words "altogether incredible—or else reduce them to the common level of banality at which they can no longer be distinguished from pseudo-events."[8] Merton later invoked Herbert Marcuse to warn a gathering of contemplative nuns that despite thinking ourselves "informed," we remain at the mercy of "language being compressed into little capsules so that it cuts down on any length or development of thought. You get the facts through the impact of these small packets thrown at you. The rest is by implication. . . . You don't actually think about what's said."[9] Merton could scarcely have better described the twenty-first-century practice of reporting (and governing) by "tweet."

Merton considered genuine communication a prerequisite for action with integrity. As Clement of Alexandria had said: "Reasonable speech, *logos* regenerates the soul and orients it toward the noble and beautiful act.... The word prepares the way for action...and justice does not take shape without *logos*."[10] Merton conceded that he did not have a clear answer to the problem of communication, but he suspected its root lay with recognition that "if we love our own ideology and our own opinion instead of loving our brother, we will seek only to glorify our ideas and our institutions and by that fact we will make real communication impossible."[11]

His essay "Peace and Revolution: A Footnote from *Ulysses*" shared how James Joyce's novel addressed "the breakdown of language and communication as part of the disruption of Western culture." Merton's remedy invoked Gandhian nonviolence as a "kind of language," a "purification of language, a restoration of true communication on a human level, when language has been

7. Merton, "Auschwitz: A Family Camp," *The Nonviolent Alternative*, 155; "War and the Crisis of Language," *The Nonviolent Alternative*, 239–40.

8. Merton, "Events and Pseudo-Events," *Faith and Violence*, 150, 162–63.

9. Merton, *The Springs of Contemplation*, 120–21.

10. Merton, *Conjectures of a Guilty Bystander*, 93.

11. Merton, "Pseudo-Events," *Faith and Violence*, 163.

emptied of meaning by misuse and corruption." This language is meant to "communicate love not in word but in act, . . . to convey and to defend truth which has been obscured and defiled by political doubletalk." But Merton cautioned against a "language of spurious nonviolence [that] is merely another, more equivocal form of the language of power" and reflects "one's will to power . . . used and conceived pragmatically, in reference to the seizure of power."[12] In "Events and Pseudo-Events" he offered similar warnings against misguided nonviolence in acts of protest, resistance, and a quest for "newsworthiness"—despite sincere "ideals" and "purity of heart." "When protest simply becomes an act of desperation, it loses its power to communicate anything to anyone who does not share the same feelings of despair." Isolated within "a closed realm of images and idols which mean one thing to us and another to our adversaries[,] *we no longer communicate. We abandon communication in order to celebrate our own favorite group-myths in a ritual pseudo-event.*"[13]

Merton's experimentation with "anti-poetry," such as *Cables to the Ace* and *Geography of Lograire*, reflect another venue through which he expressed waning faith in the capacity of language to adequately communicate. As he wrote in a 1967 letter to Hiromu Morishita, a Hiroshima nuclear blast survivor who had visited Merton, his *Cables* poem was "full of ironies and ambiguities appropriate to the moment when we are saturated with the wrong kind of communication. It is perhaps a time of 'anti-poems.'"[14] Regarding advertising, he lamented to Czeslaw Milosz its "images that society fills [one] with," "a very fine picture of hell" that made him "want to curse them" and "so sick." He offered as evidence a TV ad with "two little figures . . . dancing around worshiping a roll of toilet paper, chanting a hymn in its honor."[15] After noting *Scientific American*'s well-done articles to Jacques Maritain, he added: "But the *advertising* is phenomenal! What naked hubris! Advertising is one of the great *loci classici* for the theology of the devil."[16]

Other letters echoed published concerns. A 1961 letter to the Brazilian writer Alceu Amaroso Lima expressed the need for "communication between the hearts and minds of men, communication and not the noise of slogans or the repetition of clichés. Communication is becoming more and more difficult, and when speech is in danger of perishing or being perverted in ampli-

---

12. Merton, "Ulysses," *The Nonviolent Alternative*, 74–75.

13. Merton, "Pseudo-Events," *Faith and Violence,* 147, 159–60. Emphasis in the original.

14. Merton to Morishita, August 6, 1967, *HGL* 461.

15. Merton to Milosz, March 28, 1961, *CT* 72.

16. Merton to Maritain, June 11, 1963, *CT* 38. Emphasis in the original.

fied noises of beasts, perhaps it becomes obligatory for a monk to try to speak."[17] In a dialogue with the British intellectual Lord Northbourne about the Second Vatican Council's Pastoral Constitution on the Church in the Modern World, Merton described its purpose as: "the maintaining of reasonable communicating between the Church and the world of modern technology. If communication breaks down entirely, and there is no hope of exchanging ideas, then the situation becomes impossible."[18]

Regarding violence and language, he shared with Louis Massignon in 1960 his recent reading of Gandhi's writings and a growing need for world peace: "In the presence of the darkness, the cloud of falsity and pretense, of confusion, of evasion, of desecration, one grows more and more to distrust words, to distrust even human communication itself. There grows in my heart a need to express something inexpressible."[19] To the historian of religion Martin Marty, he asserted that nonviolence must not be used "for the interests of the white against the Negro. We must use it, as it is meant to be used, for truth, and for the good of everybody. To begin with, it must be used to keep open possibilities of authentic human communication when the bullets are flying."[20]

In these ways, clear communication of Truth and Love served as a foundation of his social vision, and as his comments to Lima and Massignon attest, he began in the early sixties to see pursuing it as part of his monastic vocation. Recognizing Merton's concern with language and communication underscores how seriously he approached constructing his letters to others, how he saw his communications as laying groundwork needed for fruitful action. It elevates the significance of his letters as vessels to help transform society.

Modern Technology[21]

Modern industrial technology reflected another dynamic that shaped Merton's vision for social transformation. From the early 1950s, as master of scholastics, Merton sensed a threat to Trappist contemplative priorities in the noise and functional rigidity of abbey mechanization. His 1953 letter to the

---

17. Merton to Lima, November 1961, *CT* 165.

18. Merton to Lord Northbourne, February 23, 1966, *WF* 314–15.

19. Merton to Massignon, October 29, 1960, *WF* 279.

20. Merton to Martin Marty, September 6, 1967, *HGL* 458.

21. See also William H. Shannon, "Technology," *ME* 466–70. *The Merton Annual* 24 (2011) devotes eleven articles to Merton and technology.

superior of a Benedictine monastery in Cuernavaca, Mexico, shows this. The Benedictine sought Merton's counsel about introducing machinery to anchor a new thread-dyeing operation, wondering if it might degrade their monastic life even as it offered the monastery financial self-sufficiency. Merton named this as a concern "close to my heart." He conceded the inevitability of machinery in modern monasteries and offered no specific advice without knowing more details of their context. But he shared his own experience where mechanization introduced problems. "As soon as one has machines one enters into the technological attitude of mind that is eating the heart out of modern life." Machines introduce "a constant expansion of activity," and coupled with their noise, can lead monks to cultivate "a pure illusion of the contemplative life . . . which deludes itself." It makes a monk "careless about the way he walks, how he handles things," replacing the Holy Spirit with a spirit "tense, hard, complicated, cold."[22]

Merton later grew concerned about the Pandora's Box of destruction beyond the monastery that modern technology had opened through the nuclear arms race. He observed in a 1961 Cold War Letter how in that race people align with a "godless and pragmatic power bloc, the immense wealth and technical capacity of which is directed entirely to nuclear annihilation of entire nations, without distinction between civilians and combatants."[23] Another letter from that collection addressed the "tragedy" that an enormous "lack of balance between technology and spiritual life" thwarted the "amazing power of science" for potential good.[24]

Merton's concerns over technology blossomed further in late 1964 when "Ping" Ferry sent him a copy of Jacques Ellul's *The Technological Society*,[25] which Ferry had sponsored for English translation. Earlier that year, Ferry had shared his own policy paper, *The Triple Revolution*,[26] which named "cybernation" as an emerging challenge for U.S. society. Though Merton acknowledged it with appreciation, its focus on social/political policy failed to capture his sustained attention. In contrast, Merton rhapsodized about Ellul's book in his journal, assured that it figured prominently in discussion at a retreat of peace activists he hosted that November, and reviewed it in a Decem-

---

22. Merton to Dom Gregorio Lemercier, OSB, October 3, 1953, *SCH* 68–69.

23. Merton to Josiah G. Chatham, December 1961, Cold War Letter #13, *WF* 26.

24. Merton to Elbert R. Sisson, February–March 1962, Cold War Letter #44, *WF* 38.

25. Jacques Ellul, *The Technological Society* (New York: Knopf, 1964).

26. "The Triple Revolution," (Santa Barbara, California: The Ad Hoc Committee on the Triple Revolution, 1964), http://scarc.library.oregonstate.edu/coll/pauling/peace/papers/1964p.7-02-large.html.

ber 1964 *Commonweal* issue.[27] That same December he recommended it to a key figure in the drafting of the Vatican Council's Pastoral Constitution on the Church in the Modern World.[28] Merton also drew from writings by Lewis Mumford on "technics."[29]

Echoing such writers, Merton's critique during the mid-sixties expressed concern not so much with specific "technologies," but with the mindset that accelerating technological advances elicited. In practice, technology did not merely provide new tools to serve genuine human needs. It functioned as an autonomous force that shaped human perceptions. It elevated efficiency and quantification of human activity into fundamental social values, independent of its concrete impact on lived experience. Beyond that, this technological mindset—which Ellul termed *technique*—now assumed a self-perpetuating life of its own that human reason no longer controlled. Humans were now compelled to develop new technologies simply for their own sake or for financial profit, not for any considered human impact or higher value. In the acceleration of technology at a pace too fast to rationally process, technique usurped human freedom. Its mantra: "What can be done must be done." Despite his general agreement with Ellul, Merton resisted his fatalistic determinism—the inevitable victory of technique over human freedom. Merton better appreciated Mumford's optimism that technology might still be brought under the control of human intention to serve human needs.

Merton's most public expression of these views appeared scattered through the pages of *Conjectures of a Guilty Bystander*. There he connected the disintegration of communication and the power of propaganda with the ubiquity of the technological mindset: "Action is not governed by moral reason but by political expediency and the demands of technology—translated into the simple abstract formulas of propaganda."[30] Had Merton lived, one would anticipate his even greater alarm over today's fusion of communication and technology (together with free-market economics) into current social media platforms. On one hand, those platforms offer amazing opportunities to document oppression for rapid dissemination, connect over distance, and rally people for events and actions. Yet at the same time they offer un-

27. See Gordon Oyer, *Pursuing the Spiritual Roots of Protest: Merton, Berrigan, Yoder, and Muste at the Gethsemani Abbey Peacemakers Retreat* (Eugene, OR: Cascade, 2014), 54–65.

28. Merton to Bernard Haring, December 26, 1964, *HGL* 383–84.

29. Lewis Mumford, *Technics and Civilization* (New York: Harcourt, Brace & Co., 1934); Lewis Mumford, *The City in History: Its Origins, Its Transformations, and Its Prospects* (New York: Harcourt, Brace & World, 1961).

30. Merton, *Conjectures of a Guilty Bystander*, 65.

precedented opportunities to surveil and co-opt those activities, including the rise of "surveillance capitalism" that tracks our movements and choices to subtly craft personally targeted marketing efforts. These platforms also brew a perfect storm of partisan "bot" programming that channels disinformation into echo chambers and diffuses possibilities for the rational human dialogue Merton championed. As one opinion writer expressed: "Unfortunately, the moral arc of the internet bends toward polarization."[31]

As a whole, then, Merton's mid-century concerns expressed in *Conjectures* remain prescient:

> Technology and science are now responsible to no power and submit to no control other than their own. . . . Even the long-term economic interests of society, or the basic needs of man himself, are not considered when they get in the way of technology. . . . It is by means of technology that man the person, the subject of qualified and perfectible freedom, becomes *quantified*, that is, becomes part of a mass-man—whose only function is to enter anonymously into the process of production and consumption. He becomes on one side an implement, . . . a "bio-physical link" between machines: on the other side he is a . . . digestive system . . . *through which* pass the products of his technological world.[32]

Conjectures also quotes Mumford that: "Too many thought not only that mechanical progress would be a positive aid to human improvement, which is true, *but that mechanical progress is the equivalent of human improvement*, which turns out to be sheer nonsense."[33]

Several months before he published *Conjectures* Merton had also penned an obscure essay on this topic titled "The Angel and the Machine." It couched modern technology in lyrical or whimsical terms that described the replacement of "angels" with "machines" in human encounters with the cosmos. Merton portrayed the "angel" in a role similar to contemplative awareness of the divine, which offers a voice that speaks "more by sudden and significant silences than by clear and probative statements." Humans once turned to angels as they now turn to machines: "at the limit of our own strength, at the frontier of our natural capacity." But unlike angels, machines,

31. Charlie Warzel, "We Are Watching History Unfold in Real Time," *New York Times*, June 2, 2020, https://www.nytimes.com/2020/06/02/opinion/floyd-protest-twitter.html?

32. Merton, *Conjectures of a Guilty Bystander*, 75–76. Emphasis in the original.

33. Merton, *Conjectures of a Guilty Bystander*, 222. Emphasis in the original.

as "extensions of our own intelligence, our own strength," now place us "safe in the world of technique that surrounds" us and "render it spiritually unlivable for ourselves."[34]

But Merton did not advocate an attempted return to simpler times. In an August 1966 letter he reflected on the dilemma to Walter James, the fourth Baron Northbourne, commonly known simply as Lord Northbourne. James promoted a "Traditionalist/Perennialist" view that pursued threads of universal or "perennial" truths found in the world's major religions. Merton's response to Northbourne's *Religion in the Modern World*[35] sparked their exchange. Northbourne viewed the Pastoral Constitution on the Church in the Modern World skeptically, and Merton's letter gently asserted that we need its guidance to adapt to rather than escape from modern realities.

> Much as we appreciate the great value of ancient and traditional cultures, the coming of the industrial and technological revolution has undermined them and in fact doomed them. Everywhere in the world these cultures have been more or less affected—corrupted— by modern Western man and his rather unfortunate systems. It is not simply possible to return to the cultural stability and harmony of these ancient structures. But it is hoped that one can maintain some sort of continuity and preserve at least some of their living reality in a new kind of society.[36]

Merton not only dismissed a literal return to the past, he in fact voiced appreciation for technology in the abstract. He conceded that despite his concern, he remained "as ready as the next man to admire the astonishing achievements of technology," which "taken by themselves" are "magnificent."[37] It "could indeed serve to deepen and perfect the quality of [human] existence and in some ways it *has* done this."[38] The exclusion of angels "is no fault of the innocent machine. It is our own choice."[39] But Merton had

---

34. Written November and December of 1965, first published in the Austrian periodical *Seckauer Heft* [Styria, Austria] 29 (1966): 73–79; first published in English in the short-lived Dominican magazine *Season* 5 (Summer 1967). Republished as Merton, "The Angel and the Machine," *The Merton Seasonal* 22, no. 1 (Spring 1997): 3–6, cited here.

35. Lord Northbourne, *Religion in the Modern World* (London: J. M. Dent, 1963).

36. Merton to Lord Northbourne, August 30, 1966, *WF* 316.

37. Merton, *Conjectures of a Guilty Bystander*, 72.

38. Merton, *Conjectures of a Guilty Bystander*, 222. Emphasis in the original.

39. Merton, "Angel and Machine," 4.

published his qualified technological commentary in the midst of a race to the moon, a Cold War for technical (as well as military) supremacy, and a cacophony of "Mad Men" hawking the newest and shiniest gizmos that U.S. industry could offer. Consequently, in published reviews and personal letters, Merton heard from several who found his view naïve, backward, and unappreciative of the many marvels technology had bestowed. He did not bother to publicly rebut them, but in their wake he sometimes addressed them in letters.

In January 1967, for example, Merton responded to Jim Forest's request for clarification as he prepared a review of *Conjectures*. Merton's reply emphasized the provisional, journal-derived nature of *Conjectures* and assured he was not saying technology was "bad," but that "the myths around it are not as simple and as glossy and as hopeful as some want them to be." He felt no need to "be a part of anybody's in-group and keep up with the cosy [sic] current opinions," he explained. Rather, he recognized value in "uttering opinions that are a bit divergent and that come from an unexpected angle."[40] Two months later Merton further explained to Catholic theologian Rosemary Radford Ruether his view that technology "is not evil, but it is not beyond all criticism either." When "used cynically and opportunistically for power and wealth," it "becomes a disastrous weapon *against* humanity" such that "the problem of getting technology back into the power of man so that it may be used for man's own good is by all odds the great problem of the day."[41]

Sandwiched between those letters, during early Lent, Merton packed his most extensive response to the backlash into eight paragraphs of a circular letter to friends. His published comments did not advocate a return to primitive practices, he explained, they just questioned "the universal myth that technology infallibly makes everything in every way better for everybody." Penicillin saved lives, but "society then allows [them] to starve." Advanced technology injected into a "backward" country "is not in the service of people but in the service of profit.... What I am 'against' then is a complacent and naïve progressivism which pays no attention to anything but the fact that wonderful things can be and are done with machinery and electronics." He summarized: "Technology has given us the means to alleviate human misery, but the profit system makes it practically impossible to use the means effectively."[42] This letter helps unpack his sense of modernity's attitude of deferential mystique toward its technologies, elevated

---

40. Merton to James H. Forest, January 28, 1967, TMC/BU.

41. Merton to Ruether, March 19, 1967, *HGL*, 506–507. Emphasis in the original.

42. Merton to Friends, Lent [February 22 1967], *RJ* 98–99.

from a practical tool into a revered social value. Despite their theoretical potential to serve humanity, they defaulted into serving modern trends that dominate and commodify human persons as economic resources and social machinery cogs.

Anthropology and the Natural World[43]

Another facet of Merton's critique of technology involved how it alienates humans from their place within the natural world—a third dynamic beyond language and technology that underlay his vision for social transformation. A lost sense of connection to and placement within the flow of Creation skewed the balance of human activity and empowered war and racial oppression. Modern technology "chang[ed] the natural environment into an artificial environment," he lectured his fellow monks, or at least engineered it for human convenience, as on their monastery grounds, where "we used to have many creeks... and now we have one creek."[44] Machines "stand between us and nature," creating space where "we are isolated from the rest of material creation" and from "terrestrial events, to which man's own nature has its ancient replies." Their quest to merely "save time" had created a new "spiritual measurement," a "machine time" that replaced not just contemplative "angelic time," but also the "natural time" of daily and seasonal rhythms.[45] For Merton, "when technology merely... exploits and uses up all things in pursuit of its own ends,... then it degrades [humanity], despoils the world, ravages life, and leads to ruin."[46] It drives humanity to "a climate of moral infancy, in total dependence not on 'mother nature'... but on the pseudonature of technology, which has replaced nature by a closed system of mechanisms with no purpose but that of keeping themselves going."[47]

Nature figured prominently in Merton's consciousness from birth; his mother recorded his spontaneous delight in natural elements during his earliest

---

43. See also Thomas Merton, *When the Trees Say Nothing: Writings on Nature*, Kathleen Deignan, ed. (Notre Dame, IN: Sorin Books, 2003); Patrick F. O'Connell, "Creation" (91–93), Ecology" (125–27), "Nature" (319–22) in ME; Monica Weis, SSJ, *The Environmental Vision of Thomas Merton* (Lexington, KY: University of Kentucky Press, 2011).

44. Paul R. Dekar, *Thomas Merton: Twentieth-Century Wisdom for Twenty-First-Century Living* (Eugene. OR: Cascade, 2011), 208, 209.

45. Merton, "Angel and Machine," 4, 5.

46. Merton, *Conjectures of a Guilty Bystander*, 253.

47. Merton, *Conjectures of a Guilty Bystander*, 77.

years.[48] Patrick O'Connell nicely summarized Merton's adult awareness of nature into four dimensions: fascination with the particulars of natural phenomena; gleaning moral or spiritual lessons from a natural fact or situation; awareness that nature requires human participation beyond detached empiricism; and as a foil to the "post-Cartesian technologism that separates man from the world."[49] The last two aspects form the core of nature's relevance for Merton's vision of social transformation. He recognized our challenge to restore balanced human/nature interdependence in different ways. These included appreciation for indigenous—"primitive" he often called them —peoples who lived outside of industrial technological dependence or before the emergence of imperial city-states. The value of engaging their experience went beyond challenging racial oppression; their traditions illuminated a sense of human Being deeply integrated within Earth's life and landscapes.

Ernesto Cardenal and Latin American Poets

The 1957 arrival of Ernesto Cardenal at Gethsemani Abbey as a novice launched one of Merton's earliest segues into this realm—interaction with Latin America poets and their indigenist poetry. The Nicaraguan poet remained only two years before his return to Latin America, but while at Gethsemani he introduced Merton to this poetry and discussed with him the indigenous peoples of both Americas. This helped set Merton on a course of expansive correspondence with these poets and translation of their poetry into English. The two maintained substantial correspondence following Cardenal's departure. Together with Merton's other Latin American literary interactions of the late fifties and early sixties, this enhanced his appreciation for the region's native peoples and nurtured his respect for the wisdom expressed in their spirituality and history. Cardenal in turn credited Merton with sparking his own awareness: "I owe you for my ability to begin to understand and love the Indians, and most of all for being able to see in them the religious and spiritual values that I did not see before."[50]

Malgorzata Poks's groundbreaking *Thomas Merton and Latin America: A Consonance of Voices*,[51] provides masterly insight into this underappreci-

---

48. See Weis, *Environmental Vision*, 29–33.

49. O'Connell, "Nature," *ME* 320–21, quoting Merton in *TTW* 312.

50. *From the Monastery to the World: The Letters of Thomas Merton and Ernesto Cardenal*, trans./ed. Jessie Sandoval (Berkeley, CA: Counterpoint, 2017), Cardenal to Merton, November 13, 1963, 151–52.

51. Malgorzata Poks, *Thomas Merton and Latin America: A Consonance of Voices* (Saarbrucken, Germany: LAP LAMBERT Academic Publishing, 2011).

ated aspect of Merton's later social and literary development during his last decade. She reveals how the indigenist poetry Merton read and translated relied upon imagery from nature and sought to re-create the lens of Latin America's original inhabitants. Merton wished to harmonize that "poetic and spiritual vocation" with his own, one that, as he wrote to poet Pablo Antonio Cuadra, would express "the Christ that was born among the Indians already many centuries ago, who manifested himself in the Indian culture, before the official coming of Christianity,"[52] or, as he shared with Cardenal, would "enter into the thought of primitive peoples...to live that thought and spirit as Christians."[53] Poks eloquently summarizes: "Merton believed that if they and their spiritual heirs remained faithful to this vocation, the joyful dance of the Lord in the garden of His creation would not be a forgotten game. This universal dance, restoring the original harmony of the created world, is suggestive of the final restoration of all things in Christ in the eschatological kingdom of peace."[54]

Laurens van der Post and Africa

The Africa-born explorer and writer Laurens van der Post played another inspirational role for Merton. His Dutch ancestors had settled in South Africa, and though he served the British government in military and other capacities, he deeply respected native Africans and opposed European colonial policies. Carl Jung's thought influenced van der Post's writing, which often channeled Jungian concepts of unconscious human connection and converging experience.

Merton corresponded with van der Post between 1959 and 1961, having first read his books *Venture to the Interior*[55] and *The Dark Eye in Africa*.[56] Merton initiated contact in response to the first book's account of exploring Mlanje (or Melanje), a mountain in southern Nyasaland (now Malawi), on behalf of the British government. It described being trapped atop the mountain during late May 1949 when a brutal storm swept a party member over a waterfall to his death on the 28th. Merton's letter praised van der Post's writing as "a real recovery of a lost dimension in the contemplative life. A

---

52. Merton to Cuadra, December 4, 1958, *CT* 182.

53. Merton to Cardenal, November 23, 1963, *CT* 143.

54. Poks, *Thomas Merton and Latin America*, 174.

55. Laurens van der Post, *Venture to the Interior* (New York: Morrow and Co., 1951).

56. Laurens van der Post, *The Dark Eye in Africa* (New York: Morrow and Co., 1955).

human dimension, which is also historical and concrete." He also commended van der Post's "love for Africa which has now become, in some
measure, my own."[57] But especially, Merton was:

> extremely moved by your account of the exploration of Mt Mlanje
> because, in a strange way,... I think I was somehow involved in it.
> The 26th, 27th and the 28th of May, 1949, were three of the most
> important days of my life. On the 26th I was ordained a priest and
> on the following two days I offered my first Masses, the first one
> simple and the other solemn. On all these days I felt deeply con-
> cerned with prayers and desires beyond words for people every-
> where and especially for those in peril or special need.... When I
> read your book it immediately struck me ... that this was one of the
> things I had been praying about.[58]

Van der Post described Mlanje as:

> a world of its own, a very ancient, lost world of trees that grew
> nowhere else[,] ... a conifer of a unique and very ancient sort.... If
> you laid your ear to a trunk, it was almost as if you could hear this
> vital, this dark, secret traffic drumming upwards, skywards, from
> the deep, ancient soil, the original earth perhaps of Africa.[59]

By then Mlanje's once expansive forests had been assaulted as an economic
resource, leaving "a world of unique and irreplaceable living trees, fighting a
desperate rearguard action against fire and rapacious human beings."[60]

One suspects that Merton's reading of the book and his letters with van
der Post helped inspire one of his earliest published works to touch upon
modern human estrangement from nature. "Atlas and the Fat Man," written
during 1959–60, provides an allegorical, poetic narrative of the titan Atlas—
representative of nature itself[61]—in the form of an African mountain that
holds up the sky and regulates the planet's rhythms. The narrator reaches
"the shores of a sentient mountain" where "stood the high African rock in the

57. Merton to Laurens van der Post, September 18, 1959, Rare Book and Manuscript Library, Columbia University.

58. Merton to Laurens van der Post, September 18, 1959.

59. Van der Post, *Venture*, 117–18.

60. Van der Post, *Venture*, 119.

61. Merton identified it as such in *Raids of the Unspeakable*, 1.

shadow of the lucky rain: a serious black crag, at the tip of the land mass, with a cloud balanced on his shoulder," one who rang a "dim bell in the heavens that moved the weather and changed the seasons." Atlas "wish[ed] well to mankind" and "want[ed] him to rest at peace under a safe sky knowing ... that the ends of the world are watched over by an overseer." However, "up jumped a great fatman" who "thought that he was god and that he could stop everything from moving." A representation of modern, industrialized humanity and named after the atomic bomb that leveled Nagasaki, this fat-man has "a clockwork mind in order to make a lot of money" as he claims supremacy over Earth's rhythms. But the fatman ultimately implodes in im-potence and "the clear bell of Atlas rings once again over the sea and the ani-mals come to the shore at his feet. The gentle earth relaxes." Now, "the pris-ons are open. The fatman is forgotten. The fatman was only his own nightmare. Atlas never knew him."[62]

Merton first published "Atlas and the Fatman" in his 1961 anthology *The Behavior of Titans*, dedicated to van der Post, and republished five years later in *Raids on the Unspeakable*.[63] Van der Post's March 1960 letter ex-pressed excitement over the "Atlas notes" Merton shared, how they re-minded him of the Portuguese poet Camões's tale of Vasco da Gama encoun-tering "Ardamastor, the last of the Titans" as the navigator rounded Africa's southern tip. Van der Post felt that "Atlas and the Fatman" had captured the same judgment upon colonial domination of "the natural man of Africa" as the Portuguese poem.[64]

Merton also drew upon van der Post for "Gandhi and the One-Eyed Giant," his introductory essay to *Gandhi on Non-Violence*. It opens:

> The white man, says Laurens Van Der Post [in *The Dark Eye in Africa*] came into Africa (and Asia and America for that matter) like a one-eyed giant, bringing with him the characteristic split and blindness which were at once his strength, his torment, and his ruin. With his self-isolated and self-scrutinizing individual mind ... the one-eyed giant had science without wisdom, and he broke in upon ancient civilizations which (like the Medieval West) had wisdom

62. *Behavior of Titans*, 24–26, 29, 31–32, 47.

63. *Behavior of Titans*, 24–48; *Raids of the Unspeakable*, 91–107. The most no-ticeable changes in the 1966 edition include capitalization of "Fatman," reference to drawing "Negro blood" rather than "Jewish blood," and a closing line that portrays Atlas watching the "African sun" rather than the "rising sun."

64. Laurens van der Post to Merton, March 25, 1960, and April 7, 1961, TMC/BU.

without science: wisdom which ... dwells in body and soul together
and ... opens the door to a life in which the individual is not lost in
the cosmos and in society but found in them.[65]

Elsewhere Merton also affirms van der Post's *Lost World of the Kalahari*,[66] which recounts his quest to find a society of "bushmen" commissioned
for a 1956 BBC documentary. In his writing and correspondence, van der Post
nurtured Merton's insights into the clash between modernity and a more integrated indigenous African experience of human interaction with nature.

Native Americans, Cargo Cults, and The Geography of Lograire

Those insights deepened even further during Merton's final two years. Completion of his essay "Ishi: A Meditation" in early March 1967 launched an extended study that would refine his anthropological awareness and inspire much
output of prose and poetry. That July he shared in a letter to Lewis Mumford:
"I have no part in a 'humanism' which submits man to his machines. I think I
will finally have to become an amateur anthropologist in order to bring out the
truth that primitive man was not simply some kind of beast, and that he was in
many ways more human than we are. Though he did not have our 'advan-
tages.'"[67] Three weeks later he wrote to Rosemary Radford Ruether:

> I have suddenly got engrossed in a whole new line of study, a new
> approach (for me)—the anthropological one, the question of the
> clash between cultures (white and advanced with nonwhite and
> more or less primitive) which has produced all sorts of strange
> things by which people have tried to cope with the trauma. So I am
> involved in looking up eschatological cults in Africa, Melanesia,
> among American Indians, and so on.[68]

This expansive pilgrimage of study would lead Merton through an array of
anthropological material on indigenous peoples of both Americas, cargo cults
of the Pacific, and emerging "post-structuralist" theory.

Merton's engagement with writings on America's indigenous peoples
yielded the five essays which constitute his posthumously published anthol-

---

65. Merton, *Gandhi on Nonviolence* (New York: New Directions, 1965), 3.

66. Laurens van der Post, *World of the Kalahari* (New York: William Morrow
and Co., 1958); Merton to Dona Luisa Coomeraswamy, February 12, 1961, *HGL* 129.

67. Merton to Lewis Mumford, July 12, 1967, TMC/BU.

68. Merton to Ruether, August 4, 1967, *HGL* 514.

ogy, *Ishi Means Man*. He crafted these commentaries in 1967—three on nineteenth- and twentieth-century North American Indians (written between March and October) and two on nineteenth-century and pre-contact Mayans (written in October and November). As noted in chapter 8, Merton was reading Lanternari's study of "modern messianic cults" when Vincent Harding visited in early July 1967. But his first recorded mention of cargo cults during this period[69] appears later that month in a letter to the Brazilian nun, Sister M. Emmanuel de Souza e Silva: "At the moment I am beginning to do some work on primitive messianic and prophetic cults in Africa, Melanesia, etc....The Cargo cults of Melanesia are a fantastic eschatology. Very revealing."[70] From then through February of 1968, his journals and correspondence are peppered with references to "cargo," and during September through November 1967 he devoted an unpublished reading notebook to the topic.[71] In the wake of that exercise, on November 11, 1967, Merton dictated into his recorder: "I would like to put on tape some of the ideas that are coming together in my mind on the question of Cargo cults and their relevance to us."[72] Merton later edited and expanded a transcript of that tape to produce a sixty-page typed document,[73] which was in turn posthumously edited and condensed into an essay less than one quarter its length.[74]

As for post-structuralism—which looks beyond our limited, constructed linguistic/conceptual frameworks to better explore the fluid nature of human experience and culture—Merton referenced works by theorists Claude Lévi-Strauss[75] and Roland Barthes.[76] He also explored George Steiner's *Language and Silence*,[77] a book more critical of the theory. Merton refers to his epic

---

69. Merton's only known mention of cargo cults before 1967 appears in speaking notes for his November 18, 1964, "peacemaker retreat" discussion. See Oyer, *Pursuing*, 84, 114–15, 247.

70. Merton to M. Emmanuel, July 31, 1967, *HGL* 199.

71. Malgorzata Poks, "With Malinowski in the Postmodern Desert: Merton, Anthropology, and the Ethnopoetics of *The Geography of Lograire*," *The Merton Annual* 25 (Louisville, KY: Fons Vitae, 2012): 59–60 and note 39.

72. "Cargo Movements and Their Implications," tape transcript, C.2, TMC/BU.

73. "Cargo Theology," 1968, typescript, D.2 manuscript file, TMC/BU.

74. "Cargo Cults of the South Pacific," first published in *America* 137, no. 5 (August 1977), 90–94; also in Merton, *Love and Living*, 80–94.

75. Readings of Lévi-Strauss spanned August through November 1967: *CT* 253; *LL* 285, 299–300; *OSM* 15.

76. Poks, "With Malinowski," 58, note 36. "Roland Barthes—Writing as Temperature," *The Literary Essays of Thomas Merton*, 140–49; first published in *Sewanee Review* (Summer 1969).

77. Read on the days surrounding New Year's Day 1968, *OSM* 32, 34.

anti-poem, *Geography of Lograire*, in terms of an "urbane structuralism,"[78] and it is no coincidence that its writing overlapped these months of Merton's anthropological and post-structuralist study.[79] Unpacking this poem and its fragmented, allusive language is best left to other venues and more qualified scholars, but Merton's study of cargo cults was central to his construction of the poem with its many mentions of American and Pacific island indigenous experience.[80]

Taken together, the fruit of this season of study suggests his deepening grasp of "whiteness" and illuminates concurrent comments on race made in letters to Robert Williams and Vincent Harding. His prose from this period explored how "primitive"[81] encounters with Western, white, colonial powers left their nonwhite subjects groping to retain or regain their sense of identity as fully human beings. Merton suggests that our white dominant culture, as constructed by the global West, permits only one avenue for others to attain full humanity: embracing the supremacy of a Western worldview. This theme of lost identity echoed through his Native American quintet of essays (see "The Shoshoneans" recap in Chapter 8), but he expressed it most clearly in the sixty-page "Cargo Theology" tape transcript and posthumously compiled essay. There Merton relied on anthropologist Kenelm Burridge's concept of "myth-dream," an unconscious, unquestioned paradigm that drives social mores and behavior. Myth-dreams are centered on commonly revered symbols that need constant "readjusting, reshaping, putting together in a new form."[82] They appear most transparently in less developed cultures, but also in highly developed ones, though in more nuanced or rationalized form.

Merton considered a core Western myth-dream to be our self-perception as a "totally objective, scientific people," which fosters our myth that "we have no myths" and remain innately superior to those we consider nonobjective and nonscientific. Many "primitive" cultures, in contrast, maintain myth-dreams grounded in the primacy of direct relationship and the role of reciprocity within it. Because "our myth-dream demands *nonreciprocity* with

78. Merton, *The Geography of Lograire* (New York: New Directions, 1969), 2.

79. Draft first mentioned October 1967 (*LL* 297); completed June 1968 (*OSM* 132); submitted for publication September 1968 (*OSM* 167).

80. The work of Malgorzata Poks proves especially relevant. Besides "With Malinowski" and "Borderlands," see also her "*Geography of Lograire* as Merton's *Gestus*—Prolegomena," *The Merton Annual* 22 (2009): 150–69.

81. Merton's use of the term "primitive," acceptable when written, now casts a negative tone he would not wish; "non-modern" might better reflect his intent.

82. Merton, "Cargo Theology," 19.

nonwhite people" and "*takes as its axiom our total superiority over every-body else*," these divergent myth-dreams clashed when Pacific islanders encountered Western colonizers and missionaries. Confronted with the marvels of Western industrial production, or "cargo," the islanders expected reciprocal access to it as fellow humans. Though Westerners may acknowledge this right in theory, "in fact we believe that a certain kind of know-how, a certain kind of business acumen...gives a person a higher right to appropriate to himself what others might be expecting." Our unconscious paradigm was incomprehensible to those immersed in a "relationship of exchange," which grounded "all social order in native thought." The result: "failure of communication between two sets of needs and desires expressed on two entirely different levels." In the islanders' failure to attain reciprocity and full acceptability as human beings on white culture's terms, they lost their innate sense of value and identity.[83]

Merton recognized similar "cargo cult" dynamics playing out among modern conflicts. "White European, White Anglo-Saxon, Protestant and Catholic too: we are all living by a myth-dream which is essentially racist and we do not realize it....Even when we think we are being nice and fair and just and so forth, we are living and acting by a dream that makes fairness and justice impossible. Even when we are being kind and liberal our kindness and liberality are tinged with unconscious racism. And Black Power, among other things, is trying to tell us so." He also saw reaction and resistance to self-recognition. "The white myth-dream of absolute white supremacy...sees all kinds of opposition before it ever happens." It fosters a "self-fulfilling prophecy" that "creates the opposition it fears" and "*needs* to find opposition and rebellion in order to act out its fears and hostilities by forceful suppression."[84] Here Merton's analysis hauntingly echoes aspects of Vincent Harding's "Uses of the Afro-American Past" recapped in chapter 8.

Beyond academic curiosity, Merton studied the topic "to reach the heart of our own problem, our universal problem of communication. Our communication with...primitive society demands an ability to communicate also with something deeper *in ourselves*, something with which we are out of touch. Our inability to communicate with [these others] (which to us are repellant, absurd, and threatening), is due to the fact that we are out of contact with our own depths." The answer lay not with the "primitive" other "dominated by the white man...[nor with getting] rid of the white man in order to be fully human: both need each other, and need to cooperate with each other

---

83. Merton, "Cargo Theology," 10, 43, 37, 40, 57. Emphasis in the original.
84. Merton, "Cargo Theology," 43, 56. Emphasis in the original.

in the common enterprise of building a world that is adequate for the historical maturity of man."[85]

Merton's interpretation of cargo cults as a "millennial" mentality that sought reciprocity, manifested less transparently in modern cultures, anticipated a position anthropologists embraced decades later. The forward to proceedings of the 1990 symposium *Cargo Cults and Millenarian Movements* notes that "It was the monk Thomas Merton who back in the sixties saw something of the underlying unity between aspects of the modern American scene and the cargo cults of Melanesia," adding hopes the symposium would extend Merton's insight.[86]

Although in this work Merton focused mostly on human identity and interrelationships, our relationship to nature also hovered at its margins. His reflections in "Cargo Theology" noted how relationship to traditional lifeways factored in. Melanesian islanders destroyed their crops and livestock in anticipation of modern "cargo's" arrival, while the Native American Ghost Dance (to Merton, a cargo theology variant) sought the reverse—the disappearance of whites and their commodities coupled with the return of buffalo and other game. "The Shoshoneans" observed how North Americans considered the continent's original inhabitants as "property owners" only in some "very mystical, primitive, irresponsible way," as "squatters on land which God had assigned to us."[87] In "Ishi: A Meditation" he commented how Ishi's last tribal remnant had "systematically learned to live [on the land] as invisible and unknown," and suggested that "the reader should reflect a little on the relation of the Indian to the land on which he lived."[88]

But this connection comes through strongest in his study of the precontact Mayan ceremonial site of Monte Albán. In "The Sacred City," he observed how "by liturgy and celebration, the lives of men, cultivators of maize, were integrated into the cosmic movements of the stars, the planets, the skies, the winds and weather, the comings and goings of gods." Here, "at the intersection of culture and nature" they lived "between complimentary opposites which balanced and fulfilled each other (fire-water, heat-cold, rain-earth, light-dark, life-death)." They existed in an "entirely different conception of man and life... as a network of living interrelationships," distinguished from ours today by its "indifference to technological progress, the lack of history, and the almost total neglect of the arts of war." Its "ar-

---

85. Merton, "Cargo Theology," 59, 60.
86. As cited in Poks, "Borderlands," 170.
87. Merton, "The Shoshoneans," 6.
88. Merton, "Ishi: A Meditation," 28–29.

chaic . . . *sense of identity*" linked it to the "close, ever-present and keenly-sensed world of nature." Though re-creating this life for modern people had become "practically unthinkable," knowing that it had once been "possible, indeed normal," might "help to tone down a little of our aggressive, self-complacent superiority, and puncture some of our more disastrous myths," including one that cultures of "'colored' races were always quaintly inferior, mere curious forms of barbarism." If we are to survive our modern culture of "artifice, abstraction, and violence," Merton concluded, we must "recover at least something of the values and attitudes" of Monte Albán.[89] For Merton, the benefits of understanding indigenous worldviews centered on gaining insight and wisdom for modern life, on not imitation or appropriation of their practices.

The Wild Places

When one thinks of Merton's view of human/nature interaction, his classic essay "Rain and the Rhinoceros" often comes to mind. First published in May 1965[90] and reprinted in *Raids on the Unspeakable*,[91] it merges his perception of the rain falling on/around his hermitage and the narrative of Eugene Ionesco's play *Rhinoceros* to contrast the freedom of nature with the oppressive conformity of mass society. The surrounding rain reminds him "that the whole world runs by rhythms I have not yet learned to recognize, rhythms that are not those of the engineer." In contrast, "rain brings no renewal to the city, only to tomorrow's weather, and the glint of windows in tall buildings will then have nothing to do with the new sky. All 'reality' will remain somewhere inside those walls, counting itself and selling itself with fantastically complex determination."[92]

But Merton's reflections on Roderick Nash's *Wilderness and the American Mind*, penned in late February 1968, provided his best published expression of how an integral relationship with nature is required for genuine social transformation—a springboard through which Merton speaks to our own imminent climate crisis. "The Wild Places"[93] summarized Nash's account of

---

89. Merton, "The Sacred City," *Ishi Means Man* 57–58, 63–65, 68, 70–71. Emphasis in the original.

90. *Holiday* (May 1965).

91. *Raids on the Unspeakable*, 9–23.

92. *Raids on the Unspeakable*, 9, 11–12.

93. First published in *The Catholic Worker* 34 (June 1968): 4, 6. Patrick O'Connell annotated it, unabridged, in Merton, "The Wild Paces," *The Merton Annual* 24 (2011): 15–28, cited here with Merton's emphases.

views on wilderness held by Henry Thoreau, John Muir, and Aldo Leopold. From it, Merton summarized Muir's realization of "other living beings, especially wild things" as not just "good for *him*, but as *good for themselves*" and highlights Muir's reminder "that man is *part of nature*. He must remember the rights of other beings to *exist on their own terms*," since "*unless man learns this fundamental respect for all life, he himself will be destroyed*." Merton noted how Kentucky's deforestation by mining industries was motivated by "a quick return on somebody's investment—and a permanent disaster for everybody else." Aldo Leopold had acknowledged this mentality, and Merton shared Leopold's rejection of "*preserving American institutions without giving so much as a thought to preserving the environment which produced them and which may now be one of the effective means of keeping them alive.*" Merton also seized upon Leopold's expression of an "ecological conscience ... centered in an awareness of *man's true place as a member of a biotic community*" and our need to "become fully aware of [our] *dependence* on a balance which [we are] not only free to destroy but which [have] already begun to destroy." Merton reproduced with strongest emphasis Leopold's "basic principle of the ecological conscience: A THING IS RIGHT WHEN IT TENDS TO PRESERVE THE INTEGRITY, STABILITY AND BEAUTY OF THE BIOTIC COMMUNITY. IT IS WRONG WHEN IT TENDS OTHERWISE."[94]

Nash's work emphasized Americans' historic view of pristine wilderness, which at its best excluded human presence. Conservationists valued wilderness as a separate resource to which civilized humans might escape to gain respite from urban civilization and return to it more content and productive. Significantly, Merton's review emphasized human balance with the whole of nature rather than conserving pristine wilderness patches while civilized humanity pillaged the remainder for economic gain. Merton emphasized our human need to participate in nature and Leopold's ecological conscience, asking us to resist the "artificial value of inert objects and abstractions (goods, money, property)" that modernity mistakes for "the power of life itself."[95]

---

94. "The Wild Paces," 23–25.
95. "The Wild Paces," 25.

In the months surrounding his anthropological study and reading Nash's book, Merton's letters hint that he recognized a "millennial" mindset at work in modern culture and saw both people of color *and* nature as targets of Western whiteness. This inclination is explored further in chapter 10, but his April 1968 response to Agnes Smith offers one brief example. Smith sought his counsel about human suffering at the hand of others. As a Native American, she understood discrimination, citing the skid row destiny of two alcoholic brothers along with slavery's legacy and observed how even repressed animals could not function normally under prolonged misery.[96] In response, Merton connected with her feelings, since "recently I have been doing some work on the Indians in the Northwest." His counsel echoed comments to Harding and Williams coupled with Leopold's insight: "Just as the Negro had been injured in his sense of his own worth, so too with the Indian. You Indian people have to recover a real sense of your own value, and not see yourself through the eyes of the white man." They must "resist with dignity and love." But one needs to comprehend the disease before finding its cure, and "the sickness is in history. The sickness is in this country itself, in the injustices committed against the Negro, the Indian, *against the wildlife of the country, the beautiful nature God made*" [emphasis added].[97]

---

96. Agnes Smith to Merton, n.d., TMC/BU.
97. Merton to Smith, April 28, 1968, *WF* 339–40.

10

AN ECOLOGICAL CONSCIOUSNESS

"Wisdom" and "wholeness" demand that man sanely integrate
his technics into their natural environment instead of using his
technology to ravage and exploit nature without regard for the
future.

> — *Thomas Merton*
> *Response to Walter A. Weisskopf's letter*
> *in* Forum for Correspondence and Contact
> *January 1968[1]*

In December 1967, when accepting an invitation to join a published forum of exchanges with other scholars, Thomas Merton listed out his primary areas of interest. Most of the topics he named would not surprise anyone familiar with Merton: "war and peace; relation of modern literature to religious wisdom; significance of the contemplative life today; psychology of religious experience; eastern and western mysticism, and their relevance to each other." But the Trappist added a topic some may not expect as primary. "Also," he continued, "nonprofessionally—questions related to ecology and the disturbance of ecological balance by ill-considered use of technology."[2] As discussed in chapter 9, Merton was by then immersed in anthropological readings and reflections, but he had not yet crafted his review essay "The Wild Places," with its concluding emphasis on Aldo Leopold's ecological conscience. But as that chapter also notes, Merton's technological concerns surfaced early in his monastic career, and his appreciation of nature began in childhood and continued thereafter. By late 1967, he grasped the danger in how these dynamics intersected and its implications for society. This final

---

1. "Comment on Charlotte Buhler, Tom Stonier, Walter A. Weisskopf," *Forum for Correspondence and Contact* 1, no. 2 (March 1968): 13.

2. Merton to Erling A. Thunberg, December 24, 1967, TMC/BU.

chapter reviews three sets of letters that demonstrate this grasp and how his concern related to the "millennial" features of the cargo cult mentalities he had studied.

Postscript to the Cold War Letters and
Prelude to an Ecological Consciousness
Thomas Merton's Letter to Rachel Carson

In tracing Merton's thread of ecological awareness, Merton's January 1963 response to reading *Silent Spring* provides a crucial marker. That letter to its author, Rachel Carson (1907–1964), tied his resistance to nuclear war with her groundbreaking study of DDT's harmful effects and captured his sense of a broad cultural pattern that "threatens not only civilization but life itself."[3] In it, he presciently connected important threads of Western domination and its need to "conquer" human and nonhuman alike. Since this letter has inspired considered reflection by others on Merton's grasp of environmental crises,[4] only a brief summary is offered here.

Merton told Carson that her study of the pesticide's deadly consequences provided "a most valuable and essential piece of evidence" to diagnose "the ills of our [technological] civilization." *Silent Spring* "makes it clear to me that there is a *consistent pattern* running through everything that we do, through every aspect of our culture, our thought, our economy, our whole way of life." He confessed that he could not clearly define what the pattern entailed, but he considered it vital that we understand it. He speculated we might owe it to "pitiful and superficial optimism about ourselves" and the "thought processes of materialistic affluence." But for the most part, his reflections tended more toward the metaphysical than the social, as he emphasized humanity's special and elevated role in the cosmos. The created world represents "a 'paradise' of [God's] wisdom, manifested in all [God's] creatures, down to the tiniest, and in the most wonderful interrelationships between them." Humans are to serve as the "eye in the body" of creation that both is "part of nature and . . . transcends it," called to maintain a "delicate balance" of relating self and nature to the "invisible." But "in gaining power and technical know-how," this "eye" had lost its sight—its "wisdom and . . . cosmic perspective." He felt Laurens van der Post's work on "South African

---

3. Merton to Carson, January 12, 1963, *WF* 70.

4. See especially Monica Weis, *The Environmental Vision of Thomas Merton* (Lexington, KY: University of Kentucky Press, 2011), 9–21, for a careful study of this letter.

Rachel Carson testifying before Congress, 1963 (Courtesy of Linda Lear Center for Special Collections and Archives, Connecticut College)

Bushmen" documented one example of this lost wisdom. Though "technics and wisdom are not by any means opposed," what Carson exposed reflected "exactly the same kind of 'logic'" that plagued the "vastly more important problem of nuclear war." To reinforce this connection, Merton later jotted on his copy of the letter, "Appendix to Cold War Letters."[5]

Merton crafted this letter hoping to launch a relationship of dialogue with Carson, sharing his wish to consult her on managing Abbey flora. She failed to respond, though, and died just fifteen months later after a bout with cancer. Thus, Merton's letter serves mostly to document what Monica Weis has called a "defining moment"[6] in his evolving environmental thought. Its nine paragraphs capture how *Silent Spring* helped Merton expand his insight into ways Western culture's pathologies worked themselves out in behaviors beyond warfare. And though Merton had positioned humanity in a privileged position within/over nature, Carson helped him more clearly see how our assault on nature for economic gain and personal ease reflected more than an isolated sin against God and God's creation. He came to see how it expressed the same self-destructive assault on life confronted in his Cold War writings. Her book's impact remained with him. In "The Wild Places," he invoked it to underscore human blindness to their own actions: "When people like Rachel

---

5. Merton to Carson, January 12, 1963, *WF* 70–72.

6. Weis, *Environmental Vision*, 19.

Carson try to suggest that our capacity to poison the nature around us is some indication of a sickness in ourselves, we dismiss them as fanatics."[7]

Choosing a Millennial or Ecological Consciousness:
The Merton-Hubbard Letters

In William Shannon's 1994 collection of Merton's "letters in times of crisis," he placed his letter to Rachel Carson in a short section that he titled "Postscript to the Cold War Letters." The section's only other content features two of Merton's three letters to a unique and fascinating figure, Barbara Marx Hubbard (1929–2019).[8] Her father, toy magnate Louis Marx, instilled in her his sense of self-made American pragmatism and urged that she follow his credo to "do your best" and maintain faith in our ability to realize what we pursue. At age six, Barbara's inability to grasp a reason for her mother's untimely death from cancer sparked her ongoing search for meaning. When she was a teenager, images of atomic detonations led her to begin asking how the nation's immense technical power might be used toward good ends. At twenty-two, she married artist Earl Hubbard, whose desire to create imagery of emerging human potential resonated with her own outlook.

Hubbard spent the next decade raising their family, but beginning in the early sixties, she began to publicly promote her sense of humanity's positive future. Appalled at the despair she perceived in a 1962 exhibit at New York's Museum of Modern Art, she asked her father to establish a foundation that would support optimistic artistic expressions of human fate. In 1964, Jonas Salk's holistic vision for his Salk Institute captured her imagination and led to several years of supportive interaction with him. Although then a Republican (her name would be considered for nomination as vice-president on the Democratic ticket two decades later), she opposed the destructive impulse of the party's 1964 presidential nominee, Barry Goldwater, and initiated a movement of "Lincoln Republicans" to offer an alternative.

The year 1966 proved especially pivotal for Hubbard when she experienced a mystical vision that shaped her remaining life. Through it she was transported into the near future where, after a period of intense pain, humanity

---

7. Merton, "The Wild Places," *The Merton Annual* 24 (2011), 18.

8. Compiled from Barbara Marx Hubbard, *The Hunger of Eve: A Woman's Odyssey toward the Future* (Harrisburg, PA: Stackpole Books, 1976); "Barbara Marx Hubbard, 89, Futurist Who Saw 'Conscious Evolution,' Dies," *New York Times*, May 15, 2019, https://www.nytimes.com/2019/05/15/obituaries/barbara-marx-hubbard-dead.html; *American Visionary: The Story of Barbara Marx Hubbard* (2018 documentary).

232 RE-VISIONING A FRAGMENTED WORLD

would emerge into a new era guided by love and awareness of oneness with all being. In her vision, she was called to nurture this impending "planetary birth experience" into reality. She established a publication to connect with others of like mind, and she distributed her first "Center Letter"[9] in August 1967 to more than a thousand people. This "Letter" ended in December 1968 after only eight issues. It had connected her with many but failed to inspire the convergence of consciousness she sought.

An important feature of her vision involved human entry into space. She saw that as "the natural organic step if man is to become operative in the universe, the outer expression of the inner state of cosmic consciousness" and the "effort to become a universal species."[10] Hubbard was disappointed that few agreed with her on the space program's evolutionary significance, but her vision to birth a new consciousness endured. "Conscious evolution," the idea that humanity embodies the process of evolution consciously choosing its path, remained a central feature of her quest. In addition to producing nine published books, Hubbard's sustained outreach during her remaining years included active engagement with numerous organizations and presentations in diverse venues.

Merton's Letters with Barbara Marx Hubbard

Thomas Merton was apparently not on Hubbard's initial "Center Letter" distribution list, since she failed to send him the first issue until late October 1967. With it she enclosed a personal letter saying that she had "deeply admired" his writing for "many years," especially his recent article, "The Self of Modern Man and the New Christian Consciousness."[11] She saw that essay as a "beautiful description of the result of our self-consciousness."[12] It described modern consciousness as one that prioritized "self-awareness as a thinking, observing, measuring and estimating" subject "over-against objects" to be manipulated for one's own interests. To Merton, this left modern people in a "solipsist bubble of awareness—an ego-self imprisoned in its own consciousness, isolated and out of touch with other selves in so

---

9. Initially published by the Center of American Living, established by Hubbard's colleague, Lady Malcolm Douglas-Hamilton; later published by the Hubbards' Deerfield Foundation. Barbara Marx Hubbard Correspondence, TMC/BU.

10. Hubbard, *Hunger of Eve*, 105, 107.

11. First published in *Newsletter-Review* 2 no. 1 (April 1967) of the R. M. Bucke Memorial Society. An abridged version appears as "The New Consciousness" in Merton, *Zen and the Birds of Appetite* (New York: New Directions, 1968), 15–32.

12. Barbara Marx Hubbard to Merton, October 26, 1967, TMC/BU.

far as they are all 'things' rather than persons."[13]

Hubbard described how she had lived and "almost died" in such a "bubble" of isolation but escaped by "finding a role within the whole body of Mankind" and the company of like-minded others, also "liberated-in-action." These "siblings" acted for the sake of all rather than self. They "loved," "knew," were "intimately connected," and "needed" each other to "fulfill their own aspiration." She rejected a pervasive "self-contempt" that blamed humanity for personal suffering, and she sought others "who in modern, secular society have become free of this egocentricity." Hubbard was then wrapping up her second "Letter," focused on an "Evolving Awareness" of a "Pattern in the Process" that surely reflected "what was once called God's will." That pattern needed broad discussion.[14]

Barbara Marx Hubbard, late 1960s (Courtesy of Suzanne Hubbard)

Merton's brief response nearly a month later thanked her but begged off directly addressing her thoughts, as he was "rather swamped with mail." Since a meaningful reply "cannot simply come from the top of one's head,"[15] he could not then do justice to her material but opted to forward three essays of possible interest: "Blessed Are the Meek: The Christian Roots of Non-Violence," "Day of a Stranger," and "The Sacred City," his just-completed essay on the Mayan city of Monte Albán. Hubbard replied promptly, enthusiastically, and "deeply moved," especially by "Day of a Stranger," which she found "'strange' and yet profoundly familiar." She saw Merton "headed for the eye of the hurricane which blows us all into a new age" and appreciated his "serenity-in-action." His "clear, pure and witty voice from amidst the thrilling winds of change" helped renew her contact with "the source of all this 'action.'" Hubbard anticipated reading his recent essay on Teilhard de Chardin,[16] whom she felt shared much with Merton while also

---

13. Merton, *Zen*, 22.

14. Hubbard to Merton, October 26, 1967, TMC/BU.

15. Merton to Hubbard, November 20, 1967, TMC/BU.

16. Merton, "Teilhard's Gamble: Betting on the Whole Human Species," *Commonweal* (October 27, 1967); also in Merton, *Love and Living*, 185–91.

differing, with greater emphasis than Merton on the "evolutionary process" to gain spiritual freedom. Hubbard enclosed her second "Center Letter," which explored "organic and cultural" evolutionary processes that had created humanity from within Earth and now sent it "forth into the universe to seek new life." She invited Merton to offer a religious perspective on that topic for her third "Center Letter."[17]

Merton indeed offered it after a month's delay "in the midst of the welter of Christmas." He enumerated four points on the matter. He first concurred that humanity stood at the threshold of a momentous decision about its fate, which we must make without fully knowing its consequences. Second, although humanity has always faced such choices, our modern decisions now determined not just the fate of individuals within a clan or nation but that of the whole species. For the first time humans could "commit the future to a certain quality of life—or no life at all."[18] Third, humanity must not forget lessons from the past about our still-present inclination to act destructively. We must make consciously "life-affirming and loving" choices that embrace:

> a few vital and by no means new imperatives: to refrain from the wanton taking of life, to avoid selfish greed and the exploitation of others for our own ends, to tell the truth (and that goes for governments and corporations as well as individuals), to respect the personal integrity of others even when they belong to groups that are alien to us, etc., etc.[19]

Merton's final point, "where the religious dimension enters in," involved a capacity for "radical self-criticism and openness and a profound ability to *trust* . . . in an inner dynamism of life itself, a basic creativity, a power of life." This required awareness that beneath our positive words may lie contradicting "destructive undertones we don't hear." Merton ended his letter with a caution to avoid "little tight systems and cliques, little coteries of gnostic experts," and he commended her for trying to bring together interdisciplinary voices, which reflected "one of our greatest needs: a real expansion of communication to its worldwide limits."[20] He did not, however, explicitly address human ventures beyond Earth.

---

17. Hubbard to Merton, November 28, 1967, TMC/BU.

18. Merton to Hubbard, December 23, 1967, *WF* 72–73.

19. Merton to Hubbard, December 23, 1967, *WF* 73.

20. Merton to Hubbard, December 23, 1967, *WF* 73. Emphasis in the original.

Hubbard published those comments in her third "Letter," but did not reach out to him again until mid-February 1968. She shared her interest, upon reading his piece on Teilhard, in Merton's mention of Teilhard's prediction that in 1957 the "Noosphere"—a new realm of evolved consciousness—would ensue. Hubbard connected this prediction with Russia's launch of its Sputnik satellite that year, marking the onset of human incursion beyond Earth's atmosphere. She cast this as an "evolutionary event" and "the moment when . . . we became *conscious* of ourselves as one body in space." She wondered how in its wake humans might understand themselves as the "culmination" of a vast cosmos beyond comprehension and then seek "relationship with the Creative Force" in this "thrilling and dangerous moment, like all births are."[21] In this, she probed more pointedly for Merton's views on space exploration.

Ecological Consciousness

This time, Merton responded immediately. His reply seeks to gently challenge some of her assumptions while retaining a sense of respect for and connection with her. This letter is especially helpful in highlighting how both his study of cargo cults, with their "millennial" aspirations, and his appreciation for Aldo Leopold's "ecological conscience" had come to frame his vision for the transformation that modern society desperately needed. It can also be read as something of a preamble to "The Wild Places," which he completed six days later. In this dialogue around Hubbard's quest for a "cosmic consciousness," he morphed Leopold's "ecological conscience" into an "ecological consciousness."

Merton opened with pleasantries, offering thanks for her third "Center Letter," requesting more copies, and—perhaps hoping to personally connect before suggesting an alternative reading of the times—commending her connection of Teilhard's "Noosphere" with Sputnik. But in comments she would ultimately find somewhat off-putting, he claimed ignorance in his ability to address the meaning of Hubbard's "birth into space" or join the celebration of "a space age mystique," given his sporadic access to popular media perused in doctor's waiting rooms. He suggested she might help him remedy that ignorance. Merton acknowledged that space exploration entailed a "sense of immense technical skill and virtuosity and the opening of fabulous new horizons." Though his intermittent scanning of magazines left "an impression of commercialism, hubris and cliché" that did not interest

---

21. Hubbard to Merton, February 12, 1968, TMC/BU. Emphasis in the original.

him, he nonetheless glimpsed "a sort of cosmic and ritual shamanic dance" that could intrigue him.[22]

From that demurral, Merton segued to expound upon an aspect he addressed with greater confidence: its implications for a "perhaps new and offbeat approach" to current ethical thought. He elaborated on "two broad kinds of ethical consciousness" that he detected currently at play. The first, a "*millennial* consciousness," reflected insights gleaned from the "Cargo Theology" notes he was then revising. He described this as a consciousness that viewed our human past as "at best provisional and preparatory" for a "new creation" about to happen. But in this view, reaching that new creation required both "acts which destroy and repudiate the past (metanoia, conversion, revolution etc.)" and "acts which open you up to the future." Echoing his anthropological conclusions, he saw this in "Marxism, in Black Power, in Cargo Cults, in Church aggiornamento [renewal], in Third World revolutionary movements, but also doubtless in movements within the establishment, management, science, etc."[23]

The emerging alternative he recognized was an "*ecological* consciousness," adapted from his concurrent reading of *Wilderness and the American Mind*. This consciousness instead emphasized: "We are not alone in this thing. We belong to a community of living things and we owe our fellow members in this community the respect and honor due to them. If we are to enter a new era, well and good, but let's bring the rest of the living along with us." It guides us to not seek renewal "by immolating our living earth, by careless and stupid exploitation for short term commercial, military, or technological ends which will be paid for by irreparable loss in living species and natural resources." Anticipating his review of Nash's book (though not mentioning it), Merton shared its quote of Albert Schweitzer on the sacredness of life and cited Leopold's "ecological conscience" principle.[24]

With this foundation, Merton closed his reflection by returning to Hubbard's musings about human entry into space. That venture was of itself "neutral," he postulated, "*outside* the natural ecological environment." Though it was as yet inherently neither millennial nor ecological, he advised that it should proceed with a "deepening of the ecological sense," and "restraint and wisdom in the way we treat the earth we live on and the other members of the ecological community with which we live." In doing so we

---

22. Merton to Hubbard, February 16, 1968, *WF* 73–74.
23. Merton to Hubbard, February 16, 1968, *WF* 74.
24. Merton to Hubbard, February 16, 1968, *WF* 74.

might "avoid a shallow millenarianism as we enter the space age, and retain a solid ecological consciousness." He closed with irony-tinged wit to suggest they might distribute buttons that advocated (in homage to countercultural imagery) that we "Put Flower Power into Space."[25] This February 1968 letter provides a concise summary of where Merton then stood in relation to conclusions drawn from recent months of reading and reflection on human experience and its relation to the natural world.

In the final letter of their exchange, Hubbard responded respectfully though not enthusiastically or in depth. She thanked Merton for his "most interesting letter," excerpted in her fourth "Center Letter." Intrigued by his "evolutionary-ecological synthesis which would recognize the fact of newness as well as continuity," she at least concurred that a focus on "responsibility of the whole of body of earth" would yield a "wholesome and good" future. Playing off his lead with equally ironic humor, she closed by predicting his Flower Power slogan would "surely spread like dandelions!"[26] Eight years later, however, her 1976 autobiography more clearly expressed her ultimate disappointment in his response, paraphrasing the essence of what she had heard as: "Frankly, Mrs. Hubbard, I never think about the space program except occasionally when I pick up a magazine in the dentist's office. I don't think it has any relationship to religious development."[27]

Merton's letters to both Rachel Carson and Barbara Hubbard were written in response to specific people regarding specific questions in specific contexts—one in response to *Silent Spring* and the other in response to visionary cultural optimism in the midst of his cargo cult reflections and reading of *Wilderness and the American Mind* (and having just engaged Walter Weisskopf's compatible reflections, reviewed next). But comparing these responses suggests how his thoughts on human/nature relationships had developed. Both his final letter to Hubbard and the one to Carson share his awareness of the need to consider all forms of life in our decisions. But although *Silent Spring* is not a religious book, he framed his letter to Carson more theologically than the one to Hubbard, despite Hubbard's previous request for his religious perspective. Also, his letter to Carson framed humanity as more of a hybrid between nature and the "invisible" divine—something significantly above the rest of nature though still a part of it—whereas his letter to Hubbard expressed a greater sense of humanity in partnership with

---

25. Merton to Hubbard, February 16, 1968, *WF* 74–75.
26. Hubbard to Merton, February 18, 1968, TMC/BU.
27. Hubbard, *Hunger of Eve*, 104.

other elements of nature. In fact, this latter aspect also contrasts with his letter to Hubbard three months earlier. That "religious dimension" of "the relationship between Man and the processes of organic and cultural evolution"[28] failed to mention nature or ecology as in his final letter. Together these responses suggest that Nash's book, in tandem with Merton's anthropological studies (and perhaps his reading of Weisskopf), seem to have nudged Merton to more clearly recognize our partnership within an "ecological community" than in his earlier emphasis to Carson on humans as an "eye in the body" to watch over that community.

Existential Balance:
The Merton-Weisskopf Letters

Like Merton's exchanges with Barbara Hubbard, our final set of letters revolves around a periodical to foster interdisciplinary dialogue. In mid-December 1967, Merton was invited to participate in recurring informal exchanges within the pages of the *Forum for Correspondence and Contact*, published by the International Center for Integrative Studies (ICIS). When Merton received his first *Forum* issue in early January, he was struck by economist Walter A. Weisskopf's "letter" within it. Merton's January 1968 response to Weisskopf (reproduced below) offers an especially remarkable synthesis of his conclusions about anthropology and the relationship of humanity and its technology to nature. The personal letters he and Weisskopf exchanged in March and April, together with their January and March *Forum* contributions, model Merton's ideal of meaningful communication and dialogue. Through them, he articulated a concise and sagacious summary of his vision for human life on Earth and the role of contemplative engagement in modern times.

Merton and ICIS

Merton received his invitation to *Forum* participation from Erling Thunberg, the Swedish-born educator who founded ICIS[29] in 1962. Thunberg described the new periodical as a venue for "dialogue—or rather multilogue —on human levels among innovative thinkers and humanistically oriented persons" about "contemporary issues and problems and the fu-

---

28. Hubbard to Merton, November 28, 1967, TMC/BU.

29. ICIS disbanded in 2014; its successor organization, Rivertides, originated as an ICIS project.

ture of man." The ICIS letter-head listed a Board of Sponsors that included thirty-one individuals from thirteen countries —half from the United States— with disciplines spanning the humanities and social sciences. The list included Merton's correspondents Amiya Chakraverty and Rollo May and well-known personalities Viktor Frankl and Abraham Maslow.[30] As noted at this chapter's outset, Merton's acceptance, sent just days later, offers a helpful window into how he defined his focus and framed his place in this mix of scholars. He asked not to be listed "simply as a theologian or something professionally religious," but for this audience he named his profession as "author and poet," though his "off beat explorations in the neighborhood of philosophy might be most relevant."[31]

Walter A. Weisskopf, ca. 1971
(Courtesy of Roosevelt University Archives)

Merton's copy of the initial *Forum* arrived the first week in January 1968, and he submitted his response a week later. He remarked that although he could not then provide an article, he actually found "this kind of informal exchange" to be "rather more fruitful."[32] Though he never submitted a full article, he continued to read the periodical. In August he submitted two more comments on *Forum* material, and he discussed meeting with Erling Thunberg after returning from his Asian journey.[33] In his only letter sent directly to Weisskopf, Merton also vetted his idea to edit an anthology of essays by men with Weisskopf's "scientific training" and concern for "restoration of balance." He asked Weisskopf to give thought to the idea and consider potential contributors, noting that "It could be very important, and this is the time

30. Erling A. Thunberg to Merton, December 15, 1967, TMC/BU.

31. Merton to Erling A. Thunberg, December 24, 1967, TMC/BU.

32. Merton to Donald F. Keyes, January 19, 1968, TMC/BU.

33. Irene Seeland [Erling Thunberg's widow], email to Gordon Oyer, June 26, 2020; Laraine Mai [past ICIS president], email to Gordon Oyer, June 25, 2020.

for it."[34] In light of our emerging climate crisis, Merton's anthology could have provided a truly prophetic voice had he returned from Asia to pursue it.

Merton's Exchanges with Walter Weisskopf

Walter A. Weisskopf (1904–1991) was born in Austria, received his PhD from the University of Vienna, and worked as a lawyer and labor relations advisor in that city. He escaped after the 1938 Nazi annexation of Austria and immigrated to the United States in 1939. Weisskopf then spent a few years teaching economics in temporary university roles and consulted in labor relations during the latter years of World War II. In 1945 he became a founding faculty member and Department of Economics chair at Chicago's newly established Roosevelt College (later University). He retired from there in 1974 and held "visiting" status at Stanford University between 1977 and 1979. Though economics became his primary discipline, he also published on psychology and social philosophy. Weisskopf synthesized concepts from all three disciplines in his two books, *The Psychology of Economics and Alienation* and *Economics*.[35]

Forum *Exchanges*

Weisskopf's initial *Forum* contribution, published under the heading "Existential Balance and Evolution," excerpted his musings in a letter originally sent to his brother, Victor Weisskopf, then chair of the Physics Department at MIT. Weisskopf's fascinating letter echoes certain aspects of Barbara Marx Hubbard's vision: his deep concern for humanity's future; insistence that evolution operates in "human culture, society, and history... as much as in nature"; and faith that humans, through "consciousness and awareness," can discern and adapt for our "survival" and "well-being." But he departed from Hubbard in his dedication to a human future that survived on Earth rather than extended into the universe. Also unlike Hubbard, he viewed a modern overemphasis on technology and business[36] as highly problematic, not birth pains of a positive new evolutionary stage. He linked those trends with overpopulation as key forces that "are interfering with the ecological

---

34. Merton to Weisskopf, April 4, 1968, *WF* 336, 338.

35. Walter A. Weisskopf, *The Psychology of Economics* (Chicago: University of Chicago Press, 1955), and *Alienation and Economics* (New York: Dutton, 1971).

36. These included: "our efforts in space, our splitting of the atom, our poisoning of the atmosphere with radiation...[and] with smog, smoke and other chemicals, etc." Walter A. Weisskopf, "Existential Balance and Evolution," *Forum for Correspondence and Contact* 1, no. 1 (January 1968): 53.

balance of man and environment" and require conscious human mitigation. Failure in this would "'force' nature and history to restore [balance] by catastrophic methods"—the "destruction of the imbalancing forces through atomic war." That self-correction would not only destroy a large swath of humanity, but also "most of our business and technological civilization."[37] Today we would add the re-balancing force of catastrophic climate crisis to his warning.

Rather than "fatalistically accept" this outcome, Weisskopf advocated countering those trends with our conscious choice to "turn towards the inner world" of "contemplation," to grow more "receptive to inner voices, to beauty in nature and art." He sought a restored rhythmic balance "between activity and rest, between doing and being, . . . between activity and receptivity" to earlier agrarian rhythms, also accessible in nonagricultural work. "Today, everything that happens in the world is influenced by Western ideas and institutions" and needs to be counterbalanced by "a more worshiping attitude towards nature and recognizing our limitations. It is the original sin of natural science and technology that it has generated a Promethean spirit of hybris [*sic*] in us: we believe that we can interfere with nature without any limits." To divert nature's catastrophic remedy, Weisskopf looked to "knowledge, wisdom, insight, and wise planning. Planning, however, is not only a matter of political and administrative measures; it requires foremost a change in spirit and attitudes; and this requires a change in outlook and in the way we see things."[38]

Merton's *Forum* "Comment" (reproduced below) in response to this letter commended Weisskopf's pursuit of "'wisdom' embracing all ends and means," rather than a narrow technical focus on specific ends that other *Forum* contributors emphasized. He cautioned against "solipsistic" educational goals to form "self-sufficient" and "coldly rational" beings.[39] Merton instead sought to nurture self-awareness of our personal gifts and limitations with interdependent reliance on the complementary abilities of others. In this, he again drew from his anthropological reflections:

> The study of primitive man shows that this sense of fellowship and reciprocity extended to all nature and all other beings. Man was whole in so far as he recognized not only what he was in himself as individual, as member of clan and tribe, but also what he owed others and what he owed the rest of natural creation. In the highly

---

37. Weisskopf, "Existential Balance," 51–53.
38. Weisskopf, "Existential Balance," 52–54.
39. Merton, "Comment," 11–12.

complex and sophisticated world view of totemism (see Lévi-Strauss) he developed an all-embracing "wisdom" in which every-thing could be maintained in a vital (basically ecological) balance.[40]

Merton contrasted this nature-based self-awareness with modern re-liance on technology and organizational structures that "master" nature and alienate us from it. He drew support from an unlikely source: Dietrich Bon-hoeffer, who observed that "our immediate environment is not nature as for-merly but organization," within which "[t]he spiritual power (by which we once coped with nature) is now lacking." This suggested to Merton that if humanity "replaces an immediate integration in nature with a technological organization that destroys this ecological balance and immediacy, [humans] can no longer be fully whole and fully [themselves]."[41]

Regarding solutions, it seemed unlikely that "letting the technological organization blow itself up" would ever restore human balance through a re-turn to pre-modern lifeways. Merton also questioned the value of trying to "program the right ideas and directives into the organization" and force the "unbalanced organization to balance itself." Our task instead requires us "go deep into the very structure of organization itself, i.e., the very nature of our 'civilized' existence." We might then consciously begin to "use our organiza-tion and technology to re-harmonize the natural and the human, to restore and maintain an ecological balance.... 'Wisdom' and 'wholeness' demand that [we] sanely integrate [our] technics into their natural environment in-stead of using [them] to ravage and exploit nature without regard for the fu-ture." Technology must foster "communion with the natural world" not isola-tion from it. Merton closed by noting that his comments, written in his wooded and isolated Kentucky setting, "emanate from a concrete experiment in living as a non-organization man."[42]

Weisskopf's Personal Response

Weisskopf did not wait to respond in the next *Forum*. He promptly whisked off a two-page letter directly to Merton that showed the monk's response had connected with and moved him. He thanked Merton "from the bottom of my heart" for sharing his views, which came "closest to what I was trying to say, and you say it better than I did," and he seemed to sense in Merton's "Com-ment" a source of insight that could benefit his own personal searching be-

---

40. Merton, "Comment," 12.

41. Merton, "Comment," 12.

42. Merton, "Comment," 12–13.

yond academic inquiry. He affirmed Merton's view that we must seek to counterbalance the lopsided forces of modern hyper-activism with more "receptive" and "contemplative" approaches to life.[43]

Weisskopf also endorsed Merton's skepticism that we might tweak modern organizational trends to help them self-balance. He resisted optimistic views of "Utopian technologists" who presumed that once "our enormous productive machine capacity" was fully realized to meet our material needs, a society "imbued with the spirit of love, beauty, tenderness, gentleness" would emerge. He suspected the very process of seeking that end through a technological path would destroy our very capacity for later contemplative engagement with the world. In the current battle between forces of love and organizational control, the latter was winning. Given this, the pessimistic alternative pointed toward destruction of our hyperactive culture so "the forces of contemplation, receptivity and love can be victorious." But this created a personal dilemma: "Being in the world of organization and technology makes it impossible to develop those faculties which are necessary for the new holistic and contemplative society." Perhaps the only moral choice in the modern world then became one of "withdrawal" like Merton's "non-organization man," and possibly "the Hippies" as well. Though Merton may not have time to respond, he would be "deeply grateful of any reaction."[44]

Weisskopf also enclosed some of his recent journal articles for Merton to consider, and one of them, "Repression and the Dialectics of Industrial Civilization," "forcibly" struck Merton enough to inspire his vision for the proposed anthology mentioned earlier. Merton's copy of this offprint survives in his archival collection, filled with his underlinings and markings. It offers a more academically sophisticated version of Weisskopf's original *Forum* letter, framed around themes of our psychologically repressed inner, contemplative human needs. As a result, "[t]he psyche re-appeared in a distorted form; the explosion of irrational forces in technology, in the economy, and in politics." Weisskopf insisted that human "religious experience is also part of nature," and he rejected separation between humans and the natural world: "The distinction between an exclusively human world quite different from the rest of the universe appears as a mixture of sick arrogance and alienated despair."[45]

---

43. Walter A. Weisskopf to Merton, March 19, 1968, TMC/BU.

44. Walter A. Weisskopf to Merton, March 19, 1968, TMC/BU.

45. Walter A. Weisskopf, "Repression and the Dialectics of Industrial Civilization," *Review of Social Economy* 23, no. 22 (September 1965): 119, 123; quotes are among many that Merton underlined/highlighted.

Existential Balance: In Harmony with Life

As he had with Barbara Marx Hubbard, Merton responded to Weisskopf's request for insight with warmth and substance. Before addressing Weiss-kopf's quest for moral integrity amid modern complexities, Merton elaborated on what motivated his vision for the anthology Weisskopf's article had inspired. Although current religious and Catholic trends appropriately looked to secular life for perspective and meaningful engagement, Merton felt that in doing this Catholicism tended to overcompensate for its stagnant contemplative practices. It did this through an "exaggerated emphasis precisely on the technological, the sociological, the economic, and a very aggressive, almost bitter repudiation of the 'interior,' the contemplative dimensions of existence." His Church needed the voice of those "like yourself with *scientific* training" who stated the "urgent need for a restoration of balance ... [and] recovery of man's self as part of nature and as a contemplative as well as active being." These voices might convince the Church better than trained churchmen "that we are repressing a most vital element in our lives in order to promote a meaningless economic development, and [that] in the end this may prove suicidal."[46]

Merton then turned to the question Weisskopf had raised about whether "withdrawal" to hasten the collapse of a hyper-organized society offered our choice of greatest integrity. His reply navigated between Barbara Hubbard's unbridled optimism regarding modern human society and Weisskopf's temptation to view it with hopeless pessimism. He first commended Weisskopf as "remarkably perceptive" in rejecting the assumption that technological progress would culminate in contemplative utopia. He also agreed that our current dilemma begged for some sort of dialectical resolution between the competing forces of technology and love. But he did not feel that only destruction of the former could permit the latter to emerge—though others presumed he felt this way. Rather than either optimistic embrace of technological proliferation or pessimistic pursuit of its destruction, Merton described his outlook as "basically *eschatological*" in a "fully Christian sense." In this he did not refer to the world's impending end but to a "decisive and critical breakthrough in man's destiny" as envisioned in the New Testament. But we cannot anticipate what form that will take, let alone plan for it. To pursue it, we must instead embrace things as they are—whether "with us or without us,

---

46. Merton to Weisskopf, April 4, 1968, *WF* 336–37. Emphasis in the original.

in us and beyond us"—rather than simply repudiate what we dislike.[47] Merton continued:

> My "eschatology" says that underlying all of it, in the deepest depths that we cannot possibly see, lies an ultimate ground in which all contradictories are united and all come out "right."...[T]his ultimate ground is personal..., a ground of freedom and love, not a simple mechanism or process. But since we are all in potentially *conscious* contact with this deep ground (which of course exceeds all conscious *grasp*) we must try to "listen" to what comes out of it and respond to the imperatives of its freedom. In doing so, we may not be able to direct the course of history according to some preconceived plan, but we will be in harmony with the dynamics of life and history even though we may not fully realize that we are so. The important thing then is to restore this dimension of existence.[48]

As for his own life choice, it was simply that—a personal choice, not a "program" he recommended for all.

This exchange with Walter Weisskopf nicely brings together Merton's views on the primacy of balanced human integration with nature and the role of contemplation in pursuing it. As Merton would tell his fellow monks later in the summer of that year, "Contemplation does not mean prescinding from present material reality for some other reality. There is only one reality....It means *penetrating* the only reality we've got."[49] Our capacity to penetrate and connect with this reality, this "ultimate ground"—and to live out the implications of that connection in relation to others—provided Merton's foundation for us to seek a social transformation that permits our species' survival. It grounds the formation of an ecological consciousness with which to engage our world—a task even more urgent now than in 1968.

---

47. Merton to Weisskopf, April 4. 1968, *WF* 337. Emphasis in the original.

48. Merton to Weisskopf, April 4, 1968, *WF* 338.

49. Merton, "Aesthetic and Contemplative Experience—James Joyce," recording at the Abbey of Gethsemani, summer 1968, transcribed by Paul Pearson, *The Merton Annual* 27 (2015): 41.

Published here for a general audience for the first time, the following document[50] *provides a unique summary of Merton's developed thought on the relationship of humans and their technology to nature. Though not a personal letter, it offers Merton's response to Walter A. Weisskopf's letter in* Forum for Correspondence and Contact. *He wrote it sometime between January 6 and 19, 1968.*

"Comment on Charlotte Buhler, Tom Stonier, Walter A. Weisskopf"

This is an entirely spontaneous reaction to the first three items I have read in the *Forum*. First "Charlotte Buhler on "The Role of Psychotherapy," then, Tom Stonier on "Education for Peace," finally, Walter Weisskopf's stimulating letter on "Existential Balance and Evolution." These three clicked in nicely with some of my own current preoccupations.

They all point in one way or other to the need for educating and forming the whole man. As novice master for ten years in a Trappist monastery I saw more and more the crucial importance of this. (I don't claim to have succeeded in doing much about it!) Buhler advances bringing a new dimension of psychiatric insight into education: systematically training people in deeper levels of interpersonal awareness. Stonier wants to see a more explicit orientation toward the solution of the problem of war, in all educational disciplines. Weisskopf shows how we need to restore the balance between an activistic philosophy of production and a more contemplative nonproductive kind of creativity which lets things happen naturally. He does not spell this all out fully (it is only a letter to someone who knows how to fill in the gaps) but there are lots of important intuitions there.

Here is my own reaction to these three.

I am nearest to the standpoint of Weisskopf who sees the whole area in the broadest perspective—that of "wisdom" embracing all ends and means (rather than the particular means to particular ends sighted in the other two pieces).

Dietrich Bonhoeffer said: "It is with what we are in ourselves and what we owe to others that we are a complete whole." Education of the whole man means, therefore, not the formation of a tight, self-enclosed, self-sufficient and perfectly solipsistic unit, a coldly rational subject able to fight his way alone through the technical jungle and come out (where?) more or less unscathed. It means educating a man to value and appreciate his own capacities as they really are, to honor what others have that he does not have: to know his own limits and accept them gladly in the confidence that others will supply what he lacks since he is ready to give them what is his.

---

50. Merton, "Comment," 11–13.

Now the study of primitive man shows that this sense of fellowship and reciprocity extended to all nature and all other beings. Man was whole in so far as he recognized not only what he was in himself as an individual, as a member of clan and tribe, but also what he owed others and what he owed the rest of natural creation. In the highly complex and sophisticated world view of totemism (see Lévi-Strauss) he developed an all-embracing "wisdom" in which everything could be maintained in a vital (basically ecological) balance. (Even though the relationships themselves were spelled out in terms of fantasy and myths.)

Now, with the development of an extremely complex and highly organized technological civilization, we have so completely "mastered" nature that, in fact, we no longer live in direct contact with it. We have replaced nature by technics and organization. Bonhoeffer says of this situation: "Our immediate environment is not nature as formerly but organization. But this bulwark against the threat of nature produced a new danger, viz.—the very organization. The spiritual power (by which we once coped with nature) is now lacking. The question is: what protection is there against the danger of organization? Man is once more faced with the problem of himself. He has coped with everything, excepting only himself. He can safeguard himself from everything excepting only from man. In the last resort it all turns upon man."

Reflecting on the two quotations from Bonhoeffer I would remark: the problem seems to be this. Man is whole in his ecological interrelation with nature. If he replaces an immediate integration in nature with a technological organization that destroys this ecological balance and immediacy, he can no longer be fully whole and fully himself. Enclosed within his own organizational machinery (extension of himself and of his organs and faculties) he is a solipsist and faces his own desperation as such. This solipsism of encapsulated man can eventually lead to self-destruction (as we are aware in the atomic era). Weisskopf remarks shrewdly that "nature" might break open the capsule by letting the technical organization blow itself up, while the "primitive" will restore the natural balance. . . . [Merton's ellipses] I am not so sure of this scenario. It might just happen that the technologically advanced people might use their technology to ravage and destroy the last remaining primitive and natural societies (Vietnam is a portent of this!).

Here is the problem as I see it.

Buhler and Stonier both assume that what we need to do is to program the right ideas and directives into the organization (specifically into organized education). But I wonder if this assumption is too facile. Is there a deeper and more critical problem in the organization itself? If the organization is basically inhuman, does it not have to be humanized first, before we can work with it to solve our deepest human needs? If so, what does this involve? Where do we begin? Can we use the unbalanced organization to balance itself? (This is the problem Weisskopf faces.) What is our own relation to the organization? Is it a "thing" or a "system" objectively existing and working entirely apart from us? Or is it our own selves extended with all our neuroses and our pathology, so that it surrounds us with our own self-defeating, self-deceiving impulses, and imprisons us most firmly when we imagine we are set free? I honestly think that our investigations have to go deep into the very nature of organization itself, i.e., the very nature of our "civilized" existence.

Obviously we cannot put the machine in reverse and go back to nature (unless, as Weisskopf suggests, the bomb simply wipes out the organized technical world and leaves the rest to the primitives). What matters is to use our organization and technology to re-harmonize the natural and the human, to restore and maintain an ecological balance appropriate to our new condition (after the ecological chaos of the last hundred years!). In other words, "wisdom" and "wholeness" demand that man sanely integrate his technics into their natural environment instead of using his technology to ravage and exploit nature without regard for the future. Technics must become a creative bond and source of communion with the natural world rather than a means to isolate man from nature so that he can play havoc with it according to his individual or collective whims (some of which may well be pathological). Technics must bring us back into a vital relationship with the natural world which will restore our sanity, instead of being used by us to designate the natural world with the projections of our own pathology.

I do not know how strange these reflections may sound. Perhaps I might explain that they are being written about five a.m. on a zero winter morning in a hermitage in the Kentucky woods, in which the writer enjoys the technological benefits of gas heat and electric light (but not much else) together with the more primitive blessings of solitude, silence, and the sight of the friendly constellations (stars, not planes) and the sound of the wind in the pines. In other words, for better or for worse, these remarks emanate from a concrete experiment in living as a non-organization man.

POSTSCRIPT

This book was conceived and written in the comfort of a quaint, century-old sublet just inside the Old Louisville neighborhood of Kentucky's largest city. As I walked the area, ghosts of voices for social transformation hovered. A half block away stands the gym in which an adolescent Cassius Clay, later Muhammad Ali, first donned boxing gloves. Five blocks farther, the street that now bears Ali's name, originally "Walnut Street," intersects with Fourth Street—a juncture also named Thomas Merton Square to commemorate his famed 1958 epiphany at that site. Nearly a century earlier, in the wake of Civil War social unrest, newly freed slaves initially settled in the adjoining neighborhood to the east, named Smoketown for the wood-burning brickyard kilns originally sited there. Kentucky's first Black public high school and its first historically Black college were established in the Limerick neighborhood that adjoins to the west, named for the Irish railroad laborers who founded it. I could scarcely have asked for a more inspirational setting in which to work on this particular book.

But the effort that began in this pleasant setting took on new poignancy as I drafted its final chapters. Earlier in the process, when a friend suggested the word "precarious" to describe the era that spans Merton's time and our own, I wondered if that word might be hyperbolic. But as the draft neared completion in the spring and summer of 2020, it seemed almost tame. This was a season of global pandemic, sustained protest over police killings of unarmed Blacks (including Louisvillian Breonna Taylor), extreme wildfires and hurricanes, and intensified polarization from election year onslaughts by chaotic incumbents clinging to power. During these months, each of the book's three parts assumed fresh urgency.

Merton's exchanges with Jim Forest and Dan Berrigan in Part 1 increasingly spoke timely wisdom, as images of frustrated protest played across media screens, the sounds of sirens and surveillance helicopters echoed through Louisville's late night skies, and increasingly authoritarian edicts emanated from federal leadership. Merton's personalist emphasis on movements that pursue refinement of conscience and invitation into spaces of connection through a shared "Ground of Love" seemed terribly urgent. So did Berrigan's drive to openly resist the work of a civic conscience that seemed either undeveloped or grounded in fear-driven self-interest. Was this a moment when Merton's caution against provocative action gave way to confrontation that, he hedged, at times becomes necessary?

On the one hand, widespread protest in the wake of those killings prompted immediate commitments to reform by public officials and commercial sponsors alike. On the other hand, they intensified rationalization for oppressive "law and order" and strengthened the faith of many in authoritarian control. These days begged for a balance of both priorities— person-centered appeals to refinement of conscience and open resistance to manifestations of fear and hate. Both, after all, meld conscience and resistance —just with different focal points. Perhaps the key to that balance lies with advocates for one refraining from making their posture absolute, from turning it into a "program," as Merton would say, that compels others to uncritically adopt their particular practice.

Directly related to those questions, the searing images of George Floyd's life evaporating under a white knee insultated within a police uniform—reinforced by similar images from elsewhere and the race-baiting of civic leaders— blatantly exposed how topics Merton explored with Black correspondents in Part 2 remain unresolved. Vincent Harding's "scandal of whiteness" remains scandalous. Marlon Green's hard work for employment justice, August Thompson's relentless truth-telling in word and deed, and Robert Williams's collaborative vulnerability with Merton all remain crucial models to consider.

Finally, scanning COVID-19 rates under "lockdown" and viewing western landscapes in flames added exclamation points to the reflections in Part 3 on the environmental consequences of our modern hubris. As science writer David Quammen explains, once humans shifted from a low-impact environmental presence into a ubiquitous force of ecosystem disruption, we began to "shake loose" viruses that mutate from their original hosts into ourselves. Our destruction of habitats enables them to "seize a huge opportunity" with their new host to "ride on airplanes [and] get around the world in twenty-four hours."[1] Quammen attributes modern zoonotic pandemics to our industrialized, overpopulated quest for planetary dominance—the same behavior that has induced climate crisis and its many consequences. Quammen's cautions

---

1. "Shaking the Viral Tree: An Interview with David Quammen," *Emergence*, posted March 26, 2020, https://emergencemagazine.org/story/shaking-the-viral-tree/.

echo the unheeded, decades-old prescience of Walter Weisskopf, with his warnings about overpopulation and the destruction of nature, and of Thomas Merton, with his call for an ecological consciousness.

Merton further observed how our narrow economic priorities simultaneously impair peace, cross-racial connection, and ecological balance. Coupled with disdain for the collective myths and illusions that misdirect us, Merton often voiced concern—marbled throughout all three parts—over our preoccupation with affluence, individual wealth, and maximized profits at the expense of persons. Now our gaps in wealth and wages dwarf those of his era. Merton and Weisskopf alerted us fifty years ago of our need for "balance" to restore the world we have fragmented. Such warnings came not only from them, but also from others like the Club of Rome, whose 1972 "Limits to Growth" models predicted climate changes that remain squarely on target today.[2] We have known what we are doing to ourselves for decades, yet we still mostly bluster along in collective denial. Perhaps we need Merton's voice here regarding these modern cultural dynamics, most of all.

Regardless of who succeeded in 2020's U.S. elections or when a COVID-19 vaccine became available, this book will be read in the midst of times that may appropriately be described as "precarious." As the introduction notes, threads of continuity firmly connect Merton's times with ours and render many of his reflections relevant for our pilgrimage into coming decades. Throughout those decades, these letters of Thomas Merton on social transformation will continue to embody signs of hope for us to draw upon. They do not signal a hope that passively reclines in anticipation that some transcendent force, whether of God or technological wizardry, will swoop in to salvage or alter our destructive habits for us. Rather, they invoke a hope that our ongoing active responses, grounded in the dictates of a well-formed conscience and respect for shared human personhood and ecological balance, may coalesce in unforeseen ways to transform humanity's global presence: a social transformation that mutually sustains and values human beings of all shades together within our interdependent habitat of Earth.

Gordon Oyer
September 2020

---

2. Asher Moses, "'Collapse of Civilisation Is the Most Likely Outcome': Top Climate Scientists," *Voice of Action*, posted June 5, 2020, https://voiceofaction.org/collapse-of-civilisation-is-the-most-likely-outcome-top-climate-scientists/.

BIBLIOGRAPHY

"Alexander Peloquin." *Liturgical Pioneers: Pastoral Musicians and Liturgists*. http://liturgicalleaders.blogspot.com/2008/09/alexander-peloquin.html.

Apel, William. "Out of Solitude: Thomas Merton, John Howard Griffin, and Racial Justice." *The Merton Seasonal* 36, no. 3 (Fall 2011): 17–22.

———. *Signs of Peace: The Interfaith Letters of Thomas Merton*. Maryknoll, NY: Orbis Books, 2006.

Asbury, Edith Evans. "David Miller and the Catholic Workers: A Study in Pacifism." *New York Times*, October 24, 1965, 76.

"Father August Thompson." *Avoyelles Today* online. August 12, 2019. https://www.avoyellestoday.com/obituaries/father-august-louis-thompson.

Berrigan, Daniel. *Essential Writings*. Edited by John Dear. Maryknoll, NY: Orbis Books, 2009.

———. "The Monk." Chapter 1 in *Portraits of Those I Love*. New York: Crossroad, 1982.

———. "The Peacemaker." In *Thomas Merton/Monk: A Monastic Tribute*, edited by Br. Patrick Hart, enlarged edition, 219–27. Kalamazoo, MI: Cistercian Publications, 1983.

———. "Thomas Merton, Nonviolence, and Me: A Conversation with Thomas Merton," interview by Terry Taylor, April 16, 2004. *The Merton Seasonal* 41, no. 3 (Fall 2016), 6–17.

———. *To Dwell in Peace: An Autobiography*. San Francisco: Harper and Row, 1987.

Berrigan, Daniel, and Philip Berrigan. *The Berrigan Letters: Personal Correspondence between Daniel and Philip Berrigan*. Edited by Daniel Cosacchi and Eric Martin. Maryknoll, NY: Orbis Books, 2016.

Bonazzi, Robert. *Man in the Mirror: John Howard Griffin and the Story of "Black Like Me."* Maryknoll, NY: Orbis Books, 1997.

Boston Pilot. "Boston Clergy, Laymen Join Selma Protest." March 13, 1965.

Catholic Online. "Final Perseverance." https://www.catholic.org/encyclopedia/view.php?id=4677.

Clarke, John Henrik, ed. *William Styron's Nat Turner: Ten Black Writers Respond.* Boston: Beacon Press, 1968.

Collins, John P. "Thomas Merton and the PAX Peace Prize." *Merton Seasonal* 33, no. 1 (Spring 2008): 3–14.

Corbman, Marjorie. "'Welcome Brother Merton': The Challenge of the Black Power Movement to Thomas Merton's Thought on Non-Violence." Paper presented at the 16th General Meeting of the International Thomas Merton Society, Santa Clara, CA, June 29, 2019.

Daggy, Robert E. "Thomas Merton's Critique of Language." *The Merton Seasonal* 21, no. 1 (Spring 2002): 11–15.

Davis, Cyprian, OSB. *The History of Black Catholics in the United States.* New York: Crossroad, 1990.

Day, Dorothy. *All the Way to Heaven: The Selected Letters of Dorothy Day.* Edited by Robert Ellsberg. Maryknoll, NY: Orbis Books, 2012.

———. *The Duty of Delight: The Diaries of Dorothy Day.* Edited by Robert Ellsberg. Maryknoll, NY: Orbis Books, 2008.

———. "On Pilgrimage." *The Catholic Worker* 27, no. 10 (December 1961): 2.

———. "Thomas Merton, Trappist, 1915–1968." *The Catholic Worker* 34, no. 10 (December 1968): 1, 6.

Dear, John. "The Life and Death of Daniel Berrigan." *Waging Nonviolence*, May 2, 2016. https://wagingnonviolence.org/2016/05/the-life-and-death-of-daniel-berrigan/.

Dekar, Paul R. "God's Messenger: Thomas Merton on Racial Justice." *The Merton Annual* 32 (2020): 137–54.

———. *Thomas Merton: Twentieth-Century Wisdom for Twenty-First-Century Living.* Eugene, OR: Cascade, 2011.

Dorothy Day Papers. Special Collection and Archives. Marquette University, Milwaukee, WI.

Douglass, Jim. "Acts of Resistance and Works of Mercy: *Street Spirit* Interview with Jim Douglass, Part 2." *Street Spirit* 21, no. 7 (July 2015): 10–14.

———. "Confronting the 'Auschwitz of Puget Sound': *Street Spirit* Interview with Jim Douglass." *Street Spirit* 21, no. 6 (June 2015): 7–10, 12.

————. Foreword to *Cold War Letters*, by Thomas Merton, x–xvii. Edited by Christine M. Bochen and William H. Shannon. Maryknoll, NY: Orbis Books, 2006.

————. *Gandhi and the Unspeakable: His Final Experiment with Truth.* Maryknoll, NY: Orbis Books, 2012.

————. *JFK and the Unspeakable: Why He Died and Why It Matters.* Maryknoll, NY: Orbis Books, 2006. Reprint, New York: Touchstone Books, 2010.

————. *Lightning East to West: Jesus, Gandhi, and the Nuclear Age.* New York: The Crossroads Publishing Co., 1983.

————. *The Nonviolent Coming of God.* Maryknoll, NY: Orbis Books, 1992.

————. *The Non-Violent Cross: A Theology of Revolution and Peace.* New York: Macmillan Publishing Co., 1968.

————. *Resistance and Contemplation: The Way of Liberation.* New York: Dell Publishing Co., 1972.

Elie, Paul. *The Life You Save May Be Your Own.* New York: Farrar, Straus and Giroux, 2003.

Ellul, Jacques. *The Technological Society.* New York: Knopf, 1964.

Everett, Karen, director. *American Visionary: The Story of Barbara Marx Hubbard.* 2018 documentary distributed on Amazon.com.

"Father August Thompson." *Avoyelles Today* online. August 12, 2019. https://www.avoyellestoday.com/obituaries/father-august-louis-thompson.

Fikes, Robert. "Marlon Dewitt Green." *Blackpast.* September 24, 2017. https://www.blackpast.org/african-american-history/green-marlon-dewitt-1929-2009/.

Forest, Jim. *All Is Grace: A Biography of Dorothy Day.* Maryknoll, NY: Orbis Books, 2011.

————. *At Play in the Lions' Den: A Biography and Memoir of Daniel Berrigan.* Maryknoll, NY: Orbis Books, 2017.

————. *Living with Wisdom: A Life of Thomas Merton.* Maryknoll, NY: Orbis Books, 2008.

————. "Meeting Thomas Merton." Posted February 2, 2011. http://jimand-nancyforest.com/2011/02/meeting-thomas-merton-2/.

————. *The Root of War Is Fear: Thomas Merton's Advice to Peacemakers.* Maryknoll, NY: Orbis Books, 2016.

————. *Walking Straight with Crooked Lines: A Memoir.* Maryknoll, NY: Orbis Books, 2020.

———. "Work Hard, Pray Hard: On Dorothy Day and Thomas Merton." Interview by *US Catholic*, published online at USCatholic.org, October 10, 2011. https://www.uscatholic.org/culture/social-justice/2011/09/work-hard-pray-hard-dorthy-day-and-thomas-merton.

Francis, Pope. "Visit to the Joint Session of the United States Congress: Address of the Holy Father." September 24, 2015. Vatican website. http://w2.vatican.va/content/francesco/en/speeches/2015/september/documents/papa-francesco_20150924_usa-us-congress.html.

Gates, Henry Louis, Jr. *Stony the Road: Reconstruction, White Supremacy, and the Rise of Jim Crow*. New York: Penguin Press, 2019.

Gay, Roxane. "The Case Against Hope." *New York Times* online, June 6, 2019. https://www.nytimes.com/2019/06/06/opinion/hope-politics-2019.html.

Genovese, Eugene D. "The Nat Turner Case." *New York Review of Books* online, September 1968. https://www.nybooks.com/articles/1968/09/12/the-nat-turner-case/.

Greco, Charles P., D.D. "Pastoral Letter on Race Relations." Alexandria, LA: Alexandria Diocese, June 3, 1965.

———. "Pastoral on Race Relations." Alexandria, LA: Alexandria Diocese, August 4, 1963.

Griffin, John Howard. "August Thompson and John Howard Griffin: Dialogue with Father Thompson." In *Black, White, and Gray: 21 Points of View on the Race Question*, edited by Bradford Daniel, 148–62. New York: Sheed and Ward, 1964.

———. "Dialogue: Father August Thompson." *Ramparts* 2, no. 3 (Christmas 1963), 24–33.

———. *Follow the Ecstasy: The Hermitage Years of Thomas Merton*. Maryknoll, NY: Orbis Books, 1993.

Hall, Gary Peter. *Communing with the Stranger: Relational Dynamics and Critical Distance between Thomas Merton and His Readers*. Unpublished PhD dissertation draft, University of Birmingham, n.d.

Harding, Rachel. Foreword to *Remnants: A Memoir of Spirit, Activism, and Mothering* by Rosemarie Freeney Harding. Durham, NC: Duke University Press, 2015.

Harding, Rosemarie Freeney, with Rachel Elizabeth Harding. *Remnants: A Memoir of Spirit, Activism, and Mothering*. Durham, NC: Duke University Press, 2015.

Harding, Vincent. "First Annual Thomas Merton Black History Month Lecture." February 22, 2007. Recording CD-0220, TMC/BU.

———. *The Movement Makes Us Human: An Interview with Dr. Vincent Harding on Mennonites, Vietnam, and MLK*. Edited by Joanna Shenk. Eugene, OR: Wipf and Stock, 2018.

———. "Uses of the Afro-American Past." Typescript, 1967. Spelman College, Stuart A. Rose Archives and Rare Book Library, Emory University, Vincent Harding Collection #868, Box 42, Folder 16. First published: *Negro Digest* XVII, no. 4 (February 1968): 4–9, 81–84.

Havel, Václav. *Disturbing the Peace: A Conversation with Karel Hvížďala*. Translated by Paul Wilson. New York: Vintage Books, 1990.

Haywood, Tom. "25 Years in 'Integrated-Segregated' Church." *The Town Talk* (Alexandria, LA), June 5, 1982.

Hennessy, Kate. *Dorothy Day: The World Will Be Saved by Beauty. An Intimate Portrait of My Grandmother*. New York: Scribner, 2017.

Hillis, Gregory K. "Letters to a Black Catholic Priest." *The Merton Annual* 32 (2020): 114–36.

———. "A Sign of Contradiction: Remembering Fr. August Thompson." *Commonweal* 146, no. 9 (October 2019): 29–31.

Hubbard, Barbara Marx. *The Hunger of Eve: A Woman's Odyssey toward the Future*. Harrisburg, PA: Stackpole Books, 1976.

Imperato, Robert. *Merton and Walsh on the Person*. Brookfield, WI: Liturgical Publications, 1987.

John Howard Griffin Papers. Rare Book and Manuscript Library, Columbia University, New York, NY.

Joseph, Rita. "Student Nurse." *Jubilee* 3, no. 5 (September 1955): 32–37.

Klejment, Anne, and Nancy L. Roberts, eds. *American Catholic Pacifism: The Influence of Dorothy Day and the Catholic Worker Movement*. Westport CT: Praeger, 1996.

Kosicki, Piotr H. *Catholics on the Barricades: Poland, France, and "Revolution," 1891–1956*. New Haven: Yale University Press, 2018.

Labrie, Ross. "Thomas Merton and Existentialism." *The Merton Seasonal* 43, no. 3 (Fall 2018): 10–13.

———. "Thomas Merton on the Unspeakable." *The Merton Seasonal* 36, no. 4 (Winter 2011): 3–12.

Malin, Brendan. "Green Patch." *Boston Globe*, October 21, 1965.

"Marlon D. Green—Biography." In Marlon Green correspondence file, TMC/BU.

"The Marlon Green Case." *America* (March 3, 1963): 285.

McClellan, Joseph. "Music." *Boston Pilot*, May 15, 1965.

Merriman, Brigid O'Shea, OSF. *Searching for Christ: The Spirituality of Dorothy Day*. Notre Dame, IN: University of Notre Dame Press, 1994.

Merton, Thomas. "Aesthetic and Contemplative Experience—James Joyce." Transcribed recording from summer 1968. *The Merton Annual* 27 (2015): 35–44.

———. "The Angel and the Machine." *The Merton Seasonal* 22, no. 1 (Spring 1997): 3–6. First published in *Seckauer Heft* [Styria, Austria] 29 (1966): 73–79. First published in English in S*eason* 5 (Summer 1967).

———. *The Behavior of Titans*. New York: New Directions, 1961.

———. "Cargo Movements and Their Implications." Tape transcript, November 11, 1967. C.2, TMC/BU.

———. "Cargo Theology." Typescript, 1968. D.2 manuscript file, TMC/BU.

———. *Cold War Letters*. Maryknoll, NY: Orbis Books, 2006.

———. *The Collected Poems of Thomas Merton*. New York: New Directions, 1977.

———. "'Comment' on Charlotte Buhler, Tom Stonier, Walter A. Weisskopf." *Forum for Correspondence and Contact* 1, no. 2 (March 1968): 11–13.

———. *Conjectures of a Guilty Bystander*. Garden City, NY: Doubleday, 1966. Image Edition, 1968.

———. *The Courage for Truth: Letters to Writers*. Edited by Christine M. Bochen. New York: Farrar, Straus and Giroux, 1993.

———. *Dancing in the Water of Life: Seeking Peace in the Hermitage. The Journals of Thomas Merton: Volume Five, 1963–1965*. Edited by Robert E. Daggy. New York: HarperCollins, 1997.

———. *Disputed Questions*. New York: New Directions, 1960.

———. "Eight Freedom Songs." N.d., typescript. Robert Williams correspondence file, TMC/BU.

———. *Faith and Violence*. Notre Dame, IN: University of Notre Dame Press, 1968.

———. *Gandhi on Non-Violence*. New York: New Directions, 1965.

———. *The Geography of Lograire*. New York: New Directions, 1969.

———. *The Hidden Ground of Love: Letters on Religious Experience and Social Concerns*. Edited by William H. Shannon. New York: Farrar, Straus and Giroux, 1985.

———. *Ishi Means Man: Essays on Native Americans*. Greensboro, NC: Unicorn Press, 1976.

————. *Learning to Love: Exploring Solitude and Freedom. The Journals of Thomas Merton: Volume Six, 1966–1967*. Edited by Christine M. Bochen. New York: HarperCollins, 1997.

————. *A Life in Letters: The Essential Collection*. Edited by William H. Shannon and Christine M. Bochen. Notre Dame, IN: Ave Maria Press, 2008.

————. *The Literary Essays of Thomas Merton*. New York: New Directions, 1981.

————. *Love and Living*. New York: Farrar, Straus and Giroux, 1979.

————. *The Monastic Journey of Thomas Merton*. Edited by Brother Patrick Hart. Kansas City: Sheed Andrews and McMeel, Inc., 1977.

————. "Neither Caliban nor Uncle Tom." *Liberation* VIII, no. 4 (June 1963): 22.

————. *New Seeds of Contemplation*. New York: New Directions, 1961.

————. *The Nonviolent Alternative*. Edited by Gordon C. Zahn. New York: Farrar, Straus and Giroux, 1980.

————. *The Other Side of the Mountain: The End of the Journey. The Journals of Thomas Merton: Volume Seven, 1967–1968*. Edited by Lawrence E. Cunningham. New York: HarperCollins, 1998.

————. *Peace in the Post-Christian Era*. Maryknoll, NY: Orbis Books, 2004.

————. *Raids on the Unspeakable*. New York: New Directions, 1966.

————. *Redeeming the Time*. London: Burns and Oates, 1966.

————. "Retreat (Day of Recollection) given to the sisters at Anchorage, Alaska." Recording 201-2-2, TMC/BU. Recorded September 29, 1968.

————. *The Road to Joy: Letters to New and Old Friends*. Edited by Robert E. Daggy. New York: Farrar, Straus and Giroux, 1989.

————. *The School of Charity: Letters on Religious Renewal and Spiritual Direction*. Edited by Brother Patrick Hart. New York: Farrar, Straus and Giroux, 1990.

————. *A Search for Solitude: Pursuing the Monk's True Life. The Journals of Thomas Merton: Volume Three, 1952–1960*. Edited by Lawrence E. Cunningham. New York: HarperCollins, 1996.

————. *Seeds of Destruction*. New York: Farrar, Straus and Giroux, 1964.

————. *The Springs of Contemplation: A Retreat at the Abbey of Gethsemani*. Edited by Jane Marie Richardson. Notre Dame, IN: Ave Maria Press, 1992.

—————. *Thomas Merton in Alaska: The Alaskan Conferences, Journals, and Letters*. Edited by David D. Cooper and Robert E. Daggy. New York: New Directions, 1988.

—————. *Turning Toward the World: The Pivotal Years. The Journals of Thomas Merton: Volume Four, 1960–1963*. Edited by Victor A. Kramer. New York: HarperCollins, 1996.

—————. "The Wild Paces." *The Merton Annual* 24 (2011): 15–28. First published in *The Catholic Worker* 34 (June 1968): 4, 6.

—————. *Witness to Freedom: Letters in Times of Crisis*. Edited by William H. Shannon. New York: Farrar, Straus and Giroux, 1994.

—————. "Workshop given at Precious Blood monastery in Alaska." Typescript transcript. Item 4, subsection E.1, TMC/BU.

—————. *Zen and the Birds of Appetite*. New York: New Directions, 1968.

Merton, Thomas, and Ernesto Cardenal. *From the Monastery to the World: The Letters of Thomas Merton and Ernesto Cardenal*. Edited and translated by Jessie Sandoval. Berkeley, CA: Counterpoint, 2017.

Moses, Asher. "'Collapse of Civilisation Is the Most Likely Outcome': Top Climate Scientists." *Voice of Action* online, posted June 5, 2020. https://voiceofaction.org/collapse-of-civilisation-is-the-most-likely-outcome-top-climate-scientists/.

Moses, John. *The Art of Thomas Merton*. Columbus, OH: Franciscan Media, 2019.

Mounier, Emmanuel. *Personalism*. Translated by Philip Mairet. London: Routledge and Kegan Paul Ltd., 1952.

New York Times. "Barbara Marx Hubbard, 89, Futurist Who Saw 'Conscious Evolution,' Dies." *New York Times* online, May 15, 2019. https://www.nytimes.com/2019/05/15/obituaries/barbara-marx-hubbard-dead.html.

Oyer, Gordon. *Pursuing the Spiritual Roots of Protest: Merton, Berrigan, Yoder, Muste at the Gethsemani Abbey Peacemakers Retreat*. Eugene, OR: Cascade Books, 2014.

Patriquin, Lane. "The Zeitgeist of Grief." *Geez* 54 (Fall 2019): 31.

Phelps, Jamie T. "African American Catholics: The Struggles, Contributions and Gifts of a Marginalized Community" In *Black and Catholic: The Challenge and Gift of Black Folk*, edited by Jamie T. Phelps, 17–28. Milwaukee: Marquette University Press, 1997.

Poks, Malgorzata. "Borderlands of Cultures, Borderlands of Discourse: Cargo Cults and Their Reflection in Thomas Merton's Poetry." In *Representing and (De)Constructing Borderlands*, edited by Weronika Laszkiewicz, Gregorz Moroz, Jacek Partyka, 167–83. New-castle upon Tyne, UK: Cambridge Scholars Publishing, 2016.

———. *"Geography of Lograire* as Merton's *Gestus*—Prolegomena." *The Merton Annual* 22 (2009): 150–69.

———. "Home on the Border in Ana Castillo's *The Guardians*: The Colonial Matrix of Power, Epistemic Disobedience, and Decolonial Love." *Revista de Estudios Norteamericanos* 21 (2017): 119–43.

———. *Thomas Merton and Latin America: A Consonance of Voices.* Saar-brucken, Germany: LAP LAMBERT Academic Publishing, 2011.

———. "With Malinowski in the Postmodern Desert: Merton, Anthropology, and the Ethnopoetics of *The Geography of Lograire.*" *The Merton Annual* 25 (2012): 49–73.

Polner, Murray, and Jim O'Grady. *Disarmed and Dangerous: The Radical Lives of Daniel and Philip Berrigan.* New York: Basic Books, 1997.

Pramuk, Christopher. *Sophia: The Hidden Christ of Thomas Merton.* Collegeville, MN: Liturgical Press, 2009.

Quammen, David. "Shaking the Viral Tree: An Interview with David Quammen." Interviewed by *Emergence* online, posted March 26, 2020. https://emergencemagazine.org/story/shaking-the-viral-tree/.

Régamey, Raymond. *Non-Violence and the Christian Conscience.* Translator not credited. London: Dartman, Longman & Todd, 1966. Originally published as *Non-Violence et Conscience Chrétienne*, Paris: Les Editions du Cerf, 1958.

Romero, Thom I., II. "Turbulence a Mile High: Equal Employment Opportunity in the Colorado Sky." *The Colorado Lawyer* 32, no. 9 (September 2003): 71.

Ross, Loretta. "I'm a Black Feminist. I Think Call-Out Culture Is Toxic." *The New York Times* online, August 17, 2019. https://www.ny-times.com/2019/08/17/opinion/sunday/cancel-culture-call-out.html?

Sanders, Katrina M. "Black Catholic Clergy and the Struggle for Civil Rights: Winds of Change." In *Uncommon Faithfulness: The Black Catholic Experience*, edited by M. Shawn Copeland, 85–89. Maryknoll, NY: Orbis Books, 2009.

Shannon, William H. Preface to *The Hidden Ground of Love: Letters on Religious Experience and Social Concerns* by Thomas Merton. Edited by William H. Shannon. New York: Farrar, Straus and Giroux, 1985.

———. *Silent Lamp: The Thomas Merton Story.* New York: Crossroad, 1992.

Shannon, William H., and Christine M. Bochen. Introduction to *A Life In Letters: The Essential Collection* by Thomas Merton. Edited by William H. Shannon and Christine M. Bochen. Notre Dame, IN: Ave Maria Press, 2008.

Shannon, William H., Christine M. Bochen, and Patrick F. O'Connell. *The Thomas Merton Encyclopedia*. Maryknoll, NY: Orbis Books, 2002.

Shenk, Joanna. Introduction to *The Movement Makes Us Humans: An Interview with Dr. Vincent Harding on Mennonites, Vietnam, and MLK*. Eugene, OR: Wipf and Stock, 2018.

Shetterly, Robert. "James Douglass." *Americans Who Tell The Truth* website. https://www.americanswhotellthetruth.org/portraits/james-douglass.

Solnit, Rebecca. *Hope in Dark Times: Untold Histories, Wild Possibilities*. 3rd ed. Chicago: Haymarket Books, 2016.

Terlizzese, Lawrence J. *Hope in the Thought of Jacques Ellul*. Eugene, OR: Cascade Books, 2005.

The Town Talk (Alexandria, LA). "Rev. Thompson Cited at Convention." August 25, 1973.

Thomas Merton Center. W. W. Lyons Brown Library, Bellarmine University, Louisville, KY.

"The Triple Revolution." Santa Barbara, California: The Ad Hoc Committee on the Triple Revolution, 1964.

van der Post, Laurens. *The Dark Eye in Africa*. New York: Morrow and Co., 1955.

———. *Venture to the Interior*. New York: Morrow and Co., 1951.

Vatican Council II. Pastoral Constitution on the Church in the Modern World (*Gaudium et Spes*). December 7, 1965.

Veterans of Hope website. "About Veterans of Hope." http://www.veterans ofhope.org/about-us/.

Warren, Louis S. *God's Red Son: The Ghost Dance Religion and the Making of Modern America*. New York: Basic Books, 2017.

Warren, Robert Penn. *Segregation: The Inner Conflict in the South*. New York: Random House, 1956.

Warzel, Charlie. "We Are Watching History Unfold in Real Time." *New York Times* online, June 2, 2020. https://www.nytimes.com/2020/06/02/opinion/floyd-protest-twitter.html?.

Weis, Monica, SSJ. *The Environmental Vision of Thomas Merton*. Lexington, KY: University of Kentucky Press, 2011.

Weisskopf, Walter A. "Existential Balance and Evolution." *Forum for Correspondence and Contact* 1, no.1 (January 1968): 51–53.

———. "Repression and the Dialectics of Industrial Civilization." *Review of Social Economy* XXIII, no. 2 (September 1965): 116–26.

Whitlock, Flint. *Turbulence before Takeoff: The Life and Times of Aviation Pioneer Marlon Dewitt Green.* Brule, WI: Cable Publishing, 2009.

Wikipedia online. S.v. "National Conference for Community and Justice." https://en.wikipedia.org/wiki/National_Conference_for_Community_and_Justice.

[Williams, Robert?]. "Boston Group Plans Jordon Hall Benefit Concert to Aid Massachusett's [*sic*] African Students." Flier, n.d., n.p. Robert Williams correspondence file, TMC/BU.

———. Constitution of the Foundation for African Students. N.d., n.p. Robert Williams correspondence file, TMC/BU.

———. *Reflections on Love.* Pamphlet, n.d., n.p. Robert Williams correspondence file, TMC/BU.

———. "Singing a People Upward." Flier, n.d., n.p. Naomi Burton Stone Papers, St. Bonaventure University.

Williams, Sidney. "Local Priest Will Be Watching Merton Special with Interest." *The Town Talk* (Alexandria, LA). September 20, 1992, 32.

Williams, Thomas D., LC. "What Is Thomist Personalism?" *Alpha Omega* 7, no. 2 (2004): 163–97.

Yungblut, John. "Triple Revolution in Atlanta." *Friends Journal* 10, no. 13 (July 1, 1964): 293–94.

INDEX